Sustainable America

America's Environment, Economy and Society in the 21st Century

Foreword by Vice President Al Gore

Edited by Daniel Sitarz

EARTHPRESS
RESOURCES FOR A BETTER WORLD

Carbondale Illinois

Library of Congress Cataloging-in-Publication Data

Sustainable America: America's Environment, Economy, and Society in the 21st
Century /
          edited by Daniel Sitarz
          p.   cm.
          An abridged and synthesized version of the reports of the President's
          Council on Sustainable Development.
          Foreword by Vice-President Albert Gore.
          Included bibliographical references and index.
          ISBN 0-935755-54-3
          1. Sustainable development–United States. 2. Economic development–
Environmental aspects–United States.
I. Sitarz, Dan. 1948- . II. President's Council on Sustainable Development.
HC110.E5S87   1998   97-28607
333.7'0973–dc21   CIP

Produced in cooperation with:
          President's Council on Sustainable Development
          Martin Spitzer, Executive Director
          730 Jackson Place NW
          Washington DC 20503

          Global Research Institute
          Daniel Sitarz, Executive Director
          705 West Main Street
          Carbondale IL 62901

Published By:
          EarthPress
          1103 West College Street
          Carbondale IL 62901
          Phone: (800)748-1175

Distributed to the trade by:
          National Book Network
          4720 Boston Way
          Lanham MD 20706
          Phone: (800)462-6420

Also Available from EarthPress and National Book Network:
Agenda 21: The Earth Summit Strategy to Save Our Planet
The award-winning guide to global sustainable development
Daniel Sitarz, Editor
ISBN 0-935755-14-4; Retail price $15.95

Table of Contents

iv

Acknowledgments

I would like to thank my wife and partner, Jan Sitarz for her dedicated editorial skill and endless patience. I also would like to acknowledge all of the people who served on the President's Council on Sustainable Development and its various Task Forces and Roundtables. Thanks to Kathleen McGinty and Michael Terrell of the Council on Environmental Quality. Special thanks to the dedicated staff of the Global Research Institute: Colleen Heraty, Sanjay Sofat (and his helper Kelly Yi), and Jackie Badger. Thanks also to former U.S. Senator Paul Simon, now Director of the Public Policy Institute at Southern Illinois University, for his encouragement. Finally, I would like to thank Vice President Al Gore for his Foreword to this book. This book is dedicated to my children, Justin and Jessica Sitarz, and all of the other children of the world.

Foreword

All across America, a powerful new idea is taking root. Visionary engineers are designing cars that can run up to 80 miles on a single gallon of gas. Neighborhood coalitions are reclaiming abandoned lots to build homes and grow gardens. Farmers and conservationists are working side by side to restore vital wetlands. From the inner city to the deep wilderness, countless people are committing themselves to this new idea called *sustainable development.*

Five years ago, when I joined leaders from around the world at the Earth Summit in Rio de Janeiro, few understood, let alone embraced, the concept of sustainable development. But that historic gathering not only placed sustainable development high on the international agenda–it spawned an energetic citizen movement that is spreading the word to the far corners of the globe.

I am extremely proud of the part we are playing here at home. In June of 1993, one year after the Rio summit, President Clinton created the President's Council on Sustainable Development. Its goal, he declared, was to find ways "to bring people together to meet the needs of the present without jeopardizing the future." The Council's deliberations were themselves cause for great optimism. Drawing from the ranks of government, business, environmental, civil rights, and labor organizations, the group traveled the country gathering input from thousands of citizens and stitching together a vision of a sustainable America.

As the Council's members discovered, many people are already hard at work turning that vision into reality. Businesses of all kinds are incorporating sustainability into their philosophies and practices. They are using resources more efficiently and preventing pollution so others won't have to clean it up. Jobs are being created as new businesses pursue sustainable technologies. Communities large and small are revitalizing downtowns, rebuilding waterfronts, and enlisting citizens in efforts to chart a sustainable future. Efforts like these are laying the foundation for America's success in the 21st century. And just as the Council itself was a model of collaboration, they are demonstrating what can be achieved when cooperation takes the place of conflict.

I am especially heartened by the renaissance under way in the city of Chattanooga, in my home state of Tennessee. Once known as one of the most polluted cities in America, Chattanooga is today reinventing itself as a model of sustainability. The air is once again breathable, the riverfront is again a place where people and nature flourish, and people are being put to work building electric busses that are virtually pollution-free.

The federal government, too, is doing its part. From an ambitious forest plan for the Pacific Northwest to a long-term strategy for restoring Florida's Everglades, we are devising innovative approaches to difficult economic and environmental challenges. We have created Empowerment Zones to revive the economies of distressed urban areas. And we have launched the American Heritage Rivers initiative to help reunite people with their rivers in ways that serve the needs of both.

As more and more people join us on this path to sustainable development, they will need help along the way. *Sustainable America*, an abridged version of the Council's groundbreaking reports, is where they should start. It is an invaluable guidebook for anyone devoted to the vision of a sustainable future.

Every day, I believe, more Americans are coming to share the Council's conviction that economic, environmental, and social equity issues are inseparable threads of the fabric that binds us. The challenges ahead are significant, but if we choose the right course, we can together build an America that is not only stronger, more equitable and more prosperous, but truly sustainable.

The Honorable Albert Gore
Vice President
United States of America

Introduction

In June of 1992, at the largest gathering of world leaders in history, the nations of the Earth agreed to collectively pursue a new path–a new direction. They decided, under the terms of Agenda 21, the central agreement of the Earth Summit, to jointly pursue a path to put the world on a more sustainable course. To describe the course to be taken, the phrase *sustainable development* was used. One year later, President Clinton created the President's Council on Sustainable Development, and asked it to "develop a national sustainable development action strategy." Leaders of government, industry, and environmental, labor, and civil rights groups were given the daunting task of working together and fashioning both a vision of a sustainable society and the blueprint for achieving it. Their work is the foundation of this book!

But what is *sustainable development*? The fact that the term *sustainability* has not yet entered the mainstream of American consciousness may be due in part to confusion about its meaning. Over the years literally hundreds of definitions have been suggested. One of the earliest was proposed in 1915 by Canada's Commission on Conservation: "Each generation is entitled to the interest on the natural capital, but the principal should be handed down unimpaired." The actual term *sustainable development* was first introduced in the late 1970s and popularized in 1987 by the World Commission on Environment and Development, also known as the Bruntland Commission, which defines sustainable development as "development that meets the needs of the present without compromising the ability of future generations to meet their own needs." It was this definition that the Council adopted in their work?

3

Sustainable America

In the final analysis, however, agreeing on a formal definition of the term is not as important as coming to agreement on a vision of a sustainable world. How can sustainability be achieved? What does a sustainable society mean? What would a sustainable America be like? As conditions change, society's overall vision of sustainability will continually change. What is certain, however, is that the present course of America, and indeed humanity, is not sustainable.

Projections by the United Nations indicate that the world's human population will add an additional 3 billion people over the next 27 years. One-fifth of humanity–over 1 billion people–currently live in abject poverty–breathing unhealthy polluted air, lacking adequate food, safe water, and even the most basic health care. The average annual rate of deforestation worldwide is equivalent to an area the size of the state of Georgia. Worldwide, the ocean's fisheries are in a state of collapse. In the United States, citizens consume 25 percent of the Earth's resources although they constitute only five percent of the planet's population. In the last 20 years, per capita consumption in the United States has increased by 45 percent. Clearly, these and many other trends are not sustainable. Faced with these trends, how is it possible to put the nation and the world on a sustainable course?[3]

To achieve sustainability, indifference, lack of knowledge, and resistance to the concept of sustainable development must first be addressed. Education is the key to acceptance of sustainable development as a major goal of U.S. society. To develop a vision of a sustainable America, the President' Council crystallized a set of core beliefs that they felt were the fundamental principles of sustainable development. These beliefs served as the framework for the Council as it set about the task of developing a national strategy for a sustainable society. These beliefs are: To achieve sustainable development, some things must grow–jobs, productivity, wages, savings, profits, information, knowledge, and education. Others–pollution, waste, and poverty–must not. That change is inevitable and necessary for the sake of this and future generations and that America can choose a course for change that will lead to the mutually reinforcing goals of economic growth, environmental protection, and social justice. That steady progress in reducing the disparities in education, opportunity, and environmental risk within society is essential for America to become sustainable.

4

Environmental regulations and basic standards of environmental performance must be clear, fair, and consistently enforced. Market incentives and the power of consumers can also be harnessed to protect the environment. Economic growth can be based on technological innovation, improved efficiency, and expanding global markets, rather than the use of more energy and resources. Steady advances in science and technology are essential to help improve economic efficiency, protect and restore natural systems, and modify consumption patterns. And that a growing economy *and* a healthy environment are essential to national and global security.

America must also strengthen its communities and enhance their role in making decisions about the environment, society, natural resources, and economic progress. The people most immediately affected must be included in the decision process. Cooperative decision-making will lead to better decisions, and more sensible use of human, natural, and financial resources. A knowledgeable public and the free flow of information are critically important for open and effective decision-making.

The United States must have policies and programs that contribute to stabilizing global human population. This is critical if we hope to have the resources needed to ensure a high quality of life for future generations. With respect to global problems like climate changes–even in the face of scientific uncertainty society must take reasonable actions to avert risks where the potential harm to human health or the environment is serious or irreparable. Finally, all citizens must have access to high quality and lifelong education that enables them to understand the interdependence of economic prosperity, environmental quality, and social justice. Their education must prepare them to take individual action that supports all three of these vital national goals.

These central beliefs guided the President's Council on Sustainable Development over the course of the past 4 years as it sought to define a sustainable society. Under the able leadership of environmentalist Jonathan Lash, President of the World Resources Institute, and industrialist David Buzzelli, Vice-President of the Dow Chemical Company, the Council has developed a clear blueprint on what actions will be necessary to achieve a sustainable America. Key to their deliberations was the sense that in working together, diverse elements of American society can find common ground and common values.[4]

5

As the co-chairs stated in their Preface to the main report of the Council: "The politics of mistrust are the greatest obstacle to the process of innovation and change that we believe is necessary to achieve the goals we share. We believe that consensus will move America forward both faster and farther than confrontation. Moreover, we believe that consensus is the public's job, not the government's. Government is important in implementing what people agree on, but we all need to do the hard work of listening, learning, and finding common ground ... the work of the Council will be important only if it ignites many debates; helps to inspire independent action; and encourages business, citizens, and government to invent new forms of dialogue and interaction."[5]

Editor's Note: This book is based on various reports that the President's Council on Sustainable Development has issued over the past 4 years. Primarily, it is based on three main reports of the Council: *Sustainable America: A New Consensus for Prosperity, Opportunity, and a Healthy Environment for the Future; Building on Consensus: a Progress Report on Sustainable America;* and *The Road to Sustainable Development: A Snapshot of Activities in the United States of America.* It is also based on reports from the following Council Task Forces: Energy and Transportation; Eco-efficiency; Population and Consumption; Sustainable Agriculture; Public Dialogue, Linkage, and Education; Principles, Goals, and Definitions; Innovative Local, State, and Regional Approaches; New National Opportunities; and International Leadership.

Although numerous high-ranking federal officials served on the Council, the recommendations in this book do not necessarily reflect administration policy. Additionally, although the entire Council unanimously endorsed the recommendations in its report: *Sustainable America: A New Consensus for Prosperity, Opportunity, and a Healthy Environment for the Future,* this book contains additional policy recommendations which have been adapted from Council Task Force reports and were not the subject of endorsement by the full Council. Those portions of this book which are taken from Task Force reports only are clearly noted and detailed in the endnotes.

Daniel Sitarz, Editor

Chapter 1

Sustainable America

As America approaches the 21st century, the challenges it faces are as great as any it has faced in the past. The end of the Cold War, the emergence of a global economy, continued population growth, and the development of advanced technologies are changing the world in fundamental ways. Human impact is placing increasingly severe stress on the natural world. If, as a nation, we wish to ensure a sustainable future for ourselves and our children, we must be willing to change our strategies to cope with these changing realities. We must be willing to adopt completely new approaches to the economic, environmental, and social challenges we face. To advance and prosper, we must be willing to develop a sustainable America–an America that can survive indefinitely without harming the environmental, economic, or social bases on which it depends–an America that provides for this generation without diminishing the opportunities of future generations to enjoy resources and a quality of life at least equal to our own. Despite America's great wealth, power, and technological prowess, we cannot complacently assume that the future of our children's lives will be better than the present. There are current trends that lead in very troubling directions.

We are eroding the fertile soil that nourishes our crops and provides our sustenance. We are rapidly depleting our nation's groundwater, the ultimate source of life. We are degrading our rangelands, home to our wild animals and our livestock. We continue to pollute the air, the land, and the water around us. We are swiftly destroying our wetlands and wildlife habitat and, in the process, extinguishing species–some forever. Our chemicals are depleting the Earth's protective ozone layer. Our lifestyles are dramatically changing the Earth's climate. We are harvesting our fisheries to the point of collapse. We are producing toxic and radioactive substances that must be contained forever to be safe. And we are contaminating and diminishing the resources and ecosystems on which all of our economic activity and quality of life depend. These acts cannot be considered environmentally sustainable. Yet they all occur in the United States today. To achieve a sustainable America, we must change them.

Economically, our nation continues to buy more from other nations than it sells–continuing our negative balance of trade and payments. So too, our governments and our households continue to spend more than their income. We spend enormous sums for environmental cleanup and compliance rather than investing in preventing pollution in the first place. We are recklessly inefficient in our use of resources. As a nation, we use more than a fair share of the world's resources and its capacity to absorb waste. As the world's largest economy, we are the world's largest single consumer of natural resources and the world's top producer of waste and toxic and hazardous substances. And our nation–the world's third largest–is the only major industrialized country in the world experiencing population growth on a significant scale. All of these activities undermine the very economic success that drives the American way of life. Yet they all occur in the United States today. To achieve a sustainable America, we must change them.

In our society, there are wide and growing disparities in wealth and income that fuel mounting social tensions. We tolerate the existence of a severely disadvantaged underclass from which escape is nearly impossible. Our toxic industries have been disproportionately located in many of our minority and low-income neighborhoods. Gender and race-based discrimination continues to infect our society. And our accumulation of material goods to the exclusion of personal, family, and community connections continues unabated. These acts are not socially sustainable. They fray the fabric required for a durable society. Yet they all occur in the

8

United States today. To achieve a sustainable America, we must change them.

A constellation of social, economic, environmental, political, and cultural factors produces this litany of unsustainable conditions in the United States. If we hope to alter these unwelcome trends, we must very soon, as a nation, alter our course. The longer the delay, the more difficult the solutions will become.[1]

We live in an era of rapid and often bewildering changes in the forces and conditions that shape human life. This is evident both in the altered nature of geopolitics in the post-Cold War era and in the growing understanding of the relationship between human beings and the natural world. The end of the Cold War has been accompanied by the swift advancement of democracy in places where it was previously unknown and an even more rapid spread of market-based economies. The authority of central governments is eroding, and power has begun to shift to local governments and private institutions. In some countries, freedom and opportunity are flourishing, while in others the rapid changes have unleashed the violence of old conflicts and new ambitions. Internationally, trade, investment, information, and even people flow across borders largely outside of governmental control. Domestically, deregulation of industries and the shift of responsibilities from federal to state and local governments are changing the relationships among levels of government and between government and industry.

In the last few decades of the 20th century, communications technology has dramatically enhanced people's ability to receive information and to influence the events that affect them. This, in turn, has sparked an explosive growth in the number of organizations, associations, and networks formed by citizens, businesses, and communities seeking a greater voice for their interests. As a result, society outside of government—civil society—is demanding a greater role in governmental decisions, while at the same time impatiently seeking solutions which are beyond government's power to decide. But technological innovation is changing much more than communication. It is changing the ways in which Americans live, work, produce, and consume. Knowledge has become the economy's most important and dynamic resource. It has rapidly improved America's efficiency as information and innovation are increasingly substituted for raw materials. During the past 20 years, the amount of energy and natural resources that the U.S. economy uses to produce each constant dollar of economic output has steadily declined, as have many forms of pollution. When U.S. laws first required industry to control pollution, the response was to install cleanup equipment. The shift to a knowledge-driven economy has emphasized the positive connections between efficiency, profits, and environmental protection, and has helped launch a trend in profitable pollution prevention. More Americans now know that pollution is waste, waste is inefficient, and inefficiency is expensive.[2]

Even as their access to information and to means of communication have increased, citizens of wealthy industrialized nations are becoming more cynical about traditional political arrangements that no longer seem responsive to their needs. They are frustrated with the seeming inability of societal mechanisms to correct the obvious problems. The confidence of many Americans in the large institutions that affect their lives–such as business, government, the media, and civic organizations–is eroding. Individual citizens have increasingly lost faith in their ability to influence events and many have surrendered to apathy, or worse, to anger.

Bringing about positive change is the challenge that the United States faces. American society has long been characterized by its capacity to embrace and profit from change. But how can communities and individuals be motivated to leave future generations a cleaner, more resilient environment; a more prosperous nation; a more equitable society; and a more productive and efficient economy–one that is competitive internationally? The situation is especially difficult because the pace and extent of today's changes are unprecedented, reflecting the mounting local consequences of powerful global economic, social, and environmental forces.

Since the end of World War II, the world's economic output has increased substantially, allowing for widespread improvements in health, education, and opportunity, but also creating growing disparities between rich and poor. Even within wealthy nations, including the United States, the gap between rich and poor is widening. Tomorrow's world will be shaped by the aspirations of a much larger global population. The number of people living on Earth has doubled in the last 50 years; the equivalent of the population of the United States was added to the world total during the last 3 years. Growing populations demand more food, goods, services, and space. Where there is scarcity, population growth aggravates the scarcity. Where there is conflict, rising demand for land and natural resources intensifies the conflict. Struggling to survive in places that can no longer sustain them, growing populations overfish, overharvest, and overgraze the fragile Earth.[3]

Economic growth and innovations in agricultural technology have allowed many of the world's people to improve their lives as the global population increases, but these improvements in human lives are not without consequences to the Earth's natural systems. While plentiful, some of the resources which humanity uses—such as minerals and fossil fuels—are finite; once used, they are exhausted and cannot be renewed. The living resources that humanity uses—plants, animals, and fish—are renewable, but they can be destroyed. Human ingenuity has developed many alternatives for scarce resources, but the depletion of resources has never been—nor will it ever be—free of serious human and natural consequences. In fact, the demands of a growing human population and an expanding global economy are placing increasing stresses on the Earth's natural systems. And while the exhaustion of finite resources may result in human and economic dislocation, the destruction of renewable resources often has far broader ramifications because they are part of a dynamic and interdependent natural system. When a forest is destroyed, species lose their habitat and disappear—some forever. The resulting erosion affects river and coastal resources, and rainfall patterns may change—with dramatic and far-reaching effects.[4]

In the late 20th century, the effects of human activity on natural systems are not only visible, they are observable from year to year. In the 130 years from 1850 to 1980, about 15 percent of the world's forests disappeared. During the next 10 years, another 6 percent—an area larger than California, Texas, New York, and Montana combined—was cut and not replanted. The expansion of human population and the destruction of forests, grasslands, wetlands, and river systems bring about an accelerated loss of species diversity. This diversity is the source not only of a wide range of human benefits—25 percent of new medicines, for example—but is also the key to the ecosystem's resilience in the face of change. The pressures on natural resources are myriad. Pollution, coastal development, and intense fishing reduce ocean fish stocks. While the number and size of fishing fleets are increasing worldwide, fish harvests are falling. Human activity—primarily the burning of coal, oil, and gas—releases pollutants that are changing the chemistry of the Earth's

11

atmosphere–changes that most scientists agree are affecting the Earth's climate.[5]

The impact of each country on the global environment can be described as the product of the numbers of people, the consumption of goods and services per capita, and the degree to which inefficient and environmentally unsafe methods are used to produce and consume those goods and services. The U.S. population is large and it is growing. U.S. per capita consumption levels are the highest on Earth. Although U.S. technology is cleaner and more efficient than that of less developed countries such as China, it is generally less so when compared to technologies in Europe and Japan. Consequently, the environmental impact of the United States is enormous.[6]

Our activities harm the ability of the Earth's natural systems to absorb waste and perform the other functions on which everything that we do depends–the way that water, air, forests, and other common areas generate the clear water, blue sky, healthy soil and vegetation, and biological diversity that are the foundation of life on earth. Continued population growth and rising per capita consumption forever raise the stakes, so that technology must achieve ever greater improvements to reduce our environmental impact on the Earth's natural systems.

The rapid global economic growth of the last several decades has been accompanied by increasing pollution, affecting both human health and the environment. Even though many wealthy nations have made remarkable progress in reducing pollution, the focus of industrial expansion has shifted to developing nations where environmental protection may not always be regarded as affordable. Although pollution controls and efficiency in wealthy nations have started to offset some of the global effects of growth, overall, global pollution is increasing. Because global economic, social, and environmental trends are connected, America's hopes for the future are irrevocably linked to the rest of the world. Americans compete in a global economy shaped by global trends. American power and interests are global in nature, and the lives of Americans are affected by global environmental changes. What Americans do affects the lives of people in every nation. Moreover, the changes taking place throughout the world affect every American.

The U.S. economy, although still the world's largest, is no longer dominant. It is now part of a global marketplace. U.S. enterprises can no longer thrive by looking only to domestic markets and domestic competitors. The fastest growing markets are not in the industrialized countries, but in those countries whose economies are in the process of becoming industrialized. Banks and private investors create huge international capital flows, seeking opportunities wherever they occur. Exports represent 7.3 percent of the U.S. gross domestic product and are growing. Imports are 9.5 percent of U.S. consumption and are growing. Burgeoning international trade now exceeds $4 trillion per year and is growing. International currency trading exceeds $1 trillion per day and is growing. These global trends also place tremendous pressure on the United States to continue to provide for its citizens.[7]

The paradoxical challenge that the United States and the world face at the end of the 20th century is to generate the individual economic opportunities and the national wealth necessary for economically healthy societies while, at the same time, dramatically lessening the environmental risks and social inequities that have accompanied past economic development. Both in the world and in the United States, there will be more people, and they will aspire to better lives for themselves and their children. Responding to those aspirations, particularly if prevalent patterns of consumption continue, will require the production of more goods and services. The challenge of sustainable development is to find ways to meet those needs without destroying the resources and ecosystems upon which humanity's future progress depends.

Prosperity, fairness, and a healthy environment are interrelated elements of the human dream of a better future. Sustainable development is a way to pursue that dream through choice and policy. Work, wealth, community, and the environment are interwoven into the fabric of everyday life and the life of the nation. Sustainable development is the framework that integrates economic, environmental, and social goals in ways that enhance the prospects of human aspirations. The issue is not whether the economy needs to grow but how and in what manner. To achieve sustainability some things must grow—jobs, productivity, wages, profits, capital and savings, information, knowledge, education—and others—pollution, waste, poverty, energy and material use—must not.

13

An economy that creates good jobs and safeguards public health and the environment will be stronger and more resilient than one that does not. A country that protects its ecosystems and manages its natural resources wisely lays a far stronger base for future prosperity than one that carelessly uses its assets and destroys its natural capital. A society that invests in its children and communities, equitably providing education and opportunity, is far more likely to prosper than one that allows the gap between rich and poor to widen. By recognizing that economic, environmental, and social goals are integrally linked and by creating policies that reflect that interrelationship, Americans can regain their sense that they are in control of their future and that the lives of each generation will be better than the last. Thinking narrowly about jobs, energy, transportation, housing, or ecosystems–as if they are not connected–creates new problems even as it attempts to solve old ones. Such narrow thinking causes misleading solutions that result only in short-term remedies for symptoms, instead of long-term cures for basic problems.

Looking at the choices that confront society only in terms of what tradeoffs are required reflects a history of confrontational politics. It pits essential elements of society against each other in a false contest. The confrontational approach inhibits an active exploration of the best solutions, those that link economic gain, ecological improvement, and social equity–solutions that build common purpose from shared goals. The United States is a democracy with powerful traditions of individual liberty. What happens in American society ultimately depends on the values that guide the choices that individual citizens make. People act according to their perception of their needs and wants, their values, and the events that affect them. But the narrow and immediate interests of individuals, organizations, or government officials do not necessarily coincide with the long-term interests of a larger community at home or abroad. Although people can act in the interests of the larger community, they rarely do so alone. Because each individual fears for their own self-interest, often no action is taken for the collective interests of society.

How can more than 265 million individual Americans define and reconcile their needs and aspirations with the needs of the future? There is enormous potential power and a growing desire for processes that directly involve people in the decisions that affect them. Americans want to take back control of their lives. Individuals and communities throughout

14

the country are demonstrating that it is possible to shift from conflict to cooperation when citizens are able to find common values to guide their action. People can find ways to lead prosperous lives which are in harmony with the environment.

Throughout this book, there are recommendations to create structures that will involve more people and a broader range of interests in shaping community vision and making public policy. The process itself will begin to improve decisions, alleviate conflicts, and counteract the corrosive trends of cynicism and civic disengagement that afflict society. A cooperative approach to decision-making, however, can be arduous and time-consuming. Such an approach requires that many customary roles be changed. For government, this means using its power to convene and facilitate, shifting its role gradually from mandating behavior to supporting responsibility–by setting goals for society, creating incentives and providing information to meet those goals, and monitoring society's performance in achieving those goals.

The federal government, in particular, can help set boundaries for and facilitate policy discussions. These dialogues must give more opportunity, power, and responsibility to individuals and communities to address questions that affect them directly. For their part, businesses also need to develop the practice and skills of open discussion with communities and citizens. They must begin participating more fully in community decision-making and they must candidly make their own company's values, strategies, and performance more accessible to individuals and society. Advocates, too, must accept the burdens and constraints of rational dialogue and exchanges built on trust. Communities must also create open and inclusive debates about their future.

The call to care for the Earth is a deep human impulse. In so many modes–intuitive, aesthetic, spiritual, religious–humans know that by protecting the Earth, they find a sense of place and purpose and fulfill a moral obligation to the future. The intuitive and moral commitment Americans have to preserving the Earth's beauty and productivity for future generations is expressed in the concept of stewardship. Principles of stewardship help define desirable human interaction with the natural world–caring for and preserving life on Earth for ourselves and future generations. Stewardship is more a perspective than a science; it is a set of values that applies to a variety of decisions. It provides moral

15

standards that cannot be imposed but that can be taught, encouraged, and reinforced. Instilled in individuals and in institutions, it can motivate resolve for voluntary change. Principles of stewardship can illuminate complex policy choices and guide individuals toward the common good.

Stewardship is a workable perspective for all professions. For government, it can refocus policy on the long-term needs of the economy and society. For advocates, it can mean embracing the needs for prosperity, environmental protection, and social equity and well-being. For corporate America, it can profitably shape a business' strategic vision and guide decisions on the shop floor. For families, it can provide a framework for rethinking customs of consumption. This book suggests a variety of means to encourage, reward, and support stewardship.

However, no set of policies, no system of incentives, no amount of information can counteract apathy or substitute for individual responsibility. Information can provide a basis for action. Vision and ideas can influence perceptions and inspire change. New ways to make decisions can empower those who seek a role in shaping the future. But the recommendations in this book will be meaningless unless individuals acting as citizens, consumers, investors, managers, workers, professionals, educators, and politicians decide that it is important to them personally to make choices on the basis of a broader, longer view; and that it is vital to turn those choices into action; and, most importantly, that they are individually responsible for that action and the changes that it can achieve.

The combination of political will, technological innovation, and a very large investment of resources and human creativity in pursuit of environmental goals has produced enormous benefits for Americans. This is an achievement to celebrate. Despite such progress, however, our world and our nation steadily use more of the Earth's resources to make more goods for more people. For the sake of future generations, much more must be achieved. The future must become one in which zero waste of resources becomes an ideal for society even as zero defects has become so for manufacturing.

Changes in the form and nature of civic discussion can make the issues of sustainability a bridge between people and institutions. That is the essence of sustainable development: the recognition that our common economic, environmental, and social goals must become our common policies.

A common set of goals emerged from the work of the President's Council on Sustainable Development. These goals express in concrete terms the elements of sustainability. They are interdependent and they reflect the belief that it is absolutely essential to seek economic prosperity, environmental protection, and social equity together. The achievement of any one goal is not enough to ensure that future generations will have at least the same opportunities to live and prosper that this generation enjoys: attainment of all the goals is necessary.[8]

A Clean Environment:

We must ensure that every person enjoys the benefits of clean air, clean water, and a healthy environment at home, at work, and at play. We must lower the number of people who live in areas that fail to meet air quality standards. We must decrease the number of people whose drinking water fails to meet national safe drinking water standards. We must continue to reduce exposure to toxic chemicals. We must reduce our citizens exposure to other environmental hazards (such as to lead and tobacco smoke) which also contributes to their health problems. We must lower the number of diseases and deaths from environmental exposures, including those from employment-related illnesses. Environmentally benign activities must be continued and expanded; environmentally harmful ones must be abandoned. We must redesign the way by which we preserve our environment into a system that is the most equitable and efficient possible. And we must protect the environmental standards which safeguard our air, water, land, and food.[9]

Economic Prosperity:

We must sustain a healthy U.S. economy that grows sufficiently to create meaningful jobs, reduce poverty, and provide the opportunity for a high quality of life for all citizens in an increasingly competitive world. The traditional measures of economic activity–gross domestic product and the unemployment rate–do not take into account the negative environmental impacts of production and consumption, nor do they gauge the incidence of poverty in society. We must develop and use new economic measures that reflect resource depletion and environmental costs, and that adequately gauge economic progress in the broadest sense. Beyond

17

reforming the methods of measuring economic progress, we must increase the number, wage level, and quality of jobs. We must, as a nation, decrease the number of people that live below the poverty line in America. Higher per capita savings and investment rates will allow America to make greater investments in the future. Increased per capita production per hour worked can also provide economic growth without increased environmental burdens. To move toward sustainability, the quality and composition of our economic activity must change. All of our goods and services must be produced with far more efficiency, so that the least energy and materials necessary are used. Waste must be considered a resource and be put to use in our industries. Products must be designed for durability, energy efficiency, ease of repair, and for recycling or composting. Technological innovations must drive these changes with better and smarter ways of meeting our needs—new ways that are good for the environment, the economy, people, and their communities![10]

An Equitable Nation:

We must ensure that all Americans are afforded justice and that they have an equal opportunity to achieve economic, environmental, and social well-being. Social equity is such an important goal that it must be a priority for every one of the other goals. However, measuring fairness and equality of opportunity throughout a population is complex. It requires measuring differences between rich and poor in a number of ways and it involves using yardsticks which are not yet available. Such measures should be developed to show whether the nation is steadily progressing toward greater equity. As a nation, we must reduce the disparities in risks and the differences in the access to benefits that our citizens face. We must, as a nation, change the income trends of recent years and work to increase the average income of the bottom 20 percent compared with that of the top 20 percent of the U.S. population. In the United States today there are the millions of people who need better nutrition and health care. There are millions of citizens who are functionally illiterate and who need additional education. And there are millions of unemployed and underemployed American who need jobs and job training. These are people who need to increase their consumption of goods and services and we must provide for them.

We must also alleviate the disproportionate environmental burdens–
such as exposure to air, water, and toxic pollution–which are borne by
different economic and social groups in America. We must insure that
there is equitable access to critical services–such as education, health
care, and community services. Finally, we must broaden opportunities for
individuals from different economic and social groups to participate in
decision-making at every level in society and politics.[11]

The Conservation of Nature:

We must use, conserve, protect, and restore our natural resources–our
land, our air, our water, and our biodiversity. We must do this in ways
that help ensure long-term social, economic, and environmental benefits
for ourselves and future generations. We must also develop measurements to reflect how well the nation is contributing to the protection of
natural systems worldwide. Overall, we must increase the health of
ecosystems, including forests, grasslands, wetlands, surface waters, and
coastal lands. We must decrease the amount of soil loss and the productivity loss due to erosion. We must lessen the harm we cause to natural
systems through chemical or biological changes. We must increase the
number of acres of healthy wetlands and of healthy native grasslands. We
must increase the percentage of our nation's forests that are allowed to
reach full maturity and diversity. We must insure that our nation's water
bodies are healthy biological communities. We must decrease the threats
to habitat and the extent of habitat conversion. We must decrease the
number of species which are threatened and endangered. We must decrease chemical releases which expose natural systems to toxics and excess nutrients. We must reduce the ecological impacts caused by the introduction and spread of exotic species. Finally, as a nation, we must res-
olutely address global environmental change and reduce our emissions of
greenhouse gases and compounds that damage the ozone layer.[12]

The Ethic of Stewardship:

We must create a widely held ethic of stewardship. As a society, we
must develop a central ethic that strongly encourages individuals, institutions, and corporations to take full responsibility for the economic, environmental, and social consequences of their actions. Quantitative measures of stewardship are difficult. What can be readily measured, however, is the use of natural resources within the United States–efficient use

and wise management are the keys to ensuring that such resources will be available for future generations. We must reduce our consumption of materials by increasing the efficiency of our materials usage. We must strive to eliminate waste in society, by reducing waste at the source, by reusing materials, by recovering useful material from our waste, and by increased recycling. We must strive for much greater energy efficiency by reducing our energy use per unit of output. Finally, we must change our usage of renewable resources to bring the rates of harvest into line with the rates of regeneration in fisheries, forests, soil, and ground-water.[13]

Sustainable Communities:

We must encourage people to work together to create healthy communities where natural and historic resources are preserved, jobs are available, and sprawl is contained, We must build neighborhoods where our citizens are secure, education is lifelong, and transportation and health care are accessible. We must ensure that all citizens have opportunities to improve the quality of their lives. We must promote community economic viability by working to increase local per capita income and employment in urban, suburban, and rural communities throughout the nation. We must insure that all Americans live in safe neighborhoods, with decreased violent crime rates. We must continue to develop our public parks and increase our urban green space, park space, and recreational areas. We must increase our investment in future generations by expanding the amount of public and private resources dedicated to children—including health care, maternal care, childhood development, and education and training. Nationally, our transportation patterns must change. We need to decrease traffic congestion and increase the use of public and alternative transportation systems. To make informed decisions, communities and individuals must have access to information. To provide for this, we must increase library use and the percentage of schools and libraries with access to the Internet and the National Information Infrastructure. We must decrease the number of homeless people in America by providing shelter to our citizens, community by community. In metropolitan areas, we must reduce the disparity in per capita income between urban areas and their suburbs. We must also strive to decrease infant mortality rates in all economic and social groups![14]

20

Civic Engagement:

Democratic societies rely on an engaged population of diverse individuals and institutions. We must create full opportunities for citizens, businesses, and communities to participate in and influence the natural resource, environmental, and economic decisions that affect them. We must work to increase citizen participation in decision-making at all levels. We need to strengthen cooperative decision-making while still allowing for individual leadership and creativity. We need to build on and expand successful efforts to build community values, public trust, and government responsiveness. We need to increase the percentage of eligible voters who cast ballots in national, state, and local elections. We need to expand citizen engagement and public trust–judged by the willingness of people in a community to cooperate for their mutual benefit. We need to work for increased citizen participation in community and civic activities such as professional and service organizations, parent-teacher associations, sporting leagues, and volunteer work. We need increased use of successful civic collaborations including public-private partnerships, community-based planning and goal-setting projects, and other consensus-building efforts.[15]

Education for Sustainability:

We must ensure that all Americans have equal access to education and lifelong learning opportunities that will prepare them for meaningful work, a high quality of life, and an understanding of the concepts involved in sustainable development. Education for sustainable development should be lifelong through integration into formal and non-formal education settings, including teacher education, continuing education, curriculum development, and worker training. To accomplish this goal, we need to increase the number of communities with infrastructure in place that allows easy access to government information, public and private research, and community right-to-know documents. We must also expand the number of curricula, materials, and training opportunities that teach the principles of sustainable development. We need national standards for sustainable development education and we need to increase the number of school systems that have adopted K-12 voluntary standards for learning about sustainable development similar to the standards developed under the National Goals 2000 initiative. The number of school

21

systems and communities with programs for lifelong learning through both formal and non-formal learning institutions should be expanded. We must strive to enhance the skills of U.S. students as measured by standardized achievement tests. And we must work to increase our high school graduation rates and the number of students who go on to college or vocational training.[16]

Population Stabilization:

Sustainability also requires a stable human population. If human numbers continue growing it will take ever more change in the quality and composition of economic activity to accomplish a given end. Continued population growth forever raises the stakes for achieving sustainability. To move toward sustainability in the future will require that we manage human numbers, resources, and wastes so that the total impact of activities in the United States is within the bounds of sustainability.

We must move toward stabilization of the U.S. population and a reduced rate of population growth in the United States and the world. The social and economic status of women within society is vital in stabilizing population. Evidence has shown that as the health and status of women improve, population pressures become more manageable. Nationally and globally, we must strive for increased educational opportunities for women and for increased income equality for equivalent work. We must also work to decrease the number of unintended pregnancies and the number of teenage pregnancies in the United States. To stabilize our population, our liberal immigration laws must be enforced to decrease the number of illegal immigrants.[17]

Global Environmental Leadership:

America must take a central leadership role in the development and implementation of global sustainable development policies, standards of conduct, and trade and foreign policies that further the achievement of sustainability. The actions taken by the United States have a significant effect on the world's environment, economy, and cultures. This nation has a long tradition of global leadership and responsibility. It is important to continue this tradition. The federal government must increase the level of U.S. international assistance for sustainable development, including official development assistance (federal money dedicated to international aid for developing nations). Federally, we must also act to increase the U.S.

contribution to the United Nations Global Environmental Facility and other environmentally targeted development aid. We must develop and use new measures for assessing progress toward sustainable development in countries receiving U.S. assistance. We must increase the level of U.S. exports or transfers of cost-effective and environmentally sound technologies to developing countries. We must increase the levels of U.S. research on global environmental problems. Finally, we must adopt national policies to lower the U.S. contribution to the greenhouse gasses which are changing the Earth's atmosphere and climate![18]

America faces enormous challenges as it approaches the 21st century. The accomplishment of this considerable list of goals for sustainable development may seem overwhelmingly difficult. It will certainly not be an easy pursuit, but it is, without question, a task worthy of the most powerful nation on Earth. Since America embarked on serious efforts to protect the environment 25 years ago, tremendous progress has been made in reducing pollution and enhancing efficiency. Nonetheless, with the world's largest economy, the United States still consumes enormous amounts of resources and generates vast amounts wastes. In addition, steady population growth is driving up the use of many resources. These factors make the job of protecting the environment, maintaining jobs and economic progress, and achieving greater equity extremely difficult.

The invaluable work done by the President's Council on Sustainable Development in formulating these goals has begun the mission of engaging the citizens of the United States in the monumental task of creating a nation and, indeed, a world which is sustainable. The following chapters delineate in detail the steps required to reach these broad goals. They are a blueprint for developing an America which is sustainable far into the future–a future in which our precious environment is protected and a future which holds economic and social progress for all citizens.

Chapter 2

Sustainable Consumption

America's national quality of life is built, in large part, on the unprecedented scale of U.S. production and consumption. The United States consumes more than 4.5 billion metric tons of materials annually to produce the goods and services that make up its unparalleled economic activity. Production and consumption account for the total mass of materials and energy that is used and makes its way through the economy, resulting in a U.S. gross domestic product of more than $6.4 trillion in 1994.[1]

There is nothing inherently wrong with a population–even a large one–meeting its material needs by consuming resources and creating wastes. Problems do arise, however, when the numbers of people and the scale, composition, and pattern of their consumption and waste combine to have negative effects on the environment, the economy, and society. Negative environmental impacts can occur because the use of a material, even in small volumes, is toxic, or has other harmful environmental consequences. Dioxin and chlorofluorocarbons are two examples of this effect. Negative environmental impacts can also occur because the scale of an activity severely disrupts or overuses the natural systems in which it occurs, though it is not inherently toxic. The use of wood, not harmful per se, may become so if forests are overharvested and ecosystems are severely disrupted in order to harvest timber. Similarly, nontoxic wastes

24

are not harmful in and of themselves. But when they become so volumi-nous that they blight entire landscapes, strain municipal governments, or contaminate groundwater beyond its cleansing capacity—then they are a serious problem. Negative impacts—environmental, economic, and social—reach a particular severity and importance when they undermine the ability of the environment, the economy, and society to continue as they have—in short, when the activities are unsustainable.

Because the United States has the world's third largest population and its largest economy—with an unparalleled scale of per capita consumption and waste—even slight changes in U.S. consumption patterns can have a significant impact on sustainability. Annual per capita gains in reducing wastes, improving resource efficiency, and promoting economic growth can translate into real reductions in environmental impact and real growth in the American standard of living. However, continued population growth steadily makes the job of reducing the environmental impact of American resource use and waste production more difficult. U.S. per capita consumption is not rising (except in plastic and paper usage), but because of population growth, total resource consumption in America is still increasing. Based on current trends, efficiency in the use of all re-sources would have to increase by more than 50 percent over the next four or five decades just to keep pace with U.S. population growth?

Managing population growth, resources, and wastes is essential to ensuring that the total impact of these factors is within the bounds of sustainability. Stabilizing the population without changing consumption and waste production patterns will not be enough, but it would make an immensely challenging task more manageable. However, without a change in U.S. consumption habits, stabilizing population will not have the desired effect of moving the country toward a sustainable economy.

Stabilization or reduction in population size is possible only on a time scale of several decades. Yet even if the U.S. population were stabi-lized tomorrow, degradation of the environment would continue because of the increasing amounts of materials consumed and the amounts and toxicity of the wastes produced. Fortunately, in contrast to the long time lag involved with population policies, appropriate incentives and other policy tools can promptly change the efficiency with which materials and energy are used. These tools have the ability to achieve real and nearly immediate reductions in environmental impact.

25

For the U.S. economy to utilize its resources on a sustainable basis will require a change in U.S. consumption patterns to reduce their overall environmental impact. The simple term *consumption* masks a great diversity of meanings. In everyday usage, consumption means the use of consumer goods by individuals in households. At a deeper level, consumption means all the resources used in an economy by all consumers, both individual and industrial, and the waste that accompanies that resource use. It means both end-products and their raw material and intermediate ingredients. This includes the total amount of resources used and wastes produced in the course of extracting, processing, manufacturing, packaging, transporting, selling, using, and discarding goods of all kinds—from houses, steel girders, or shipping pallets to automobiles, mattresses, and food. Also included are the resources and wastes involved in creating and delivering services of all kinds—from college educations to health care and television repair. Thus, total consumption is the aggregate mass of materials and energy sources that makes its way through the economy.

Unlike traditional environmental issues—even population growth—consumption of materials and energy is not customarily considered a problem; indeed, it is welcomed in nearly all quarters as a good thing. However, there is a growing global consensus that the unsustainable pattern of production and consumption—particularly in industrialized countries—is one of the major causes of the continued deterioration of the global environment. Facts support this assertion: approximately 20 percent of the world's population in the late 1980s lived in industrialized countries. These countries consumed 85 percent of the aluminum and synthetic chemicals used in the world; 80 percent of paper, iron, and steel; 75 percent of timber and energy; 60 percent of meat, fertilizer, and cement; half the world's fish and grain; and 40 percent of the fresh water. This scale of consumption ranges from three to 19 times the consumption levels of developing countries. Industrialized countries also generate most of the world's hazardous chemical wastes, 96 percent of radioactive wastes, and nearly 90 percent of all ozone-depleting chemicals.[3]

The United States plays a singular role in the consumption of natural resources, even among industrialized countries. As the world's largest economy, the United States is the largest single consumer of natural resources, including fossil fuels, and the greatest producer of wastes of all

26

kinds. Raw material use in the United States multiplied 17 times between 1900 and 1989, during which the U.S. population multiplied three times. To yield the 4.5 billion tons of materials actually used in the United States annually, about 10 billion tons of crude materials are handled. About half of that becomes waste, such as mining wastes, before any saleable products are made. Another billion tons of waste are generated in manufacturing and materials processing. About two billion tons of materials such as pesticides and fuels are dissipated into the environment during use. After consumers use a final product, it joins the 200 million tons of post-consumer waste produced in the United States annually. Americans produce the most municipal waste per capita of any country on earth. The United States is also the leading producer of greenhouse gas emissions (contributing 19 percent of total world emissions in 1991) and is the world's largest producer of toxic wastes[4]

Not surprisingly, American natural resource use per capita is high compared with average world consumption. In 1990, Americans used nearly seven times the world average in plastic and petroleum per capita; over six times the synthetic fibers and aluminum; nearly five times the industrial salt (used to salt roads, for example); four or more times the potash, industrial sand and gravel, and copper; around three times the nitrogen, iron, and steel; about twice the bauxite, phosphate, and iron ore; and one and a half times the cement. Except for petroleum, bauxite, and potash, 70 percent or more of the mineral and metal commodities consumed in the United States are also produced here. Thus, the environmental impacts of mining, processing, and transport take place domestically as well.[5]

As the world becomes increasingly aware of the environmental impact of natural resource consumption, it will look to the United States—with its large role in that problem—for leadership. It is also vital for the United States to address the sustainability of U.S. consumption out of sheer self-interest in its own domestic environmental quality. Further, studies indicate that consumption is not buying the high quality of life desired by Americans. In the last 20 years, personal consumption of goods and services has risen by an estimated 45 percent. But an Index of Social Health—which subtracts from the positive features of American life such things as child abuse, teen suicide, and the gap between rich and poor—has dropped by more than half.[6]

27

To address the enormous issue of consumption of natural resources, economists, environmentalists, and others often call for reducing the amount of materials and energy needed to make and do all the things that Americans use–whether it is industrial machinery, roads, computers, houses, cars, household appliances, transportation, or heat. This means getting more out of each unit of material and energy–making and doing everything more efficiently. Analysts of natural resource consumption agree that one overriding economic condition is the most powerful force encouraging inefficient use of natural resources. Throughout the entire life-cycle of natural resources, the resources themselves are nearly free of *cost* in traditional economic terms. Any harm done to the environment does not show up as a cost on any company's balance sheet (except when environmental laws impose a partial cost). Thus, the current prices of natural resources generally do not reflect their true environmental costs. Neither industries, retail firms, governments, nor individual consumers, therefore, have any incentive to use natural resources efficiently. The resources are artificially cheap in terms of their total environmental impact, and gross national product and other measurements of economic health do not measure the costs of environmental harm from their inefficient use.

In the absence of *internalizing* environmental costs (paying for them in the actual cost of products and services), Americans pay for environmental damage after it occurs, which is generally extremely inefficient and far more costly. Practical experience reinforces the adage that the cost of prevention is far less than the cost of the cure. It is widely agreed that a single strategy would–at less cost than environmental regulation–encourage the efficient use of natural resources, reduce waste and environmental harm of all kinds, and promote the development of technologies to improve efficiency. That strategy is to let the price of natural resources accurately reflect the ecological truth of their usage.

Prices are powerfully capable of changing the ways in which resources are used. As price goes up, the use of a resource generally goes down, although the precise extent varies. The American experience with energy during the 1970s and early 1980s is often offered as evidence of the way price-hikes reduce per capita use and promote efficiency and technological innovation. After years of paralleling economic activity, the rate of total energy use stabilized during the 1970s and early 1980s, even as the economy grew. Similarly, per capita use of all energy fell during that time, and average fuel economy (miles per gallon of gasoline) rose nearly 60 percent.[7]

There is an imperative need to create large-scale economic conditions that make it easy for educated consumers to exercise their consumption choices responsibly, and a concurrent need to educate consumers about the environmental impacts of their actions. If most people had readily available, easily understandable information, they would choose a less environmentally harmful product or service over a more harmful one. Yet it is often difficult and time consuming, and usually takes technical understanding that only a small percentage of consumers have, to decide which of several goods or services is the wiser environmental choice. Educating Americans about the environmental effects of their purchases is an uphill battle since the prices of goods and services send perverse signals by failing to reflect true environmental costs. If, however, unsustainable and environmentally harmful goods and services were to cost more than sustainable and environmentally benign ones, prices would educate people immediately and powerfully. It would provide an instantaneous and compelling environmental education to consumers of all kinds—from households to large industries and governments.

The tools for implementing such true cost pricing for natural resources are two-fold: imposing charges and reducing subsidies for environmentally damaging resource usage. Appropriate incentives and policy tools can change the efficiency with which Americans use materials and energy. Additionally, consumer education regarding the environmental consequences of their individual consumption choices is also required. Thus, there are three recommendations regarding shifting American consumption of resources onto a sustainable course.

• The United States should adopt a revenue-neutral change in federal tax policy which acts to shift taxes away from activities that promote economic progress—such as work, savings, and investment—and toward activities that lead to excessive environmental damage. The tax shift should not increase the overall tax burden on Americans, but only act to change the way revenues are raised.[8]

• There is an immediate need for a significant realignment of the present system of federal subsidies. The nation must redesign or eliminate federal subsidies that fail to incorporate the economic value of natural, environmental, and social resources into the marketplace and into governmental policies.[9]

• Finally, a full range of consumer educational incentives should be implemented. Environmental labeling and certification, media and advertising, and public education are ways to help people make wise consumption decisions.[10]

Federal Tax Policy

Government exerts tremendous influence over the direction of economic activity through the tax code. Currently, federal and state governments raise a significant portion of their revenue through taxes on individual and business incomes. Such taxes often discourage work and savings, thereby reducing national income. This, in turn, reduces the ability of the economy to create new jobs, invest in new technologies, and remain competitive in the global market. However, the tax code can be changed in ways that advance sustainable economic goals![11]

The free market often fails to incorporate the environmental costs of economic activities. This reduces efficiency and may allow excessive levels of environmental damage. Where such activities are dispersed among millions of households and enterprises, prices may influence behavior more effectively than direct regulation. At sufficient levels, taxes offer one way of affecting prices in order to discourage activities which are damaging to the environment. They are an effective way of influencing the behavior of hundreds of millions of citizens—motorists, water and energy uses, trash generators, and users of lawn and farm chemicals—whose activities result in significant environmental problems.

There is a pressing need for alignment of tax policy with the goals of sustainable development. Although special tax provisions may have been economically justified at some time in the nation's development, they may no longer be serving their original purposes and instead may have unintended side effects that run counter to national economic and environmental objectives. A tax system should be designed to raise sufficient revenues without discouraging capital formation, job creation, environmental improvement, and social equity. Currently, the federal government raises more than $1 trillion per year, nearly 90 percent of which is raised by taxing wages and personal and corporate income. Since tax policies influence individual and institutional investment and consumption decisions, an effective use of the tax system could be a powerful tool in meeting the challenges of sustainable development. These challenges could be met, in part, by shifting some of the nation's taxes to activities and forms of consumption that are economically bad for society—inefficiency, waste, and pollution—and away from those that are economically good—employment, income, and savings and investment![12]

Environmental fees, charges, and other economic instruments are often proposed as part of broader tax reform proposals aimed at shifting taxes from income and savings to consumption in its traditional economic sense—the use of goods and services to meet current wants. A broad *tax shift*, as it is usually called, has the benefit of encouraging savings and investment. The U.S. savings rate is currently at 3.6 percent of gross domestic product, very low in comparison with that of other industrialized nations. Savings and investment are the principal sources of funds for financing the machinery, buildings, and other capital investments that drive economic activities. Savings and investment also drive technological developments to raise productivity and develop alternatives to material uses that harm the environment. Indeed, as sustainable development depends heavily on technological innovation, it depends heavily on savings and investment.

Of all 1991 federal tax receipts, 42 percent came from payroll taxes, 41 percent from personal income taxes, and 9 percent from corporate income taxes. (Corporate income taxes ultimately tax investments and capital gains, because the costs are borne by stockholders). Nearly all taxes work to discourage the activities being taxed and encourage alternatives. Similarly, taxes on payroll make workers more expensive to employers, therefore inducing employers to find alternatives such as layoffs, heavier work loads on a smaller workforce, automation, or moving operations overseas. Taxes on income from investments lower after-tax returns, encouraging people to seek tax shelters or to invest less. Thus, taxes on income, payroll, and corporate income have economic costs in the form of lost income and investment.[13]

World Resources Institute (WRI) analysts looked at the effects of a tax shift that would tax resources and pollution instead of income and investment. They found that, for every tax dollar shifted in this manner, the economy could gain a further 45-80 cents beyond the revenue replaced—

31

in the form of additional work and investment and in environmental damages averted.

Without the disincentive from taxes on work and investment, more people would work and make investments, thus adding to income and investment. With the disincentive instead applied to pollution and resource use, pollution and environmental harm would be discouraged. The WRI study calculates benefits in the aggregate. Individuals and firms in some businesses would experience losses, as with any change in tax policy. The long-term effect, however, is decidedly positive. Thus, environmental taxes meet the requirement of all taxes that they be economically rational, or raise revenue at the least overall cost to the economy![14]

Environmental taxes must also meet standards of equity, administrative feasibility, and stability of the revenue stream required of any tax. These concerns are real. A system of environmental taxes would require a change in administration and enforcement, as well as coordination among now separate agencies dealing with natural resources, the environment, and taxes. The new taxes would, however, resemble existing excise and sales taxes, and both federal and state tax authorities have considerable experience with those. There is some criticism of environmental taxes on the grounds that stability of revenue cannot be guaranteed. But careful framing—including gradual increases in tax rates, periodic adjustments, and changes in the targets of taxes—can counter these concerns.

Similar treatment of taxpayers in similar situations and taxation according to ability to pay are also issues of particular concern. Provisions of any tax shift should compensate for *regressivity* (the higher proportional taxation of lower-income taxpayers). Rebates to individuals and businesses disproportionately affected by a tax could be offered. Income and payroll tax credits or deductions could be provided. Tax revenues could be invested in worker training or other appropriate compensatory programs, particularly for the poor who do not pay taxes. Environmental taxes imposed as part of a comprehensive tax shift should be revenue neutral, replacing taxes on income, payroll, and savings on a dollar-for-dollar basis. Environmental taxes introduced on a gradual basis should also be made revenue neutral by substituting for selected existing taxes, again dollar-for-dollar.

Such a tax shift represents a significant change in many quarters, requiring substantial consumer and taxpayer education and considerable administrative realignment. But no other single policy step could so effectively and at so low a cost move the country toward more efficient–and eventually sustainable–resource use. Since such a proposal is the most powerful option available for moving significantly toward sustainable resource use in the United States, there must be much thoughtful analysis and political discussion to work out the details and make such a policy a political possibility.

For a tax shift to become real, more fully developed rationales, public participation, and the support of the business community are required. Such a tax shift is based on the *polluter-pays* principle–that those who use the resources or benefit from the pollution created should ultimately be the ones who pay the full cost of their use. This principle receives broad public acceptance as a fair and efficient approach to environmental policy. In addition, market-based economic instruments often receive support from both sides of the political aisle.

To be able to reduce one's tax bill by saving resources or developing a new technology for increasing materials and energy efficiency–rather than by working and earning less–makes economic sense for individuals, corporations, and the nation as a whole.

Action: Change Tax Policies:

The federal government should reorient fiscal policy to shift the tax burden from labor and investment toward consumption, particularly consumption of natural resources, virgin materials, and goods and services that pose significant environmental risks. In this process, the federal government should seek replacement revenue measures that encourage maximum economic, energy, and material-use efficiency. Finally, a new system of taxation should be not be regressive, but rather be progressive–that is, not place a higher proportionate tax burden on lower income people. In order to promote a more progressive system of taxation, the federal government should offset the impact of consumption taxes on the poor with corresponding reductions in payroll taxes.

Federal market-based environmental policy instruments already exist in the United States, though they were usually adopted to raise revenue rather than to achieve environmental ends. The federal tax code currently allows tax credits for the production of ethanol and other renewable fuels. The tax code also imposes excise taxes on gas-guzzling cars and chemicals that deplete the ozone layer. There are U.S. taxes on crude oil and imported petroleum products to finance the Oil Spill Liability Trust Fund and Superfund. There are charitable deductions against income or estate taxes for donations of land or conservation easements, which work to lower income taxes. Perhaps the best-known economic instrument of federal environmental policy is the tradable permit plan for sulfur emissions developed under the Clean Air Act Amendments of 1990.[15]

State and local jurisdictions also impose a number of fees and related charges that affect the environment. Numerous states levy severance taxes on petroleum and other mineral resource extraction, have deposit-refund plans for beverage bottles, and impose packaging taxes. Many municipalities impose user fees for local solid waste disposal and offer recycling incentives. The precise forms and degree of these taxes vary greatly.[16]

At the same time, both federal and state tax codes encourage a number of environmentally damaging activities and discourage beneficial ones by lowering production costs and distorting the true price of resource-related activity. At the federal level, for example, farmers can deduct from their taxable income part of the value of groundwater which is withdrawn for irrigation usage–thus encouraging use beyond an aquifer's annual recharge rate. Employers can provide free-parking to employees as a tax-free fringe benefit–encouraging more driving. Businesses engaged principally in natural resource development or processing may avoid the corporate tax. Owners of interests in fuel and non-fuel minerals can take *percentage depletion* deductions against taxable income from resource extraction enterprises–deductions that may ultimately exceed the owner's total capital investment. The percentage depletion allowance has enormous reach. The Office of Management and Budget has estimated that the federal government loses more than $1 billion annually to this deduction, which partially pays for production of some of the country's most toxic minerals, among them lead, mercury, and asbestos.[17]

Such a tax shift–which must be designed to minimize any adverse impacts on vulnerable segments of the population–would promote sustainable development by stimulating economic growth and protecting the environment. Ideally, a tax system should promote economic growth and jobs in a socially equitable manner, while discouraging pollution and other forms of inefficiency. Substantial progress in reaching these objectives can be made through revenue-neutral improvements in the tax system—changes that shift the ways revenues are raised without increasing overall tax obligations.

Tax policy must ensure that individuals and families at different income levels are treated as fairly as possible. Taxes should not place a disproportionate burden on lower income individuals and families. There are significant limitations of some options—such as the value-added tax or a national sales tax—in meeting this criterion. Federal tax policy must address social equity to be consistent with the goals of sustainable development.

The tax system must promote savings and investment, employment, and economic growth. Any tax shift should encourage savings, private investment, and job creation. Tax-based policy should also be more skillfully employed to provide for enhanced environmental performance. Market mechanisms, such as pollution taxes and taxes on consumption, warrant further evaluation. Any tax shift will need to be implemented gradually. A shift in taxes will not eliminate the need for legally enforceable environmental standards or agreements. But such a shift in taxation should increase the overall efficiency of national efforts to improve environmental quality.

The United States must begin the long-term process of shifting to tax policies that—without increasing overall tax burdens—encourage employment and economic opportunity and discourage environmentally damaging production and consumption decisions.[18]

National Commission on Tax Shifting: Federal, state, and local governments should begin designing and implementing tax policies that better reflect environmental costs and help achieve sustainable development goals.

A national commission should be established to review the effect of federal tax policies on the goals of sustainable development. The commission should have responsibility to conduct an explicit assessment of alternative tax policies and, in particular, the assessment of opportunities for increased use of pollution taxes while reducing reliance on more

35

traditional income taxes. The commission should make recommendations to the President and Congress on tax reform initiatives that are consistent with the goals of economic prosperity, a healthy environment, and social equity.

Modifications to the U.S. Tax Code would result in short-term dislocations, but would provide long-term benefits for the nation as a whole. The commission should evaluate and act on remedial or preventive steps to mitigate any short-term effects. Although environmental taxes are not, in principle, more regressive than the existing tax structure, they should be designed to minimize adverse impacts on vulnerable segments of the population, and part of the revenue generated should also serve equity considerations. Other revenue should be used to reduce burdensome income, capital, and employment taxes.[19]

Federal Subsidy Policy

The counterpart to imposing charges or taxes is to remove subsidies that keep the price of environmentally harmful activities and products artificially low. Federal law currently encourages environmentally destructive activities with subsidies outside the tax code. Below-cost timber sales and timber road building, below-market grazing fees, the treatment of hard-rock mining under the 1872 Mining Law, below-market charges for irrigation water, below-market charges for federal power, below-cost charges for recreational uses, agricultural commodity subsidies, many subsidies for highway construction and water projects, certain energy research and development programs, and federally underwritten flood, crop, and disaster insurance are among the programs that distort the cost of natural resources. All of these subsidies shift part of the true cost of doing resource-related business from the resource developer or user to the taxpayer.[20]

Any federal subsidy program should provide a reasonable return to taxpayers. Many federal subsidy programs, however, no longer effectively serve valid public policy goals. Many are economically unjustified, no longer benefiting the target groups or activities that originally needed federal assistance. Many directly conflict with other federal policies and objectives (including that of deficit reduction) but continue to exist because of the political efforts of well-organized interest groups. At times these subsidies promote excessive, inefficient, and environmentally damaging use of natural resources.

There is an immediate need to redesign or eliminate federal subsidies that fail to incorporate the economic value of natural, environmental, and social resources into prices and governmental policies. Steps must be taken to reduce and eventually eliminate inefficient and environmentally harmful government subsidies, particularly those related to natural resource extraction and use. This will help achieve the broader national goals of minimizing subsidies, reducing the deficit, and moving private investment into sustainable processes, products, and practices.

Action: Reform Subsidy Policies:

America should establish a national commission to review all major federal subsidy programs. The commission should review all existing subsidies and determine if there remains a national need for the subsidies to continue. The commission should evaluate and examine existing federal subsidy programs related, but not limited to, agricultural support programs, energy investment and production, irrigation, transportation, timbering, mining, public lands use, and federal insurance. The commission should recommend to the President a list of subsidies that fail to meet this test and which should be phased out or rapidly eliminated. For those subsidies determined to still meet a national need, the Commission should set criteria to be used by the administering agency to bring the program into line with the goals of sustainable development. Any remaining subsidies should be made subject to a sunset or review clause that would require the appropriate government agency to ensure on a regular basis that these subsidies are consistent with national sustainable development goals; otherwise they would be eliminated. Finally, the commission should develop and publish a list—which is accessible and understandable to the public—of existing federal subsidies and their beneficiaries.

America should eliminate government subsidies that encourage activities which are inconsistent with economic, environmental, and social goals. Unlike the tax reform proposal above, subsidies have been the subject of analysis and debate. Their likely economic, environmental, and equity effects are relatively well-known. Most of these programs have been the subject of repeated critiques, reform recommendations, and proposals for change by both Congress and the Executive Branch. Proposals to reform subsidies have been blocked in the past by intractable political barriers that have proven very difficult to overcome. Hence, the subsidy commission should also evaluate alternative mechanisms for addressing these political hurdles.

The elimination of subsidies would result in short-term dislocations, but would provide long-term benefits for the nation as a whole. The commission should evaluate and act on remedial or preventive steps to lessen any short-term effects. The practical effects of various kinds of subsidies conflict directly with the goal of national sustainable development. Eliminating subsidy programs or significantly redesigning them to more accurately target beneficiaries will reduce economic waste and environmental damage. As this nation moves toward a more sustainable society, it is absolutely essential to scrutinize existing subsidies and to determine their efficiency in advancing the goals of sustainable development. In addition, the federal government could achieve billions of dollars of annual savings. These savings could be used to finance higher priority objectives, such as deficit reduction and tax relief?[1]

Consumer Education

Environmental taxes, subsidy reform, and other economic instruments, however, represent a dramatic change from the status quo and will take time to implement. To move the country toward more efficient use of resources in the meantime and to enlist the considerable power of individuals—most of them eager to do environmental good—it is important to provide clear and understandable consumer education. To enable consumers to make wise choices in the marketplace and to build popular support for difficult political changes in the future, it is important to make available the full range of information required for good environmental citizenship.

Individual Americans are eager to make a positive difference in the environment with their own actions. In recent polls, the vast majority of Americans have indicated their interest in doing more in their daily lives to protect the environment. The public also fully realizes that protecting the environment will require major changes. Thus, in addition to tax and subsidy reform, another way toward sustainable consumption is a comprehensive program to educate consumers—both individuals and businesses–of the environmental consequences of their consumption choices.

Every American can contribute to sustainable development by understanding each individual's ability and responsibility to conserve resources and prevent waste. To assist consumers, the labeling of consumer goods to explain their environmental impact–as nutritional labels now explain the dietary effect of food products–is one powerful informational technique for enabling individuals to make a difference to the environment. The establishment of federal *eco-labeling* procedures–through a nongovernmental, third-party group that would set criteria and standards for labeling certain goods as environmentally superior–is one way. Educating citizens about consumer practices and choices that will lead to sustainable lifestyles is another.

Action: Adopt Product Labeling:

Perhaps the greatest leverage individuals can have on the environment is through their hundreds of billions of dollars of annual purchasing power. According to a recent poll, 80 percent of consumers say they think of environmental considerations when shopping for groceries and household products. However, even experts have a hard time making informed choices in a clamorous marketplace. It is very difficult for an individual consumer to buy *green*. An examination of hundreds of supermarket products over the past five years revealed recently that although more companies are using labels designating products *recyclable* or *biodegradable*, the terms are used more to attract consumers than to inform accurately.[22]

Terms such as *environmentally friendly* are used a third more often in 1995 than they were in 1992, according to a recent study. And yet the precise meaning of these terms is far from clear. Norman Dean of Green Seal has found examples of telephones labeled *foam-free*, when ordinary telephones use no foam; of light bulbs labeled as *using 10 percent less energy* when they also produce 10 percent less light than the comparison light bulb. All of this contributes to enormous consumer confusion, if not cynicism.[23]

Even without confusing or deceptive claims by manufacturers, it is difficult and time consuming for an individual to make an informed choice. The complexity of weighing all the environmental issues

39

involved in whether to choose cloth or disposable diapers is a good example. Disposable diapers have a large impact in terms of materials and landfill space used. On the other hand, delivering and washing cloth diapers has other environmental impacts in the form of detergents, water use, and air pollution.

A proper analysis should consider environmental impacts from the entire life-cycle of a commodity: whether the paper used to make disposable diapers was recycled or came from virgin materials, and, if from virgin materials, whether from a forest managed sustainably; whether cloth diapers were made from cotton grown with heavy pesticide use, or in an area where water is scarce; and whether raw materials growers or processors and manufacturers have fair hiring practices. It is difficult for experts to determine the right choice, let alone a harried parent hurrying through a grocery store with no time to spare for careful thought.

Solving these problems requires holding manufacturers and advertisers to standards of honesty and fairness. Another requirement is to develop life-cycle analyses with which to judge the environmental impact of products and label them accordingly—usually by stating whether a product meets a particular standard of acceptability. Such a label would parallel the popular nutritional labels now found on food in grocery stores.

Twenty-one countries have adopted *green* or *eco*-labeling, including Germany's *Blue Angel*, Canada's *Environmental Choice*, and Japan's *EcoMark* programs. The European Union and China are both developing programs. In the United States, a fledgling private program exists under the group *Green Seal*.[24]

Labeling products so that buyers can know the full environmental impact of a product throughout its entire life-cycle is both a powerful force for wise consumption practices and desired by consumers frustrated by existing product claims. Environmental labeling programs can provide consumers with an immediately available, objective, and accurate evaluation of a product's environmental impact. They also provide an incentive to manufacturers to meet the standards—to make products with environmental impact deemed technically acceptable by an unbiased, third-party entity.[25]

Developing Eco-labeling: The United States Environmental Protection Agency (U.S. EPA) should establish a collaborative initiative to define appropriate product categories and develop criteria and standards for them, based on life-cycle analysis and assessment. The initiative would involve government experts (particularly those at the National Institute for Standards and Technology), private industry representatives, third-party entities (for example, Underwriter Laboratories and Green Seal), and the public (including representatives of environmental and consumer organizations).

The federal government should support the development of a third-party certification program capable of certifying that products meet predetermined environmental standards. The program should also be authorized to award a national seal of approval. A public-private partnership should be established to develop criteria bases for labeling certain goods and services as environmentally superior. An appropriate third-party, non-governmental entity working with public and private experts should certify these products as a voluntary incentive program. After a necessary development phase, the program would be self-financed.

Eco-labeling involves two steps. Based on life-cycle analysis, the first step involves establishing product criteria and setting standards that products must meet to be deemed environmentally acceptable or superior. Using the diaper example, analysts would choose criteria such as the percent of virgin material, the percent of secondary material, the production methods of the virgin material, and the compostability of the diapers–to name just a few. Then, analysts would set the standard that a product must meet to win approval. For diapers, these standards might be that they are composed of no more than 40 percent virgin material and that they are completely biodegradable within 10 years of disposal, under certain specified composting conditions.

For the second step, experts–often independent entities such as the International Standards Organization, the International Society for the Testing of Materials, or Underwriters Laboratory–test and certify actual products. At this stage–continuing with the diaper example–analysts would evaluate Pampers, Huggies, Luvs, and other brands of both disposable and cloth diapers to see which meet the standards and merit an environmental seal of approval. The group of experts that certifies and awards the seal of approval for products should be an independent, or third party-entity–neither manufacturers nor the government.

An effective program must also have certain other characteristics. It must involve all key interests (for example: businesses, consumer and environmental groups, and governments). Its certification and assessment processes must be open, public, and involve peer review. Its data must be independently verifiable. It must be accompanied by a public education program. Its standards and criteria must be updated as science and technology change. Finally, the cost of obtaining the seal of approval must not keep small and medium-sized companies from participating.

Additional related methods are also available for providing information to consumers about the environmental consequences of, or risks associated with, their market choices. These programs can also lead to behavioral and purchasing changes on the part of concerned consumers. Some examples of this type of program which have been used include radon and lead testing and labeling programs such as required under California's Proposition 65. Another type of program relies on public disclosure of information on facilities' environmental releases and the off-site transfer of certain toxic wastes (e.g., the Toxic Release Inventory). This information encourages continuous environmental improvement and also provides industry with a vehicle for enhancing its public image. These programs are all powerful strategies for educating the consuming public. In addition, they allow U.S. manufacturers to compete in a marketplace which increasingly emphasizes clean products, as the labeling programs of Canada, Germany, and Japan attest.[26]

Action: Assist Consumer Education:

There should be a coordinated national effort to educate society in numerous ways about consumer practices and choices that will lead to sustainable consumption patterns and lifestyles. Initiatives by the mass media to highlight sustainable lifestyles will help. Greater advertiser responsibility in the promotion of environmentally sound products and services will also assist consumers in making informed choices. Education to encourage financial literacy and community-based education initiatives will also improve the abilities of consumers to use their purchasing power to make a difference.[27]

Mass Media: Mass media powerfully drives consumption patterns in the United States and is an equally powerful force for changing consumer behavior. Stories showing wealth become models of a desirable lifestyle to many viewers. The media could instead be an influential source of education about sustainable ways of living. The media industry–through innovative partnerships with government, business, and non-profit groups–should be encouraged to incorporate sustainable lifestyle practices into storylines and advertisements.[28]

Advertiser Responsibility: In an average American life, an entire year is spent watching television commercials. By the time they graduate from high school, typical American teenagers have been exposed to 360,000 advertisements. Thousands of consumer messages a day tell Americans to buy things. Advertisements are often the only source of information a consumer has about a product and the complex information that is required for a consumer to make an informed decision about the environmental impact of a product. There is an unmet need for educating consumers to evaluate advertisers' claims so that they can distinguish emotional manipulation from objective information to allow them to make prudent, considered choices. To ensure that consumers are receiving accurate information on which to make informed sustainable choices, the print and television advertising community should be encouraged to adopt an ethic that insures the accuracy of claims regarding the environmental impact of products.

To support the honesty of eco-labeling, the Federal Trade Commission (FTC) and other appropriate federal agencies should establish the necessary means to prevent deceptive environmental marketing claims and ensure the integrity of a national eco-labeling program. In 1992, the FTC undertook to hold advertisers and manufacturers to a standard of honesty and fairness, issuing *Guides for the Use of Environmental Marketing Claims*. These guides describe various terms such as *biodegradable, compostable, recyclable,* and *ozone safe.* Marketers are asked to avoid certain claims likely to be misleading and to qualify other claims to avoid deception–the guides are not yet legally enforceable; they provide guidance only.[29]

The FTC is currently gathering public comment on whether to modify the guides. It would aid consumer education to strengthen the FTCs efforts, in particular by standardizing definitions. An internal code of

43

ethics, developed and adopted by advertisers themselves would also improve advertising's ability to educate consumers.[30]

Financial Literacy: There is also a need for formal and informal education, adult education, and other public education to teach individual fiscal responsibility. Such education will assist individuals to live within their means. A citizenry that values savings and knows how to save money can understand sustainability on a personal level.

As a matter of economic definition, whatever is saved is not used for consumption. Yet savings in the United States are abysmally low and falling, while current consumption is high and often financed with rising levels of debt. The average 50-year-old American has saved $2,300 for retirement. About half of all grocery and hardware store purchases are made on impulse. In 1990, 83 percent of disposable income was spent on personal debt payments. Consumer debt increased 140 percent in the 1980s; in 1993, 4.2 percent of disposable personal income was allotted to savings, compared to 8.6 percent in 1973.[31]

A higher savings rate would contribute not only to individual financial soundness, it would also buttress the national need to increase savings for financing economic prosperity and technological change. And it would empower individuals to live within their means–sustainably.

Education departments and educators should reform their K-12 home economics and related curricula to place a greater emphasis on time and money management. This will help Americans better understand the importance of saving and to give them the tools for sound financial management and for living within their means.[32]

Work Patterns: Another way of moderating high-consumption lifestyles in the United States would also aid in job creation, reduce employee stress, and allow Americans to turn to non-material sources of satisfaction. This innovation is modifying work schedules for greater flexibility.

Working Americans today typically spend 163 more hours on the job annually than they did in 1969, contributing to a pervasive sense of being rushed and overworked. Nearly 70 percent of Americans would like to "slow down and live a more relaxed life." Seventy percent of Americans earning over $30,000 a year say–in response to questioning–that they would give up a day's pay each week for a day of free time. Nearly half of Americans earning less than $20,000 would make the same trade. A third of American workers would forego raises and promotions to spend more time with their families. Greater flexibility in work schedules would allow workers to take their wage increases in the form of time rather than money–a trade-off that a large percentage of Americans would like to make, and one that would also contribute to a more sustainable way of life.[33]

The U.S. Department of Labor, in cooperation with the U.S. Department of Commerce, should analyze working trends in the United States and recommend options for greater flexibility and reduced hours of work. The report should explore ways that private industry could offer workers the option of wage increases in the form of time, rather than money[34]

Community-Based Education: Education programs based in communities are capable of conveying the message of sustainability particularly relevant to individuals at the local level. Landfill closings, difficulties over siting new ones, water shortages, congested highways, and fiscal constraints on new construction have already sparked programs to educate individuals about recycling, composting, water and energy conservation, ride-sharing, and other strategies for sustainable ways of living. The local results are readily apparent once programs are in place.

Further efforts at community-based consumer education are an appropriate focus of public education for sustainability. Municipal governments, utility companies, local businesses, and community-based citizen groups should expand efforts to develop information, financial incentives, educational materials, and programs to educate citizens at the community level in recycling, composting, water conservation, energy conservation, ride-sharing, and other aspects of sustainable ways of living.[35]

Initiative: Community Environmental Education:

Many of the resources consumed in the United States are used in the home. The *Global Action Plan for the Earth* (GAP) is a grassroots effort providing individuals and communities with the motivation, support, and hands-on experience they need to live their lives more sustainably. GAP believes that the primary means for shifting America onto a sustainable path is for households to make changes in the way they live.

To date, approximately 7,500 households in 12 countries have participated on GAP *Eco Teams*. GAP reports that, on average, these households sent 42 percent less garbage to landfills, used 25 percent less water, cut 16 percent of their carbon dioxide output, and used 16 percent less fuel for transportation.[36]

A powerful strategy for encouraging American efficiency is to rework economic incentives so that the environmental costs of resource use and waste production are clearly evident in the price of goods and services. Restructuring taxes and eliminating environmentally harmful subsidies are some of the policies available to the government for adjusting prices. But individual actions are also capable of mitigating the environmental impact of resource use and waste production. Consumers need information, services, and opportunities to allow them to make informed choices in their selection and use of goods and services. With these tools provided, consumers will begin to base their purchasing decisions on a clear understanding of the environmental, economic, and social implications of their choices. In doing so, they will begin personally building the foundations of a sustainable America.

Chapter 3

Sustainable Production

The environmental burden created by U.S. economic activities is not currently sustainable, neither nationally nor globally. That simple fact must serve as the foundation for the reform of U.S. economic and environmental policy. The goal of sustainable development is to attain a safe and clean environment while increasing the quality and quantity of job opportunities in all communities and protecting the health and social well-being of all people. These are not mutually exclusive goals. They can, and must, be reached together.

America's businesses face unprecedented challenges today as they compete in the global marketplace. Improved technologies, production processes, and management approaches are being developed every day; and businesses must incorporate these changes into their operations and products if they wish to remain competitive. At the same time, they are faced with meeting evolving environmental standards and with the demand to provide the public with affordable products and services that serve their needs. Many businesses and individuals have shown that it is possible to adopt environmentally responsible practices while improving their economic competitiveness. By addressing the environmental impacts of their activities as a priority in their decision-making, they have paved the way toward a new standard of responsibility.

Sustainable America

Today, many businesses are demonstrating that environmentally-sound business practices can make good economic sense. They are improving product quality and production efficiency, reducing energy needs, and minimizing the costs associated with pollution. A 1996 study by the World Resources Institute noted that electric utilities now produce twice as many kilowatt hours per ton of emissions as they did when the Clean Air Act was passed in 1972. And the pulp and paper industry produces seven times as much paper per ton of water pollution as it did before the Clean Water Act was passed in 1972. These efficiency gains have greatly improved overall productivity while also reducing the impacts of pollution on human health, the environment, and natural resources.[1]

A number of innovative economic strategies and approaches must be used in order to integrate environmental and social considerations into America's economic framework. Extended product responsibility, eco-efficient industry, and market incentives are some of the proposals that head the list. Market mechanisms are not the right solution for every problem, any more than technology-based standards are the right answer in all cases. Science, economics, and societal values must all be considered in making decisions. Problems cannot be addressed in isolation. Economic prosperity, environmental quality, and social equity all need to be pursued simultaneously. The following framework is proposed in order to bring American economic policy in line with the core concepts of sustainable development.

• America should adopt a national policy of *extended product responsibility*. Government should encourage this type of shared responsibility for the environmental impact of products. This responsibility should be shared between the designers, suppliers, manufacturers, distributors, users, and disposers of products. This new practice would enhance the current approach to waste reduction, resource conservation, and pollution prevention by treating products holistically and looking at their entire lifecycle. This approach should also incorporate innovative policies to enhance new technological ideas.[2]

• Programs to streamline packaging, to implement weight-based municipal fees for collecting garbage, and to spur proper handling of household toxics are innovative ways to address consumer waste reduction.[3]

48

- Market incentives should be used as a vital tool in environmental management. Market incentives, such as tradeable permits and environmental fees, should be used to achieve environmental goals and stimulate technological innovation. This approach can substantially influence the behavior of firms, governments, and individuals.[4]

- Government procurement policies should be developed at all levels to increase the use of environmentally preferable products and to provide an incentive for the creation of products that exceed standards for environmental superiority.[5]

- National and state policies should be developed which support the concept of *eco-efficiency* in manufacturing and industry. These concepts should be integrated into all phases of business regulation and practices.[6]

- There should be a significant increase in information collection and dissemination regarding environmental management. There must be a national effort to efficiently provide high quality information. Good information will enable informed decision-making and support the transition to a sustainable economy.[7]

- The nation needs to change the standard of economic success by improving its national income accounting. Environmental concepts must be integrated into the U.S. system of national accounting. The nation should augment the accounting of the gross domestic product by implementing a system of national accounts that measures sustainable development through the integrated tracking of the environment, economy, and the natural resource base.[8]

- The United States needs a clear and concise set of sustainable development indicators. The development of a full set of national sustainable development indicators will allow the nation to monitor the nation's economic, environmental, and social trends. This will allow the public and decision-makers to verify society's progress toward sustainable development goals.[9]

- Finally, access to capital for environmental management and protection needs to be expanded. America needs to develop innovative financing programs to improve access to capital for small businesses and communities so that they may more easily invest in cleaner and more efficient practices. Existing programs within the U.S. EPA and U.S. Small Business Administration (SBA) should be coordinated in order to foster investment in technologies and practices that improve resource efficiency, reduce waste, and add value to local economies![10]

Human well-being is affected by the availability and quality of educational and job opportunities and by environmental, health, economic, and social impacts on individuals and communities. To improve the social well-being of all its citizens, America must ensure that the negative impacts of any of these proposed changes are not borne disproportionately by any segment of society. As each of these sustainable development policies are implemented, their implementation must be done in such a way as to eliminate existing inequities; maximize the quality and quantity of job opportunities; and minimize any negative health impacts on workers, customers, and the community. The policies must be developed to maximize communication between individuals at industrial facilities, local governments and other organizations, and the general public. As they are implemented, their full social costs and benefits must be evaluated to determine their effects on society.

Extended Product Responsibility

Environmental programs that focus on one point in the product chain have often resulted in resource conservation and pollution prevention. However, further advances will be limited as long as the approach taken continues to separate all stages of economic activity, including product design, manufacture, use, and disposal. For example, when looking to reduce air emissions of a particular chemical associated with a product, the production plant is often not the only place to examine. Sometimes, more cost-effective and larger reductions can be found by analyzing emissions from the transportation and distribution of the product.

A unified system of extended product responsibility should be developed which can transform the present dispersed approach to waste reduction, resource conservation, and pollution prevention. This new approach is based on the principle of shared responsibility. Extended product responsibility is an emerging practice that considers the entire life of a product–from design to disposal–to identify the best opportunities for resource conservation and pollution prevention. Under extended product responsibility, accountability for the environmental impacts of products and waste is shared among manufacturers, suppliers, users (both public and private), and disposers of products.[11]

Such a lifecycle approach works to capture the upstream environmental effects–those associated with raw material use and the effects from production and distribution. It also reflects downstream effects–those associated with product use, recycling, and disposal. Lifecycle approaches can yield better environmental results at a lower cost. This approach also addresses the underlying influence of consumer needs and preferences, government procurement, and the role played by those in the entire chain of production and distribution. Under the principle of extended product responsibility, manufacturers, suppliers, users, and disposers of products share responsibility for the environmental effects of products and waste.

The goal of extended product responsibility is to identify those parties and actions with the greatest ability to reduce the environmental and energy impact of specific products. In some cases, this may be the producer of raw materials; in other cases, the end user![2]

Through a mix of incentives, information, education, and institutional support, this new approach would motivate individuals, governments, and corporations to recognize, understand, and act on their responsibility to advance the nation's sustainable development goals. Creating an innovative system of extended product responsibility would improve the current fragmented approach to waste reduction, resource conservation, and pollution prevention. When there are missing links in the chain of responsibility, waste and inefficiency result. Currently, communities bear the greatest burden for the disposal of hazardous products. Similarly, decisions made upstream in the chain by suppliers can reduce a manufacturer's emissions and wastes and improve profitability. Sharing responsibility implies not only understanding and communicating the environmental effects of product development but also acting collectively to reduce them. Further, government agencies–the nation's largest consumers–can use their market leverage to encourage U.S. manufacturers to increase the efficiency of their use of materials. Purchasing specifications can give manufacturers strong incentives to create products that result in fewer negative environmental effects while maintaining similar product performance.

A series of demonstration projects that illustrate new models of shared responsibility throughout different product systems could provide valuable experience with extended product responsibility. While extended product responsibility should constitute a national priority, actions of states and localities are integral to its success. Ultimately, sharing responsibility for environmental effects would transform the marketplace into one driven by more efficient use of resources; cleaner products and technologies; more efficient and more competitive manufacturing; safer storage, shipping, and handling of materials; improved relations between communities and companies; improved recycling and recovery; and responsible consumer choices.

Action: Implement Extended Product Responsibility:

The United States should adopt a voluntary system that ensures responsibility for the environmental effects throughout a product's lifecycle by all those involved in the lifecycle. The greatest opportunity for extended product responsibility rests with those throughout the commerce chain—designers, suppliers, manufacturers, distributors, users, and disposers—who are in a position to practice resource conservation and pollution prevention at a lower cost.[13]

Developing Models and Identifying Categories: Companies, trade associations, wholesalers, retailers, consumer groups, and other private parties can develop models of shared product responsibility. Industry should solicit the participation of government and environmental representatives in developing voluntary product responsibility models or demonstration project proposals. Each demonstration project proposal should identify critical links in the product chain, opportunities for significant improvements, and key participants that need to be involved to prevent pollution or conserve resources within each product category under consideration.

The following product categories should be addressed: products that utilize non-renewable/non-recoverable resources; products that pose high risks and the potential for hazardous exposure; products that contribute significantly to environmental degradation; and products that contribute significantly to waste entering the air, land, or water.

Within each product category, an effort should be made to identify the parties and links in the chain of commerce with the greatest opportunities for improvement. Where parties voluntarily assume responsibility, efforts should be made to secure protection against unjustified extensions of product liability. There is also a need to establish goals for pollution prevention, resource conservation, and waste reduction for each product category.[14]

Product Responsibility Panel and Projects: A joint committee involving industry and non-profit groups should recommend to the President individuals to be appointed to a *Product Responsibility Panel*. This panel would review and select demonstration projects, help identify appropriate participants, and provide advice on the execution of the demonstration projects themselves. Demonstrations should include companion training and educational programs to communicate the objectives of the demonstrations and principles of extended product responsibility. The Product Responsibility Panel should help identify means of conducting effective monitoring, evaluation, and analysis of the projects' progress and possible links with other sustainable development initiatives. It should also help coordinate sound economic and environmental analyses to assist in transferring the lessons from local demonstration projects to regional and national policies. The panel should have a balanced representation of all parties with interests in the lifecycle of a product, including its supply, procurement, consumption, and disposal. By immediately identifying product categories for demonstration projects, U.S. industry—in cooperation with government agencies and the environmental community—could begin to carry out the new models of shared responsibility to produce rapid and measurable results. Measures to protect against the extension of product liability would encourage the voluntary assumption of responsibility by businesses.

Demonstration projects should be undertaken to implement extended responsibility for several product categories. The goal of the projects should be to reduce the environmental impact of various stages of the product lifecycles including manufacture, transport, and post-consumer waste. Demonstration projects should be undertaken in the identified categories in a variety of regions and industries.[15]

Developing National and Regional Policy: The practice of extended product responsibility would then begin on a larger scale. Academic or institutional researchers should monitor the demonstration projects to provide an independent analysis of the projects' successes. This feedback and the lessons learned would then be utilized in developing national and regional policies. Evaluation and policy refinement would continue as the practice of extended product responsibility expands to an ever broader array of product and waste categories. Following evaluation of the projects, the federal government, private companies, and individuals should voluntarily adopt practices and policies that have been successfully demonstrated to carry out extended product responsibility on a regional and national scale. The Product Responsibility Panel should recommend any legislative changes needed to remove barriers to extending product responsibility.[16]

Action: Enhance Efficient and Clean Technologies:

In order to reduce the total environmental impact of human activities, U.S. industry must attain greater efficiency in the production of goods and services. The goal is to reduce the total amount of materials and energy used in producing what Americans consume. Achieving that efficiency depends–to an enormous degree–on technological innovations. Encouragement for the development of environmental technologies might include direct funding of research, public-private partnerships for technology transfer, and research and development tax credits for industries. A complete examination of the full range of actions required to stimulate the development and commercial availability of clean and efficient technologies should be commenced by industry/government partnerships. Civilian technology should be developed and promoted in partnership with the federal government to provide new ways to increase materials and energy efficiency and prevent pollution in the first place. The federal research establishment should assess its commitment to applied environmental research to determine whether it is laying an adequate basis for commercial technology and for assessing the environmental and social impact of technological developments. The federal government should revise the federal tax code to allow preferential tax credits to industry for research and development activities targeted at environmentally sustainable technologies. The federal government should also support partnerships that bring private firms, federal laboratories, and universities together to plan and carry out research aimed at the development of environmentally sustainable technologies.[17]

Industry Initiatives:

A number of businesses throughout the United States are already implementing extended product responsibility and making significant changes in products, waste, and their associated environmental impacts.

One approach that manufacturers can take to extended product responsibility is to assume responsibility for a product through the end of its useful life and to provide a traditional product as part of a customer service package. A good example of this is the *Evergreen* program, developed by Interface Flooring Systems, Inc., which provides a new approach to the conventional sale of carpet. Through this program, commercial and institutional customers lease the services of replaceable carpet tiles without having to take responsibility for disposal when they become worn. Instead of buying and replacing entire flooring systems every few years, customers prolong the life of the flooring by replacing individual tiles as needed.[18]

Another approach to extended product responsibility is to reclaim waste products and recycle them as inputs to the production process. For example, Georgia-Pacific Corporation is recovering, processing, and recycling urban wood waste at its particleboard production plant in Martell, California. In California, the U.S. Forest Service's timber harvest has declined, as has the residual fiber supply that results from the lumber manufacturing process. This fiber supply has been the primary resource for producing particleboard at the Martell plant. To augment the supply, Georgia-Pacific has reached agreements with recycling companies in the area to purchase the wood they recover from commercial and general urban solid wastes. This use of waste products as inputs for the manufacturing process is helping Georgia-Pacific reduce the costs of its final products and achieve its sustainability goals.[19]

Another example of recovering and utilizing wastes is the *America Recycles Aerosols* program, initiated by S.C. Johnson & Son, Inc., the Steel Recycling Institute, WMX Technologies, and others since 1991. Nearly 17,000 communities across the United States collect steel cans as part of their recycling programs, but steel aerosol cans are often not included. By recycling the 3 billion aerosols produced annually in the United States, America could potentially build 160,000 cars and save the energy-equivalency of 5.7 million barrels of oil. As a result of this recycling effort, more than 100 million Americans in 4000 local and statewide programs (e.g., Los Angeles, Chicago, Pittsburgh, Philadelphia, Houston, Boston, and Sacramento; and Michigan, Illinois, and Delaware) now recycle aerosols in their recycling programs. For every ton of steel which is recycled, over 10 million BTUs of energy are conserved; and

2500 pounds of iron ore, 1000 pounds of coal, and 40 pounds of limestone are saved. In addition, communities avoid the costs of needlessly landfilling aerosol cans and increase their revenues from the sale of recyclables–with no increase in the cost of final products.[20]

Other companies are approaching extended product responsibility by developing new institutional relationships throughout the chain of commerce. The U.S. Council of Automotive Research has established a consortia among Chrysler Corporation, Ford Motor Company, and General Motors Corporation known as the *Vehicle Recycling Partnership*. This partnership involves U.S. automotive manufacturers, as well as suppliers and vehicle recyclers. As a frame of reference, the current U.S. vehicle recycling infrastructure processes approximately 95% of all vehicles that are removed from service. Approximately 75% of each vehicle by weight is recycled, and the remaining 25%–comprised primarily of plastics, rubber, fluids, and glass–is shredded and landfilled. A primary objective of this program is to reduce the contribution of this automotive shredder residue to municipal solid waste landfills.[21]

The Xerox Corporation has initiated a corporate-wide program to minimize the environmental impacts of its products at all stages of the product lifecycle. The overall goal of the *Asset Recycle Management* program is to eliminate the disposition of materials to landfills by designing waste-free, high quality products with minimal environmental impacts. In 1995, 60 percent of the Xerox cartridges sold around the world were recycled, preventing the need to discard 1,100 tons of materials in landfills. Between 1991 and 1995, Xerox achieved a 45 percent reduction in solid wastes for its 17 largest sites. The recycled content in products has more than doubled in five years, and the company is realizing over $200 million in annual savings from the program.[22]

The Rechargeable Battery Recycling Corporation has initiated the *Charge Up to Recycle* program to educate the public about the need to recycle used nickel-cadmium (Ni-Cad) batteries. Used Ni-Cad batteries are a principal source of the toxic heavy metal cadmium in solid waste, and the program is designed to reduce environmental risk and conserve natural resources. The program is funded by over 20 companies worldwide that manufacture rechargeable batteries for sale in North America. Batteries are collected from businesses, government agencies, institutions and consumers. This program recycled over 15 percent of the Ni-Cad batteries available for recycling in 1995, the first full year of the program. By the year 2000, they hope to achieve a 100 percent collection rate and a greater than 70 percent recycling rate.[23]

Non-governmental Initiatives:

Non-governmental organizations (NGOs) and academic institutions are playing an important role in demonstrating sustainable practices. NGOs are reaching out to their members, to businesses, and to the general public to create the broad-based foundation that is essential to long-term sustainability. Small businesses provide most of the new jobs in the United States, and they are essential to the nation's economy. Yet in order to stay in business, they must comply with a maze of environmental regulations. Unlike large and mid-size companies, they often lack the resources, staff, and training they need to ensure compliance or to remain competitive. NGOs are beginning to work with small businesses to meet these challenges. The printing industry provides a good example. The printing industry is dominated by small businesses; 80 percent of the print shops in the United States employ fewer than 20 people. The printing process involves a number of potentially toxic chemicals, and printers must comply with dozens of state and federal regulations that deal separately with air, water, and land pollution.

In 1993, the Environmental Defense Fund and the Council of Great Lakes Governors joined with representatives from the printing industry to establish the *Great Printers Project*. The U.S. EPA and state regulatory agencies also participated in the project. The main objective of the project is to make pollution prevention a standard business practice for the printing industry. This is being accomplished by linking simplified compliance requirements to flexibility in pursuing pollution prevention opportunities that can save raw materials and improve product quality.[24]

Associations can also play an important role in addressing the environmental concerns of citizens and communities and in fostering environmentally-sound policies and management approaches. In 1988, the Chemical Manufacturers Association adopted the *Responsible Care* initiative which provides a framework for demonstrating corporate responsibility and environmental stewardship. All association members and partners have pledged to abide by a common set of principles. Examples include the following: recognizing and responding to community concerns about chemicals and plant operations; developing and producing chemicals that can be manufactured, transported, and disposed of safely; making health, safety, and environmental considerations a planning priority; reporting promptly on health or environmental hazards; participating with government and others in creating responsible laws, regulations, and standards to safeguard the community, workplace, and environment. Four times a year, a public advisory panel of individuals from government and private industry meets to help identify and respond to public concerns and to evaluate Responsible Care principles and management approaches.[25]

There are an increasing number of partnerships among industry and NGOs to improve environmental performance. In 1995, the Environmental Defense Fund and The Pew Charitable Trusts jointly established the *Alliance for Environmental Innovation*. The Alliance's mission is to work in partnership with major American corporations to reduce waste, prevent pollution, and conserve resources, while also enhancing business performance. Staff from the Alliance and its partner companies are conducting projects to identify key environmental issues, analyze the economic performance and functionality of potential solutions, refine new methodologies for reducing environmental impacts, and develop implementation options. The main objective is to develop innovations that significantly reduce environmental impacts and make good business sense (e.g., increasing market share and sales, improving a company's reputation, reducing costs, etc.). The Alliance is responsible for all of it expenses and receives no financial support from partner companies.

In August 1996, the Alliance and S.C. Johnson & Son, Inc. embarked on the first project to help further integrate environmental considerations into the creation and production of the company's leading household brands. A key focus of the project will be to ensure that environmental considerations and energy efficiency principles are systematically built into initial product concepts, even before product design and development begin. Another Alliance project with Starbucks Coffee Company is focused on developing ways to serve coffee that are kinder to the environment. In particular, the project is exploring ways to encourage customers to use reusable cups and has challenged the cup industry to develop a new single-use cup that lowers environmental impacts.[26]

In addition there are numerous innovative product stewardship programs and public-private partnerships dealing with production and waste issues. Stewardship programs typically deal with the downstream environmental and safety aspects of product use. Many companies and organizations already have voluntary programs of this nature. Examples include the U.S. EPAs Green Programs such as the Energy Star initiatives; Environmental Defense Fund/McDonald's partnership; and initiatives by the Business Council for Sustainable Development, Coalition for Environmentally Responsible Economies, International Standards Organization, National Association of Chemical Distributors, and Synthetic Organic Chemical Manufacturers Association.[27]

These and many other innovative programs demonstrate the tremendous potential of extended product responsibility to achieve enormous gains in the efficiency of America's production and consumption of materials. As more U.S. businesses shift to considering the entire lifecycle of products in making production, distribution, and disposal decisions, even greater reductions in material use will result.

Lessening the Impacts of Waste

Each American now produces 4.5 pounds of trash per day—by far the world's highest level. Citizens understand the problems of packaging, garbage, and household toxics, and they show strong concern about these issues in polls. The three recommendations regarding waste disposal call for streamlining packaging materials; volume or weight-based municipal garbage fees; and proper handling of household toxics. The three issues—packaging, municipal garbage, and toxics in waste—all interact in various ways. The encouragement of manufacturers to insure appropriate recycling, reuse, and disposal of all packaging will aid in making it returnable. Streamlining packaging will also reduce household and commercial waste, thereby letting consumers avoid the highest garbage collection fees. Federal guidelines and models for municipal volume and weight-based household waste collection systems and curbside recycling programs can assist municipalities in better waste handling techniques. The garbage-fee proposal, by supporting recycling, also helps to create a reliable supply of used materials. Finally, reducing packaging takes some toxic materials out of waste and the adoption of state and local programs can also begin to curb the flow of toxic materials into municipal waste.[28]

Action: Reduce, Reuse, and Recycle Packaging:

Packaging made up one-third of municipal waste in the United States in 1990 and has grown rapidly in volume in the past several decades. Today, 53 percent of municipal waste is paper or plastic; one-fourth is glass. Manufacturers, responding to current prices, have no economic incentive to reduce packaging or design it for efficiency or ease of reuse and recycling. Essentially, the cycle of responsibility is broken once a consumer buys a product. It then becomes the consumer's job to dispose of it, not the manufacturer's. This is so even though many consumers actively wish for less packaging.[29]

Consumers have no control over the design of product packaging. Making manufacturers responsible for the recycling and disposal of the packaging that they produce would put the incentive to redesign packaging just where the power to do it lies—with the manufacturers themselves. Such a program would rely on the initiative and ingenuity of manufacturers to design their own innovative methods to reduce, reuse, and recycle packaging.

Germany, which produces more than 23 million tons of household wastes annually, has nearly five years of experience with placing responsibility on manufacturers for the packaging they produce. The United States can learn from the successful and unsuccessful features of Germany's program. The German law specifically calls for manufacturers to reuse packaging or pay for recycling it. The program divides packaging into transport use (pallets, crates, corrugated containers, and the like); secondary packaging (packaging that does not directly contain the product being sold, such as outer boxes and cellophane wrapping); and primary packaging (bags, boxes, tubs, tubes, and other containers that actually hold the product being sold). Different requirements are placed on each kind of packaging—the percent of all packaging that must be reused or recycled—and are phased in gradually.

Consumers are able to leave at stores any secondary packaging they do not want, after paying for the product it held. Retailers must then pay for the removal and recycling of the discarded materials, which creates an incentive for them to press suppliers to reduce packaging. Retailers also must take back primary packaging after consumers use up the product. Mandated deposits on certain containers (beverage bottles, paint cans, and detergents, for example) create an incentive for consumers to return them to retailers.

Distributors then return the packaging to manufacturers, who are required to reuse it or recycle it privately, outside municipal waste collection systems. The law also allows manufacturers to pool resources to form a large collection and recycling system. In line with this option, German industry has established a program by which materials are certified for recyclability.

Fees from manufacturers based on the weight of the packaging that they produced has funded the certification and collection program in the first few years. But problems with markets for the large amount of plastics collected, and unanticipated collection costs, marred the German program's experience in its first few years. In response, the program shifted to a sliding fee scale based on the ease of recycling each material and is now more financially sound. As a result of the fee structure, plastic's share of the packaging market has shifted to more easily recycled paperboard and glass. In fact, the recycling fee now constitutes two-thirds of the price of plastic packaging in Germany.[30]

In 1996, the European Union also adopted packaging laws that called for 50 to 65 percent of packaging to be recovered within five years (recovery includes recycling, composting, and incineration) and established percentages of packaging waste and material that must be recycled. Standards based on life-cycle analysis are being prepared to determine packaging acceptability with regard to heavy metals content, recycled content, and recycling and composting methods.[31]

Using the lessons learned from these two major foreign packaging initiatives, the federal government should find ways to encourage U.S. manufacturers to ensure the recycling, reuse, and disposal of all packaging they produce. A public-private partnership financed by manufacturers should certify packaging for sustainability.

Options for packaging also include the collection of packaging materials by manufacturers and the ability of consumers to return packaging to retail establishments. Manufacturers, retailers, and distributors should work together to make packaging materials returnable to manufacturers and retailers. Other options are public-private partnerships–financed by manufacturers–that certify manufacturers' packaging on the basis that it is designed for materials efficiency, reuse, recycling, and remanufacture. Once certified, a packaging design could receive a stamp of approval akin to eco-labeling that tells consumers the packaging is being handled sustainably. Manufacturers could finance this partnership through fees, graduated by material type to reflect the different levels of reuse, recycling, and remanufacturing possible among glass, paper, and plastics. Policy options should also establish graduated targets for the proportion of all packaging of various kinds being recovered under the program; the proportion of packaging material of various kinds that is reused; and the proportion of packaging that is recycled. In order to avoid glutted markets and the illegal dumping of materials, these targets should be designed to track with the development of markets for each material.

Other strategies include take-back, buy-back or leasing systems where waste materials are returned to their source for reuse, recycling, treatment, or safe disposal. These alleviate downstream environmental effects and permit the recovery of valuable materials. Buy-back and take-back programs are not appropriate for all product categories, such as those that are extremely complex or where recycling infrastructure already exists, but there are many valid applications. Under leasing systems, the ownership of materials or products is never transferred to the user, thus encouraging manufacturers to extend the products life. Reuse or recycling by other manufacturers also works to bring the flow of material through the economy into line with a closed-loop system.[32]

Action: Adopt Weight/Volume-Based Garbage Fees:

Between 1960 and 1988, the volume of U.S. municipal solid waste more than doubled, while population multiplied 1.4 times. Today the average American produces 4.5 pounds of trash a day, by far the highest per capita production of municipal waste in the world. Americans could recycle or compost half this volume–yard waste, newspapers, corrugated cardboard, and beverage containers. Americans actually recycle or compost only about 13 percent currently.[33]

Municipal solid waste (residential and commercial waste, but not industrial, agricultural, or construction waste) makes up only three to four percent of total U.S. waste, but it has an enormous impact on municipalities. Three-fourths of all municipal waste is landfilled, but public acceptance and space for landfills grows ever scarcer. Many municipal garbage collection efforts are financed with flat fees or through property or other local taxes. This structure fails to alert consumers to the real costs of garbage and does not encourage them to reduce their wastes. Even where direct fees for trash collection exist, the fee may not rise with the volume of trash collected. These municipalities thus offer no financial incentive to the producers of household garbage to reduce the discardables they bring into their homes or businesses, to keep goods longer, or to recycle and compost.[34]

A number of municipalities, however, scale the charge for trash collection to the amount of waste generated–the more trash, the higher the fee. Some are able to finance recycling programs with the additional revenue. The World Resources Institute analyzed the experience of 10 municipalities that introduced volume-based collection fees between 1980 and 1989 and found that households readily accept such fee systems, that most cities reduced the amount of waste generated, that illegal dumping was rare, and that local governments increased their revenue for financing recycling programs. World Resource Institute analysts found that a municipality that raised the cost of collecting a 32-pound bag of garbage from zero to $1.50 would see an 18 percent reduction in the volume of solid waste it had to landfill. If the town introduced a curbside recycling program simultaneously, volume fell by 30 percent. Net savings reached 17 percent in areas where disposal costs were high (densely populated areas with scarce landfill space). Moderate-cost areas realized savings of six percent.[35]

Weight and volume-based garbage fees show that the use of environmental fees can achieve results superior to regulations in certain circumstances. Regulating the amount of each type of waste that each household can produce is unimaginable. Yet scaling the charge for garbage collection to the amount of trash produced is an appropriate, powerful, and efficient approach.

Decisions about municipal solid waste collection are best made at the local level. The federal government can usefully enter into partnership with local communities and serve them by sharing experiences and lessons learned in a growing number of communities experimenting with volume and weight-based garbage fees. Thus, state and local governments should adopt volume-based household waste collection systems and curbside recycling programs, with special provisions to avoid undue burdens on those with low incomes. The federal government should establish guidelines and models needed to initiate these programs.

The U.S. EPA should build on its experience and expertise in municipal solid waste management to develop a model program for states and localities in volume or weight-based garbage collection fee systems that finance curbside recycling programs. Guidelines accompanying this model should include its cost-effectiveness compared with landfilling and incineration and it should address the political costs of interstate transport of waste. The U.S. EPA should also explore possible federal incentives to states and localities for adopting the U.S. EPAs model program. Possibilities for incentives include outright grants; tying the development of such programs to highway or other grants; or conditioning permission to export trash out of state on adoption of the model program. The fee structure of the model program should also take into account the impact that a graduated fee for garbage collection would have on lower-income households and should involve a rebate or threshold mechanism to cushion that impact.[36]

Action: Improve Disposal of Household Toxics:

The average American household throws away 15 pounds of hazardous waste annually which accounts for one percent of household waste. This hazardous household waste includes paints, solvents, motor oil, electrical appliances, tires, and batteries. Batteries alone contain concentrated doses of numerous heavy metals, such as lead, arsenic, zinc, cadmium copper, and mercury. Each year, million gallons of motor oil are improperly sent to landfills or poured down U.S. drains. These hazardous materials—by definition harmful to human health—can contaminate landfills, leach into groundwater, become toxic incinerator ash, vaporize into stack gases, or concentrate in sewage treatment plants. One-fifth of the toxic waste sites placed on the U.S. EPAs priority list as national problems in 1989 were municipal landfills.[37]

As with garbage in general, economic instruments can be useful in the control of household toxics. The most appropriate form appears to be a system similar to bottle deposit/return schemes, under which buyers would pay a deposit on hazardous materials that manufacturers would redeem on return. Manufacturers would then recycle or dispose of the hazardous materials properly.

State and local governments should adopt programs to curb the flow of toxic materials into municipal waste streams, focusing on incentives for recycling, deposit or buy-back systems, procurement mandates, and finding substitutes for the most troublesome materials. This policy aims to minimize the contamination of waste that goes to landfills and incinerators. The U.S. EPA should develop a model program curbing household toxics for states and localities. The program should aim at establishing deposit-return programs for problem products including tires, used motor oil, lead and mercury batteries, and paint and solvent containers. Guidelines accompanying this model should highlight the extent and sources of these hidden polluters. The fee structures should take into account the cost of avoided pollution and the fee level necessary for motivating consumer compliance. As with existing bottle deposit bills, the deposit-return program would be implemented throughout the marketplace, with manufacturers providing incentives through prices and deposit-return systems and distributors acting as agents to redeem the used toxic products.[38]

Greater Use of Market Forces

In the American economic system, the marketplace plays a central role in guiding what people produce, how they produce it, and what they consume. The choices and decisions made by millions of consumers and firms determine prices for the wide range of goods and services that constitute the national economy. The marketplace's power to produce desired goods and services at the lowest cost possible is driven by the price signals that result from this decentralized decision process.

Despite the nation's commitment to a free market economic system, governmental policy substantially influences the workings of the marketplace. Market-based economic policy can be used to encourage economic, environmental, and social goals. In some cases, the market itself produces environmental improvements, but in others the market fails to fully value natural and cultural resources. When such market failures occur, governmental involvement may be necessary to assist in regulating the cleanliness of the environment or the rate of resource consumption. Intentional use of market mechanisms can be an efficient and cost-effective way to protect the environment, enhance social well-being, and safeguard competitive advantage. Each economic instrument has its own

65

particular advantages and disadvantages. They can be effective in dealing with some aspects of a problem and less so with other aspects. The improper use of some types of economic instruments may have the effect of legitimizing rather than stigmatizing pollution, to the detriment of the environment.[39]

To improve environmental performance, the design of environmental and natural resource programs should take advantage of the positive role the marketplace can play once environmental goals and market policies are aligned. Current policies generally do not use the power of the marketplace. At present, some environmental costs in the product chain are shifted to society at large, rather than being fully reflected in the product price. The cost of air, soil, and water pollution associated with materials and energy use as well as the expense to local communities for product disposal are examples of costs not typically included in a product's price. If these types of costs were reflected in the price of a product, the marketplace would receive an important signal. All other things being equal, consumers generally will purchase the lower priced product, creating an important incentive for a company to reconsider how it makes a product. Increasing the use of market forces can create opportunities to achieve natural resource and environmental goals in the most cost-effective way possible–by encouraging the innovation that flows from a competitive economic system.

Not only are efficiency gains important in the design of economic instruments, but so too are equity concerns. Economic and social equity–who pays the costs, who accepts the risks, and who receives the benefits–must also be considered in the design and selection of economic policy options. Examples of market incentive strategies include greater use of systems that allow regulated firms to buy and sell emissions reductions, charges, fees, deposit-return charges, or tradable-permit plans. Under these and other similar strategies, environmental harmful activities or material–such as water and air pollution, sulfur-containing materials, or toxic chemicals–could be taxed, while the purchase of potentially harmful materials, such as lead-acid batteries and automobile tires, might include a deposit that is redeemed when the products are returned safely for disposal. Similarly, emissions of pollutants could be better regulated by the use of the marketplace to place a value on efficient pollution control methods. Finally, adopting government procurement policies which call for the purchase of environmentally beneficial products can send powerful signals to industry to adopt cleaner and more efficient technology.

Action: Use Market Incentives:

Market forces offer a powerful means of affecting the decision-making of individuals, businesses, and governments. The use of market-based incentives to further environmental goals encourages the application of pollution control measures in the places where these controls will be most cost-effective. Economic instruments also provide operational flexibility and account for the need of U.S. manufacturers to remain competitive in the global marketplace. The U.S. should make greater use of market incentives as part of an overall environmental management system to achieve its environmental and natural resource management objectives. This system must provide for verification, accountability, and the means to ensure that national standards are met or exceeded. Economic incentives, regulatory flexibility, and enforcement innovations will attract business participation in the new system. Tools such as emissions reduction banking and recognition of superior performance will reduce costs and promote strategic environmental thinking in government and business. Those tools that harness the market must be designed to minimize negative impacts on health, safety, and the environment, and prevent geographic pockets of increased pollution.

The success of programs such as the sulfur dioxide trading market, lead phase-down banking and trading, and hundreds of pay-by-the-bag trash collection systems confirms that the expanded use of market incentives will help achieve environmental and economic objectives. Economic instruments have their own niches, but they can also be used effectively in combination. For example, trading or pricing approaches work better if supported by information programs–communities that adopted pay-by-the-bag systems of trash disposal found fewer problems when households were given adequate information well in advance. Similarly, environmental tax systems can incorporate trading features; for example, taxes could be levied on net emissions after trades occur.[40]

The challenge is to design the most appropriate market incentives to deal with particular environmental problems. These incentives should always reflect sustainable development ideals. They should strive for steady progress in reducing environmental risks in a cost-effective manner. They should encourage technological innovation, shared responsibility, and administrative simplicity. The justice and fairness of their application should also be considered.[41]

Emission Trading and Fees: Federal and state governments should build on existing programs to design and carry out a system that allows the buying and selling of emissions reductions, while guaranteeing that there are permanent overall reductions in emissions. Such systems should be appropriate to the environmental problems being addressed and to local conditions. If applied appropriately, this approach can reduce the costs of meeting air and water quality standards without compromising human and environmental health. Emission trading strategies are designed to allow facilities to meet their emissions obligations by using reductions in emissions from other sources which keep their emissions below legal allowance levels. By creating market structures for environmental compliance, these systems harness private entrepreneurial energies in the search for the most efficient means to achieve environmental goals.

Two existing approaches to trading are *cap and trade* and *emission reduction credit* systems. Both have produced economic and environmental benefits. The cap and trade system is exemplified by the federal Acid Rain Control Program which allows sources to trade sulfur dioxide allowances between plants.[8] The emission reduction credit system has largely been applied to the management of smog precursors in metropolitan areas. Cities failing to meet the National Ambient Air Quality Standards have used emission reduction credit trading to allow new sources of emissions to build and operate without increasing the area's overall emissions. A third approach, termed *open market trading*, has been proposed by the U.S. EPA. The open market system would allow emitters to acquire surplus emission reductions from other sources in lieu of existing regulatory requirements. This system is still under development and awaits experience in application.[42]

Care must be taken to match the program's design and application to the underlying physical nature of the environmental problem. Trading systems work best when the transactions involve the trading of *excess reductions* between the sources of pollution. By this it is meant that if one pollution source reduces its emissions below the legal requirements, it may sell or trade its excess reduction amount to another pollution source. The second pollution source may then use the acquired reduction amount to increase its own emissions allowance amount. These will work if the effort is directed toward voluntarily lowering and redistributing the costs of compliance while guaranteeing that the environmental goal of permanent reductions in emission will be met.

Emissions fees use prices to provide incentives for environmental improvement. The use of emission fees makes environmentally damaging activities or products more expensive than less polluting alternatives. Firms and individuals tend to control pollution to the level at which it is cheaper to pay the emission fee than to further reduce pollution. Emission fees can be particularly useful when pollution is due to many small sources, or where direct regulation or trading strategies may be impractical due to high transaction costs.[43]

Action: Greening Government Procurement Policies:

The federal government is the single largest consumer of goods, products, and services in the United States and spends an enormous sum every year buying goods from private industry suppliers. It is the largest single consumer of paper in the world. Harnessing the more than $400 billion the federal government spends annually purchasing goods from private industry will have a significant impact on how products are produced in America. With this purchasing power, the federal government can have a enormous impact on markets and the commercial viability of recycled and other environmentally superior goods. At the same time, the government can set a clear example for other U.S. consumers, both individual and business. It can also move toward operating at the least possible cost to society, both in economic and environmental terms.

Government procurement procedures should be reformed to increase the use of environmentally preferable products whose full life-cycle costs are the most economical. The federal government already makes some effort to buy *green*. The Resource Conservation and Recovery Act calls for the federal government to buy recycled products. Under the law, the U.S. EPA designates procurement items and their recycled content, and agencies buying these items must match or exceed the recycled content of the U.S. EPA designations—within the limits of price, competition, availability, and performance.[44]

Unfortunately, by 1993, the EPA had issued guidelines for only five products (cement, paper, lubricating oil, tires, and insulation), and the percentage of federal purchases of these commodities that were recycled was not impressive. Although 80 percent of insulation purchased met the guidelines, less than 50 percent of paper, 33 percent of cement, five percent of tires, and one percent of oil did. Since 1993, the government's green procurement efforts have been significantly strengthened with a series of six Executive Orders. They deal with recycling and waste prevention, ozone-depleting substances, alternative-fueled vehicles, energy-efficient computers, pollution prevention, energy efficiency, and water conservation. The U.S. EPA has now issued guidelines for 21 additional products, from engine coolants and plastic piping to carpeting and plastic trash bags. The federal government has also accelerated its purchase of alternative fueled vehicles and products that do not use or contain ozone-depleting chemicals.[45]

Despite these efforts, green procurement by the federal government remains a small part of the total. The process is complex and time-consuming, and the exceptions in the laws are numerous. To flex the muscle of its considerable purchasing power in favor of sustainability, the government needs to accelerate, intensify, and broaden its existing efforts. In particular, it needs to modify the requirement that goods be purchased at the lowest price.

The U.S. EPA should accelerate the process of developing guidelines for products that are or can be made with recycled goods, pursuant to the Resource Conservation and Recovery Act. Each agency of the federal government should purchase, to the maximum extent practicable, recycled products in the 26 categories already established by the U.S. EPA. After the federal government has established criteria and standards for appropriate product categories–based on life-cycle analysis and assessment–and products have been certified as environmentally superior, the Federal Procurement Council should take the necessary steps to prohibit the sale of products that do not meet the environmentally preferable standards.[46]

In addition, the federal government should join with industry in offering incentives–in the form of guaranteed purchase awards–to businesses that create new products exceeding the standards for environmental superiority. The procurement policies of state, local, and tribal governments should also reflect preferences for the resulting cost-effective, environmentally superior products. A strategy to adopt environmentally sound procurement policies by governments–particularly the federal government–would operate to send signals to manufacturers that green products are preferred and would assist in the creation of markets for recycled goods.[47]

Supporting Eco-efficiency

The current use of materials and energy in the U.S. economy is not sustainable. Production and consumption of materials now account for large shares of U.S. energy use, waste, and pollution. The transformation to sustainable development is necessary to bring U.S. industrial production in line with environmental goals. This will occur through the actions of individuals, government, and the marketplace. The concept of eco-efficiency is one method to achieve those goals.[48]

Environmental analysts have been focusing increasingly on the way raw materials are used–the consequences of extracting raw materials from the earth and of processing raw materials into products inefficiently. There is also increasing examination of the wasteful policy of designing products to be used once, sometimes briefly, and then discarded. There is also more focus on the difficulty of repairing goods and of the challenge facing those who wish to recycle materials. Finally, more attention is being given to the environmental, social, and economic costs of municipal landfills and incineration.

A new way of dealing with materials is needed that reduces the total volume handled and cuts reliance on virgin resources. The economy must begin to use both raw and secondary materials much more efficiently. It must rely more lightly on the extraction of raw materials and it must reuse and recycle materials which have already been used. Industry must design products for durability, ease of repair, and ease of recycling. This approach not only uses creatively what has until now been considered waste; it also produces less waste in the first place.[49]

Eco-efficiency is broadly defined as the production, delivery, and use of competitively priced goods and services, coupled with the achievement of environmental and social goals. The Business Council for Sustainable Development, in its 1992 publication, *Changing Course*, introduced the term eco-efficiency to describe corporations which were producing economically valuable goods while continuously reducing the ecological impact associated with the production of those goods. Some of

71

the business advantages of eco-efficiency are the use of less material, water, and energy, thus driving a reduction in the cost of manufacturing. Additionally, eco-efficient products are designed to be durable, repairable, and reusable, and therefore more attractive to consumers.[50]

An eco-efficient society—in which ecological and economic values are married—would produce cleaner, safer workplaces; healthy, vibrant communities; and greater economic opportunity for all Americans. In an eco-efficient society, market forces would be harnessed to protect the environment. Supply and demand would be influenced by better information about environmental impacts and by a heightened sense of responsibility among all. Prices would incorporate eco-efficient values. The more energy and materials used to make a product and deliver it to the consumer, and the more waste generated in its manufacture and use, the higher would be the product's price tag. This is not always the case under the present system.

An eco-efficient regulatory system would maximize environmental protection while enhancing economic competitiveness. Eco-efficient regulation would rely more on pollution reduction at the source rather than on costly controls. Eco-efficient regulation would foster trust and cooperation by inviting public participation and by recruiting industry partnerships in the discovery of cost-effective environmental solutions.

Eco-efficiency could produce a high quality environment and a robust and competitive economy while at the same time ensuring continuing improvement to both. Borrowing from our understanding of natural systems—in which waste from one process becomes fodder for the next—such manufacturing can be described not as a linear activity, but as a circular one. In eco-efficient manufacturing, the waste from one process can provide the raw materials for the next production activity. The products of eco-efficient manufacturing, once used, should be able to be disassembled or reassembled to become useful again. Eco-efficient manufacturing is a closed loop—a sustainable system. It is a whole-systems approach to manufacturing.

Action: Eco-Efficiency Study:

There should be a full study of manufacturing in the United States to determine how economic growth and environmental protection might be aligned in a domestic policy agenda. Such a study should include the full range of manufacturing-related activities in the chain of commerce—not just the actual production step. Manufacturing from the time raw materials are extracted to the time consumers finish with an end-product should be examined. Material flows should be examined to find opportunities to affect supply chain dynamics that influence raw material extraction and the use of recycled materials and products. Product storage, shipping, distribution, and use, should be studied to see how these are affected by demand and other consumer behaviors.[51]

Action: Analysis of Environmental Consequences:

To encourage and support broad, personal commitment to eco-efficiency, a number of changes must occur. Entities and individuals must strive to identify sources of environmental, economic, and social consequences associated with resource extraction, production processes, distribution, use, and subsequent disposal. This will require changes in the management practices of all business involved and improvements in individual as well as community knowledge and involvement. It will also require more efficient use of governmental regulatory and tax policies. The goal should be to act collectively and individually in ways that contribute to eco-efficiency and sustainable development through better understanding and communication of the environmental, economic, and social consequences of individual and collective actions.

Individuals, through their actions, choices, and decisions, have been and will continue to be the foundation upon which our society and economy are built. Therefore, eco-efficiency must become a widely held societal value in order to capture the significant improvements offered by sustainable development. Only when each individual and each element in society (business, government, environmental organizations, academic institutions, labor, etc.) understand and value eco-efficiency will the full impact of the concept of sustainable development be realized.

There should be efforts to broaden the scope of environmental management by involving a lifecycle perspective in order to understand the full impacts and costs of manufacturing and to arrive at an optimal plan to improve the sustainability of manufacturing. Environmental management should be integrated into central business planning and systems in order to facilitate eco-efficient manufacturing. Efforts should be made to assess and improve the environmental aspects of manufacturing and supplier relationships. There should be industry-specific collaborative efforts to develop the necessary lifecycle data base and inventories. Efforts should be instituted to combine energy planning with environmental management, and merge both into the best existing management practices. This will harness the practical aspects of environmental efficiency for economic gain.

An industry-led coalition should be formed that would review eco-efficiency in order to develop and implement a plan for extending the concept of eco-efficiency throughout the chain of commerce. The coalition should include members from the entire chain of commerce and should base its work on the lifecycle perspective. Along with this, communication should be improved to provide an exchange of information on environmental, health, and safety issues throughout the entire chain of commerce.[52]

Initiatives: Eco-Efficiency:

A comprehensive project to improve energy efficiency and cut wastes throughout the White House complex is being carried out jointly by the Department of Energy and the National Park Service. In the three years since the project was initiated, major progress has been made in reducing energy and water consumption, in minimizing and recycling the materials consumed, and in reducing air pollution. For example, the White House has upgraded most of the overhead lighting with energy-efficient fluorescent fixtures; replaced exterior lighting with more energy-efficient halogen-based fixtures; replaced 98 percent of the windows in the Old Executive Office Building with energy-efficient, double-glazed film units; installed a state-of-the-art heating, ventilation, and air conditioning system which uses no chlorofluorocarbons and contains a computerized control system to maximize the efficiency of the unit; installed a condensation heat recovery system to capture waste heat which will be used to preheat domestic hot water; installed low-flow faucets and flush valves; reduced the release of volatile organic compounds (e.g., from paints); composted organic landscape waste material; and prevented chemicals in surface runoff from entering the storm water sewer system. This project is intended to serve as a model that others—both public and private—can build on as they strive to improve the efficiency and cost-effectiveness of their own facilities.[53]

Other government agencies are also beginning to implement the principles of eco-efficiency. In January 1997, the U.S. Postal Service awarded a five-year contract to Southeast Paper Recycling in Atlanta, Georgia, to collect and recycle undeliverable junk mail. The company is collecting the junk mail from approximately 200 post offices and two mail processing plants in northern Georgia. The district's post offices are expected to generate about 500 tons of paper for recycling each month, and the recycling program should reduce disposal costs by 50 percent. In addition, the recycling program will generate over $150,000 in annual revenues. Through similar efforts across the nation, the U.S. Postal Service recycled one million tons of wastepaper, cardboard, plastic, cans, and other materials in 1996. These recycling efforts contributed $6.6 million to the nation's economy.[54]

Action: Eco-Industrial Parks:

An *eco-industrial park* is a group of businesses that work together and with the community to efficiently share resources (materials, water, energy, infrastructure, natural habitat and information), enhance economic prosperity, and improve the environment. Eco-industrial parks can be initiated by a community, local government, a non-profit organization, or a business. There are three general models of eco-industrial parks: (1) a zero-emissions eco-industrial park, in which a group of businesses are co-located and work together to reduce or eliminate emissions and wastes; (2) a virtual eco-industrial park, in which businesses are geographically separate, but work together to minimize their impact on the environment; and (3) eco-development, in which non-industrial establishments apply the principles of industrial ecology.[55]

This newly evolving area of economic development is only beginning to be tested in practice. Early experience suggests that it presents unique opportunities to link economic development, environmental protection, and social equity in communities throughout the United States.[56]

An example of the first type of eco-industrial park is the Port of Cape Charles *Sustainable Technologies Industrial Park*, located in Eastville, Northampton County, Virginia. Cape Charles is in the Chesapeake Bay coastal region, and the area serves as a critical flyway for migrating birds, with some of the highest bird counts on the entire eastern shore. In addition to its natural features, the area has a rich cultural and historic heritage, characterized by Native American archaeological sites and historic homes. The future park will provide for water recycling among the resident companies by means of a used-water collection system, a water recovery facility, and a recycled-water distribution system. In addition, a technical panel will be established to analyze and determine whether the by-products of existing and proposed companies can be used by other companies within the park.[57]

An example of the second type of eco-industrial park–a *virtual* eco-industrial park–is a project in Brownsville, Texas. Brownsville is located on the southern tip of Texas in the Rio Grande Valley. It has a rich natural environment and is considered to be one of the three top birdwatching sites in the United States. At the same time, the city has some of the most serious environmental problems in the northern hemisphere and is struggling to address its 43.9% poverty rate and 11.72% unemployment rate. If the region's industrial growth is to continue, the nature of that development must change to protect both human health and the environment. As a virtual eco-industrial park, the Brownsville project takes a regional approach to exchanging waste materials and by-products. As currently envisioned, the project will include not only industrial facilities, but also small businesses and the agricultural industry.[58]

An example of the third type of eco-industrial park is the *Riverside Eco Park* in Burlington, Vermont. This project will create an agricultural-industrial park in an urban setting which will (1) generate electricity using bio-mass technologies that utilize readily available resources (e.g., wood chips), (2) use the waste heat generated by the power plant to support the greenhouse production of fish and horticultural products, (3) use biologically-based living systems to digest liquid organic wastes (which are common in the food processing industry) to purify water and create high strength fertilizers; and (4) recycle and compost the area's waste foodstuffs and yard debris to replenish local soils, increase agricultural production, and support local organic food industries. All of these emerging technologies are being developed with the ultimate goal of transferring them to other industries and communities. This project is expected to have several positive results including reducing the waste heat that is released into the air and water, improving soil conditions and water quality, and creating sustainable jobs for the local people.[59]

The concept of eco-industrial parks is to develop centers where the concept of eco-efficiency is put to its fullest use. The challenge is to create areas where the waste products of one factory provide the input to another factory, and so on. This type of system could potentially provide for a closed-loop of manufacturing, with the result being zero waste. For such eco-industrial parks to flourish, environmental regulatory systems must be flexible enough to allow park participants to trade their waste products so that environmental goals can be reached in the most cost-effective way for the entire park. Federal, state, and local governments should coordinate and streamline their regulatory requirements to allow for the development of such parks.

One-stop networks or centers should be established so that communities interested in developing eco-industrial parks can easily obtain regulatory, technical, and financial assistance information concerning federal, state, and local requirements. Environmental goals for eco-industrial parks should be developed through a participatory process involving all interested parties in the community. Market incentives should be used widely in the encouragement and management of eco-industrial parks to enable cost-effective environmental protection within parks. Barriers to investment in eco-industrial parks, including liability and capital access, must be removed to promote ecologically sound park development. Finally, for the concept of eco-industrial parks to succeed, information must flow openly between industry, government, and the community[60]

Information Collection and Dissemination

Accurate and relevant information is essential to reaching the goal of sustainable development. It assists individuals, communities, governments, and businesses in understanding how their actions affect the environment. It increases their sense of shared responsibility. Good information allows verification of progress toward long-term goals and enables public accountability. High quality information about product lifecycles is necessary to make sound environmental management decisions, especially within corporations. It also influences the purchasing decisions of individual consumers and organizations.

Improved public participation, information, and education will play a critical role in the successful implementation of sustainable development. Interactive processes should provide the public with the opportunity to help establish environmental goals and to verify progress toward those goals over time. Once information is collected, it must also be made available in a form most useful and appropriate. Examples of such forms include environmental labeling, material flow reporting, full cost accounting, and integrated indicators.

Information is a component of the pricing of products, and pricing is important to changing the behavior of consumers and business buyers. Improving the collection and dissemination of information about the total lifecycle costs of a product should, therefore, result in a more accurate price being sent to the marketplace. To the extent that environmental and social costs begin to be more properly accounted for by this improved information flow, the development and diffusion of eco-efficient products, processes, and practices should be triggered.

Because consumer behavior is not solely based on price, information also plays a larger role in the marketplace. Emotional, philosophical, or aesthetic factors also affect choice. Therefore, providing information to consumers about the environmental benefits or risks associated with the manufacture, use, or disposal of a product may encourage a shift toward more sustainable consumption.

Information has also emerged as a key element in performance-based environmental management. Accurate and reliable information is a prerequisite for evaluating performance. Improved information about environmental performance will strengthen the partnerships recommended under the new environmental management system outlined in Chapter 7. The theme of improved information—within manufacturing entities; between sources of supply and demand; and among regulators, the public, and business—is also threaded throughout most of the other recommendations in this chapter, and, indeed, throughout this entire book[61]

Action: Improve Government Information Functions:

America must improve the nature and means of information collection and dissemination. Environmental, economic, and social information should be collected and made accessible in an efficient and coordinated manner. These improvements must take place with full protection for proprietary information. The information collected should be useful and relevant for its intended audience, and developed in the most cost-effective manner possible.

Accurate information is vital to sound decision-making, and the federal government has an important continuing role in helping to ensure the quality and integrity of public information, whether generated by government or the private sector. Citizens depend on the quality and timeliness of information to alert them to hazards and to make informed decisions that promote economic and social welfare. As sustainable development focuses attention on new environmental, social, or economic concerns, government must perform this critical management function more effectively to ensure the quality and timely availability of new kinds of information. Government already has collected an abundance of information, but often it is not available to policy-makers or the public in a form they can use. A critical management issue is thus to improve the availability and usefulness of government information. The federal government is already participating in efforts to improve information management. These efforts should be expanded to include priority setting for data collection and analysis, identification of the most useful formats for dissemination, and additional mechanisms to help ensure that communities can obtain the information needed to guide sustainable development at the local level. At the same time, the federal government should work with private industry to inform the public through disclosure of appropriate information in such areas as health, safety, the environment, and the social impact of products and services.[62]

Action should be taken to improve the collection, organization, and dissemination of information to reduce duplication and streamline reporting requirements while giving decision-makers information related to economic, environmental, and social equity goals. The federal government—working with state and local governments, private businesses, and the public—should thoroughly review and revamp how it collects, organizes, and disseminates data on economic, environmental, health, and social conditions. The outcome should be improved coordination among federal agencies to better meet the needs of information users. Federal agency information system programs should be included in agency submissions under the Government Performance and Results Act. Rather than manage their information-gathering and processing activities by such elements as cost and the number of personnel involved, agencies have been directed to manage programs according to their outcomes or products. This approach should be used to ensure that money spent by the federal government on information leads to the production and dissemination of information that meets the needs of the public and policymakers. The federal government should also lead an effort to reduce duplication of information by integrating the efforts of various authorities. All levels of government should coordinate their programs on comprehensive regional inventories and assessments of environmental, economic, and social indicators of progress.[63]

The ability to achieve sustainable development depends on scientific knowledge of the Earth's natural systems and the ways in which human activities affect these systems. Accurate information built on basic scientific research establishes the foundation of knowledge needed for sound decision-making by individuals, businesses, government, and society as a whole. It helps people understand and predict changes in the environment, manage and restore natural systems, prioritize the potential risks associated with environmental problems, and take advantage of opportunities from technological developments. Private industry uses science to develop new technologies, production processes, and goods and services. In addition, baseline scientific data are critical to developing community-based sustainable development strategies.

Major efforts must be made to strengthen the base of scientific knowledge and increase its use by decision-makers and the general public. Government, industry, the scientific community, and non-profit organizations should support or conduct long-term, independent scientific research to help decision-makers understand sustainability issues, including the relationship among human and natural systems, human health issues, and emerging global problems such as global climate change and the loss of biodiversity. Current scientific research should be disseminated broadly and in ways that help policy-makers, individuals, businesses, and communities make decisions that promote sustainable development.

Information can be a powerful tool in making institutions accountable, building trust, and empowering citizens to take greater responsibility for economic and environmental improvement. Sustainable development requires that communities have the ability to compile and link disparate sets of data to create the information bases needed for effective decision-making. For example, in the late 1980s the federal government for the first time required firms to disclose publicly the total quantities of hundreds of chemicals they released into the environment. The disclosures of toxic releases under the Emergency Planning and Community Right-to-Know Act quickly led to voluntary reductions–more than 40 percent in the first five years–and contributed to increased dialogue between companies and communities. Many companies now voluntarily report far more broadly on environmental performance and invite community representatives to observe, evaluate, and help improve company operations. Implementation of the Emergency Planning and Community Right-to-Know Act demonstrates that complex data can be made available to the public in a manner useful to society. Trust in open processes and broad disclosure and dissemination of information are central to sustainable development.[64]

The federal government should encourage agencies to ensure that the standards and formats used to provide access to public information are consistent throughout the government so that members of the public and policy-makers can effectively search within and across agencies for information. The federal government should encourage and facilitate the creation of and access to information and data on sustainable development and sustainable living, such as ways to use resources more efficiently.

Action: Integrated National Accounting:

Continued long-term economic growth is essential to the prosperity of the United States and is fundamental to sustainable development. Maintaining this economic growth as the United States makes the transition to sustainability is a critical challenge. An important component of this transition is the inclusion of previously undervalued natural, environmental, and social resources into a new definition of economic well-being.

The U.S. should establish and implement a system of national accounting to measure sustainable development through integrated tracking of the environment, economy, and the natural resource base. The goal of such an accounting system would be to maximize economic growth in the expanding global marketplace as measured through a newly established *Sustainable National Product* that fully accounts for social, economic, and environmental costs and resources.

One of the most common measures of our nation's economic health is the gross domestic product (GDP), an indicator that accounts for the dollar value of all goods and services produced in our economy. However, the GDP is an incomplete and imperfect measure of sustainable development because it does not adequately account for environmental quality and natural resource depletion. Therefore, America needs to develop a better national accounting system which accurately reflects environmental concerns as well as traditional economic indicators.

The Bureau of Economic Analysis (U.S. Department of Commerce, Economics and Statistics Administration) has designed a new set of economic accounts for analysis of the interaction of the economy and the environment. The Integrated Economic and Environmental Satellite Accounts (IEESA) will include measures of economic growth, natural resource use, and environmental quality. The satellite accounts will not interfere with the continued tracking of the GDP and other standard indicators. By recording the national stock of natural resources, these satellite accounts can, in theory, provide a better measure of sustainable economic activity than traditional accounts. Fully implemented, the accounts could also provide an improved basis for analyzing the interaction between the economy and the environment in a number of ways–by type of resource, industry, product, and region.[66]

However, the development of such integrated accounts is a difficult and challenging task. It requires methodologies and data that are not yet available. Also, to the extent that the concept of sustainability is considered to include a wider range of social issues, indicators of change in these areas are more appropriately tracked within the proposed framework of sustainable development indicators than in the national economic accounts. See the following section on *Sustainable Development Indicators*.

The Bureau of Economic Analysis has already completed the first phase of the accounts. The overall framework and prototype estimates focus on mineral resources, including oil and gas, coal, metals, and other minerals with a scarcity value. Pending completion of a National Academy of Sciences study of the IEESAs–which was requested by Congress–the Bureau will move forward with the second phase to extend the accounts to encompass renewable natural resource assets, such as timberland, fish stocks, and water resources. Development of these estimates will be more difficult than for mineral resources because they will be based on less refined concepts and less data.[67]

The third phase will involve issues associated with a broader range of environmental assets, including the economic value of the degradation of clean air and water and the value of recreational assets, such as lakes and national forests. To accomplish these objectives, significant advances will be required in the underlying environmental and economic data, as well as in concepts and methods.

The Bureau of Economic Analysis should move forward in its work with international agencies–and all other interested private and public parties–to research, develop, and implement economic accounting concepts that more fully reflect the interaction of the economy, the environment, and the natural resource base. Progress in this work will depend upon resource availability and close, continuing cooperation with the scientific, statistical, economic, and environmental communities.[68]

Action: Broaden Business Environmental Accounting:

Many businesses are integrating environmental concerns into all facets of their operations in order to increase their competitiveness in the global marketplace and to address public concerns about the environment. Environmental accounting can provide the information to help them identify opportunities to reduce both production costs and potential environmental threats through more effective environmental management. Companies must spend money to meet environmental objectives, whether on a voluntary or mandatory basis. Their environmental costs include capital expenditures for pollution control equipment and salaries for staff who specialize in this area. Companies also spend money on the environment in other areas, such as operations and maintenance, labor, research, and marketing.

Unfortunately, standard business accounting practices bury the lion's share of environmental costs in non-environmental accounts and fail to trace costs back to the activities that generate them. As a result, managers often make crucial business decisions–what products to manufacture and what technologies and materials to use–without all the relevant facts. With a better understanding of a firm's actual environmental costs, managers and workers can identify opportunities to increase profits by using materials and energy more efficiently and so better protect public health and the environment.

Those who practice environmental accounting realize it is not a one-time exercise relegated to the periphery of a company. To ensure lasting benefits, it must be incorporated into ongoing business practices, including strategic planning, product development, and capital budgeting.[69]

Businesses in all industries must develop and adopt accounting practices that link environmental costs with the products, processes, and activities that generate them to provide better information for business decisions. National business associations can work with their memberships to develop and adopt voluntary sustainable business practices, including accounting for the consequences of environmental practices and profitability. National business associations can also provide technical assistance to small and medium-sized companies that are interested in identifying the range of costs associated with environmental management and innovative ways to reduce these costs while increasing their environmental protection and economic productivity. Colleges and universities that offer degrees in accounting and business administration should offer courses on environmental accounting practices.[70]

Action: Sustainable Development Indicators:

The assessment of progress toward sustainable development is difficult because the concept integrates three complex and dynamic systems—the social, economic, and environmental. Assessment is further complicated by multiple scales and various time frames over which development occurs. Ethics and values must also be considered. These requirements go far beyond the assessment provided by national accounts. To accomplish this, new indicators are needed.

A full set of national sustainable development indicators to highlight economic, environmental, and social trends needs to be developed. This will entail developing an information access system, developing analytical techniques for constructing indicators, providing regular reports on progress toward national sustainable development goals, and encouraging the development of indicators at regional, local, and industry levels.

Significant work on environmental policy indicators has been done by the Organization for Economic Cooperation and Development, the United Nations Commission on Sustainable Development, and the Dutch government. The Dutch have developed indicators for distinct environmental issues (climate change, stratospheric ozone depletion, acidification, eutrophication, dispersion of toxic substances, disposal of solid waste, and disturbance of local environments) and for target sectors (agriculture, traffic and transport, industry, energy, refineries, building trade, and consumers). The U.S. needs to build on this work and expand the scope of indicators to include economic and social dimensions as well as environmental factors.[71]

Such indicators of progress should be designed to provide quantitative snapshots of the progress the country is making towards achieving the goals. They are not intended to be top-down mandates and they may change over time as the country moves towards these goals and learns more about the science and policy options underlying them. Further, many of the indicators of progress are currently not measurable in any effective manner and will require developing new benchmarks as the necessary first step towards their utilization.

The Federal Interagency Working Group on Sustainable Development Indicators was formed to develop a conceptual framework for indicators of sustainable development. It has participants from twelve different federal agencies. In the spring of 1997, it published an initial selection of important indicators. The proposed initial set of 32 sustainable development indicators are intended to reflect the intergenerational nature of sustainable development, as well as the integration of economic, environmental, and social issues.[72]

Initiatives: Community, Urban, and State Indicators:

The Foundation for the Future of Youth, through its *Rescue Mission Indicators Project*, is working to create partnerships among groups of students around the world to create community-level indicators to measure progress toward meeting sustainable development goals. The foundation is developing youth-run state centers to coordinate this work locally.[73]

The U.S. Department of Housing and Urban Development is working with the Rutgers University Center for Urban Policy Research to develop urban and housing indicators at the national level based on research in 77 U.S. cities. This research includes indicators in the following categories: employment and economic development; demographic factors; housing and land use; poverty and income distribution; fiscal conditions and the public sector; and environment, health, and other social indicators. HUD is also working with non-profit organizations, professional journals, and housing groups to promote further public engagement and awareness of indicators and the role they play in identifying key problems and in working toward their solution.[74]

The State of Oregon has selected benchmarks to serve as indicators of the state's well-being. Oregon's 259 benchmarks are organized as core and urgent indicators. Core indicators examine primary and long-term goals for the state: family stability, capacity, enhanced quality of life and the environment, and promotion of a strong and diverse economy. Urgent indicators examine critical issues facing the state, such as endangered wild salmon runs and rising teen pregnancy rates.[75]

Access to Capital for Environmental Management

Sixty-two percent of the net new jobs in the United States come from firms with less than 500 workers. Firms with less than 20 workers employ only 21 percent of the labor force, but provide 48 percent of new jobs. Small businesses and communities face a variety of barriers which prevent straightforward investment in environmental improvements. Without some intervention, the capital market is unlikely to drive the transformation to a sustainable economy. At the same time, the threat of environmental liability prevents some lending institutions from supporting projects that are perceived to be high-risk. Addressing these access and liability barriers will speed the infusion of capital for environmental gains. It will free up capital for eco-efficient investments and it will facilitate investors' access to such capital.[76]

Alternative capital markets may be necessary to provide capital for investment in sustainable environmental improvements. Innovative financing programs should be developed to improve access to capital for small businesses and communities so that they may more easily invest in technologies and practices that will use resources more efficiently and produce less waste. Initially, government may need to be involved to demonstrate and support methods to increase access to capital; but the use of public funds should be limited. Eventually, it is expected that the market will come to value the economic benefits of investments in sustainable development and respond accordingly.[77]

Action: Stimulate Environmental Investments:

At present, when lenders evaluate the creditworthiness of an environmental investment, they typically rely on a fixed set of qualifying ratios that are a function of the percentages of assets, inventory, and receivables held by the applicant. As a result, high-return investments that cost-effectively improve resource use and reduce pollution often do not qualify for funding because their potential benefits are undervalued in the analysis.

The creditworthiness of cost-effective, environmentally-driven investments, and the inherent value of *avoided costs* (e.g. reduced energy and material use) need to be demonstrated to the lending community. Market incentives should be used to account for these real, but currently unrecognized, attributes. The federal government could help reduce risk by providing loan guarantees for qualifying business projects. On a pilot basis, the federal government should also develop alternative underwriting standards for eco-efficient investments for small businesses.[78]

Action: EPA-SBA Partnership:

The U.S. EPA and the U.S. Small Business Administration (SBA) should identify exiting funds that could be made available for small business eco-efficiency investment. The amount of assistance should depend on the expected level of environmental improvement resulting from the project. During the development of such an EPA-SBA *environmental bank*, the SBA should also review its existing ranking system to identify opportunities for incorporating sustainable development criteria into its general granting and lending equations.[79]

Action: Community Environmental Investment:

Community-based boards should be established to help facilitate market-based environmental trades in industry and help identify non-traditional sources of capital. Trade receipts could be used in a number of ways to promote community economic development. Innovative community-based financing and trading programs have the potential to become self-financed, but could receive government support until that time. The government funding for this could be derived from a decrease in the amount of funding for non-sustainable subsidies in the U.S. economy, as explained in Chapter 2.[80]

Sustainable America

As the American economy begins the shift to sustainability, there will be many problems to work out. Different industries will be affected in different ways. However, if government, business, academia, and non-profit groups begin to work together, America can collectively bring about a smooth transition to an economy in which all aspects of U.S. economic production are sustainable.

Chapter 4

Sustainable Population

With a population of more than 265 million, the United States is the third largest country in the world. Fueled by both an increasing amount of births and record high immigration, the U.S. population is growing by 3 million people each year, over 1 percent annually—more than twice the annual growth rate in most of Europe and other industrialized countries. The U.S. Census Bureau projects that if current demographic trends persist, the U.S. population will reach 350 million people by the year 2030, and almost 400 million by the middle of the 21st century. To put these numbers in perspective, under current trends, the United States is adding the equivalent of Connecticut's population every year and California's every decade. This level of growth places an ever greater strain on America's ability to increase its prosperity, clean up its pollution, alleviate its congestion, manage its sprawl, and reduce its overall consumption of resources.[1]

Population has for many years been a sensitive subject in America, if not altogether taboo. The subject of U.S. population growth is complex and controversial, involving such difficult issues as personal childbearing decisions, contraceptive methods, teenage sexual behavior, and abortion. It raises a variety of moral and ethical concerns that must be addressed carefully and in ways that are consistent with the various religious, cultural, and ethical values and backgrounds of the American people. The issue of legal and illegal immigration is also potentially explosive and must also be addressed with sensitivity and recognition of long-standing American traditions of fairness, freedom, and asylum. (Editor's note: The President's Council on Sustainable Development did not take a position on the issue of abortion).

Currently, each year approximately 4 million children are born and 2 million people die in the United States. Thus, not including additional increases due to high levels of immigration, the U.S. population grows by 2 million people a year from the excess of births over deaths. This occurs despite an average family size of two children, slightly under what is termed *replacement-level* fertility–the level of births that just replaces parents. This annual population increase continues because the large baby-boom generation produces a large total number of babies, even though individual families are relatively small. Additionally, the older generations of Americans are small compared with the current parenting generation, and they are living longer than past generations. All this adds up to a wide gap between births and deaths and significant population growth in America.[2]

In 1992, 6.6 million women became pregnant in the United States. Americans achieve this pregnancy rate with high levels of unintended pregnancies and births. Nearly 60 percent of all pregnancies in America are unintended. Of the nearly 4 million U.S. births annually, 40 percent are unintended–either *mistimed* (the pregnancy occurred before the mother was ready–accounting for 30 percent) or *unwanted* (the woman did not wish to have the pregnancy at all–accounting for 10 percent). Some 30 million American women are estimated to be at risk for an unintended pregnancy. One third of these women do not use contraceptives, and the unhappy consequence is that half of all unintended pregnancies occur to these women. Most vulnerable are sexually active teens. More than 80 percent of the 1 million teen pregnancies every year are unintended. The incidence of unintended births has risen in the past decade, after falling between the 1960s and early 1980s.[3]

The consequences of unintended pregnancy can be tragic. They are associated with higher rates of low birthweight and infant mortality than are planned pregnancies. It is estimated that eliminating unintended pregnancies would reduce U.S. infant mortality by 10 percent and the incidence of low birthweight babies by 12 percent. Unintended pregnancies can have other disturbing consequences. They add pressure to social concerns such as poverty and abortion. Half of all unintended pregnancies in the United States that do not end in spontaneous miscarriage end in abortion. If all pregnancies were planned, demand for abortion would be lowered significantly. Women of all ages and income levels experience unintended pregnancies, but teens, women over 40, and poor women do so more often than others. Four in five adolescent pregnancies are unintended, and for women over 40 more than three-quarters of pregnancies are unintended. Poor women have the highest percentage of both. Women with family incomes below the poverty level report that three-quarters of their pregnancies are unintended. Unintended births can also have significant economic consequences for families. For example, 39 percent of new entrants onto the welfare rolls in any given year are the result of a first birth to an unmarried woman. More than half the teens who give birth receive welfare within five years–although not all of these are unintended births. In addition, because of unintended pregnancies more teens forgo furthering their education, and more children wind up raising children of their own–all of which contribute to the deterioration of American families.[4]

Fortunately, it is possible to move toward stabilizing U.S. population simply by meeting the reproductive health needs of Americans. American women today have more children than they wish to. If all U.S. births were wanted, their number would fall by 10 percent–from 4 million to 3.6 million a year. Population growth from the excess of births over deaths would fall 20 percent–from 2 million to 1.6 million. Delaying currently mistimed births–through better access to contraceptive services, education, and economic opportunities–would also reduce total births significantly. If adolescents had access to the education and services they need, a significant decline could be expected in the life-stunting childbearing that too many teens now experience too early in their lives. Alleviating the conditions that give rise to poverty and powerlessness–particularly for women and adolescents–also works to enable parents to choose the number and spacing of their children. All these strategies can work together to enable Americans to have the number of children they want. Working to eliminate unintended pregnancies and births can move the country toward two mutually reinforcing goals: meeting women's reproductive health needs and progressing toward national population stabilization. The American public strongly supports enabling parents to have the number of children that they want when they want them, as it also supports comprehensive reproductive health care services that will prevent unwanted pregnancies and abortions.[5]

Voluntarism lies at the heart of all American family planning programs. Family planning programs are both a medical enterprise–where the tradition of voluntary informed consent is strong–and a social enterprise–where freedom and choice are essential. Voluntarism also must be the foundation for promoting population stabilization. By meeting the needs of all Americans, regardless of income, and by providing the high-quality family planning and reproductive health services they already want, fertility will fall and the United States will be closer to a stable population than it is today.

The broad goal is to stabilize U.S. population as early as possible in the next century as part of similar worldwide efforts. This challenge for American health care can be met through various actions. To achieve this goal, the U.S. needs to begin providing universal access to a broad range of information, services, and opportunities so that individuals may plan responsibly and voluntarily the number and spacing of their children. These include high-quality family planning and other basic and reproductive health services. Special attention and sensitivity must be given to addressing the needs of adolescents–emphasizing abstinence and, as a precautionary measure, providing education and services that enable young people to behave responsibly. Encouraging personal and social responsibility regarding sex and fostering educational efforts about population are essential for America's future. There also needs to be increased funding for contraceptive research and development. The overall goal also requires targeted actions to eradicate poverty in America. America's overall reproductive health can be raised by decreasing the nation's poverty levels. Perhaps most importantly, American reproductive health can be significantly improved by addressing the remaining obstacles to women's full economic and social equality. Equitable educational, economic, social, and political opportunities for women must be part of the solution. Finally, there must be a national drive to reduce infant mortality and to increase male responsibility for family planning and childrearing.

While fertility is the largest contributor to U.S. population growth, responsible immigration policies that respect American traditions of fairness, freedom, and asylum will also contribute to voluntary population stabilization in the United States. Population growth in America is also based on net immigration levels. Whereas increased births supply two-thirds of U.S. population growth annually, the additional one-third of the growth comes from immigration—both legal and illegal. Illegal entry into America is now at an all-time high. As a matter of public debate, immigration is a sensitive and explosive issue. Any action on immigration must be undertaken with respect and concern for the civil and human rights of all of the individuals involved—foreign-born U.S. citizens and legal residents, as well as new immigrants. Working to ease conditions around the world that force people to leave home is also essential in alleviating immigration pressures on the U.S.[6]

U.S. Population Policy

The notion that America's best interests may not lie in continued population growth has been widely discussed only since the 1960s. Before then, population growth was generally viewed not only as necessary and inevitable but also desirable. In the 1960s, people began to examine critically the notion that all population growth is desirable. Several public interest groups were established and population issues joined environmental and social issues on the public agenda. In 1969, President Nixon issued to Congress a *Message on Population*. Referring to the expectation of the time that the U.S. population might exceed 300 million by the year 2000, he said, "This growth will produce serious challenges for our society. I believe that many of our present social problems may be related to the fact that we have had only fifty years in which to accommodate the second hundred million Americans. In fact, since 1945 alone some 90 million babies have been born in this country. We have thus had to accommodate in a very few decades an adjustment to population growth which was once spread over centuries. And now it appears that we will have to provide for a third hundred million Americans in a period of just 30 years." [7]

One result of Nixon's message was the passage in 1970 of Title X of the Public Health Service Act, providing family planning services for low-income women and men. Another was the creation of the Commission on Population Growth and the American Future, chaired by John D. Rockefeller III, which released a multivolume study of U.S. population growth and its impacts in 1972. The Rockefeller Commission's most widely cited recommendation reads: "Recognizing that our population cannot grow indefinitely, and appreciating the advantages of moving now toward the stabilization of population, the Commission recommends that the nation welcome and plan for a stabilized population."[8]

When President Nixon transmitted his message to Congress in 1969, U.S. families averaged between two and three children–the total fertility rate was 2.5–so that parents more than replaced themselves, and each generation grew ever larger. By the time the Commission released its report in 1972, the total fertility rate had fallen to two children, or replacement level. The following year, it fell below two children per family, where it stayed until 1989.[9]

Public concern for population growth in the United States waned sharply when news of the drop in fertility was confused with achievement of zero population growth. Below-replacement fertility rates do not translate into zero population growth until all age groups in a population are approximately the same size–even with zero immigration. In fact, the huge U.S. baby-boom generation entered childbearing age during the 1970s and 1980s. Such a large generation produces an enormous total number of babies even though the average family has only two children. Thus, the number of births has exceeded the number of deaths in the United States throughout the period–and U.S. population has grown significantly even without taking immigration into account![10]

Between 1972 and 1994, no sustained official conversation about U.S. population growth took place. Most citizens and most government officials assumed incorrectly that below-replacement fertility automatically meant immediate zero population growth and that the U.S. population was no longer growing. In contrast, immigration received considerable attention. Several national commissions have reviewed immigration issues, including illegal immigrants and refugees, and published reports and recommendations. The most recent effort, which was chaired by the late Barbara Jordan, is the U.S. Commission on Immigration Reform. Its work is still under way.[11]

Rapid population growth elsewhere in the world has received regular attention, especially at three United Nations international meetings in 1974, 1984, and 1994. At the most recent meeting, a broader consensus emerged on a new approach to population concerns than has occurred at these meetings before. The 1994 Plan of Action from the International Conference on Population and Development in Cairo is grounded in a comprehensive, woman-centered commitment to health, development, and education. It recognizes the complex context in which decisions about childbearing are made. Nations at the Cairo conference reached broad agreement that development (poverty alleviation, education, basic health care, and economic opportunity) and family planning each are important for reducing population growth rates–but that they work best when pursued together. Similarly, the consensus recognized that population growth is not the only driving force behind environmental concerns, and that consumption patterns also play an important role. Finally, it was widely agreed that family planning should be provided as part of broader primary and reproductive health initiatives, and that population policy should encompass economic opportunity for women and the elimination of legal and social barriers to gender equality. The United States actively participated in the Cairo process, provided important leadership, and is part of the broad consensus that now exists worldwide for this approach to stabilizing world population.[12]

The United States is today the only major industrialized country in the world experiencing population growth on a significant scale. The U.S. population grows at 0.7 percent annually when immigration is not taken into account, compared to an average annual growth rate (also without counting immigration) of not more than 0.2 percent in all of Europe. The U.S. population grows at approximately 1.0 percent when immigration is taken into account. Annual growth figures of 0.7 and 1.0 percent may seem small, but a persistent 1.0 percent growth rate translates into a doubling time (the time it takes a population to double in size) of 70 years. When the population that is doubling is the United States–the third largest country in the world–this constitutes an enormous increase. Only a handful of other countries in the world contribute more to their populations annually–all of them far less-wealthy developing countries.[13]

U.S. fertility has risen in recent years. In 1989, the average number of children born per woman in the United States exceeded 2.0 for the first time in 17 years, after remaining between 1.7 and 1.8 for 15 years. After reaching 2.1 children per woman on average for a year or two, the rate is now again 2.0. This means that current U.S. fertility matches birthrates in

95

less wealthy countries such as Ireland and Malta, rather than the birth rates of America's economic peers in Europe and Asia, such as Germany and Japan. Annual immigration to the United States is also high by historical standards, matching levels achieved during the peak immigration years of 1901-1910.[14]

The U.S. Census Bureau projects that if current mortality, fertility, and immigration patterns persist, U.S. population will reach 350 million people by the year 2030 and nearly 400 million people by 2050, continuing to grow indefinitely. This is the *medium* projection. The *low* projection forecasts that if fertility and immigration fall slightly, U.S. population will still increase until about 2030, when it will reach about 290 million people. In another decade, a slow decline in numbers would begin. The opposite assumption–the *high* projection, involving rises in fertility and immigration–would produce 500 million Americans by the year 2050, with continued growth inevitable and no stabilization in sight. Continued population growth in the United States, particularly on the scale envisioned by the medium and high projections, has enormous implications. Coupled with the resource consumption patterns that underlie the U.S. standard of living, population growth in America produces an environmental impact unparalleled by any other country in the world.[15]

Continued population growth also has the potential to overwhelm any efficiency and productivity gains in the economy, negating all of the technology-based efforts to reduce U.S. environmental impact. Population growth also challenges industry's best efforts to provide new, higher quality jobs for all Americans and to improve real wages for American workers–wages which have been stagnant for 22 years. It similarly adds to the nation's needs to reduce poverty, improve education, and provide health care for all Americans. In short, the United States is already severely challenged by the need to provide better opportunities for millions of disadvantaged citizens, and continued population growth will only increase these challenges.[16]

Economic theories about the relationship between population growth and economic prosperity vary across the full spectrum of possible opinions. There is an unwarranted belief that population increase is something essential to the maintenance of vigorous demand and economic growth. The consensus opinion, however, is that slowly shrinking populations have little negative economic impact. The effects of low fertility on labor supply, technological change, and investment and consumption are relatively slight. The Rockefeller Commission analyzed the difference between a growing and a stable U.S. population and concluded that the nation has nothing to fear from a gradual approach to population stabilization and that, in fact, from an economic point of view, a reduction in the rate of population growth would bring important benefits. The Commission report goes on to state, "In short, we find no convincing economic argument for continued national population growth." Many analysts express concern that countries with low fertility will eventually have trouble financing public old-age pensions as the ratio of workers to elderly people falls. It is possible, however, that the rising costs of supporting the elderly may be offset by declining costs of supporting children. The precise calculation for each country depends on the exact age structure of the population, the social security system, and immigration patterns. In any case, population policy is a crude tool for making social security policy, and it makes little sense to endure high levels of unwanted fertility and environmental degradation from continued population growth in the hope of affecting pension policy![17]

Action: Prevent Unintended Pregnancies:

Of the estimated 62 million women of reproductive age (15-44) in the United States in 1990, an estimated 55 million were sexually experienced. Of these, 25 million were pregnant, had just given birth, were attempting to become pregnant, or were protected from pregnancy by sterilization (either of themselves or their partners). The rest–some 30 million American women–were estimated to be technically at risk of an unintended pregnancy. It is estimated from surveys that approximately four or five million of these women did not use contraception, and just over half of all unintended pregnancies (53 percent) occurred to them. The remaining unintended pregnancies occurred to the 25 million women who used a contraceptive method other than sterilization, but for whom the method failed.[18]

The risk of unintended pregnancy is exaggerated for 15 million women who need subsidized family planning and reproductive health care. The poor are overrepresented in the ranks of these women. An estimated 56 percent of low-income women and 69 percent of sexually active teenagers in need of family planning services do not receive medically supervised contraceptive care.[19]

An effective way to reduce the number of unintended pregnancies and births in the United States is to expand access to family planning, education, and related reproductive health services, particularly for at-risk individuals. Family planning is highly cost-effective compared with the social and public costs of unintended pregnancy, and it helps ensure that every child is a wanted child. National family planning efforts are critical to preventing unintended pregnancies before they occur and to achieving national health and social aims. Governments at all levels should increase and improve educational efforts and public outreach related to contraceptive methods and reproductive health. There must also be expanded access to the services individuals need to freely and responsibly decide the number and spacing of their children. Simply addressing and ensuring access to basic reproductive health needs—such as family planning, education, and pre-natal and post-natal care—would move the United States toward population stabilization.

Other strategies also make sense for reducing unintended pregnancies and births. These include expanding the range of contraceptives available and broadening the participation of men in contraceptive and childbearing decisions. Additionally, enlisting the media to convey messages about reproductive responsibility and attempting to foster mature discussion and education related to sex, sexuality, and contraceptive issues will assist in the efforts to prevent unintended pregnancies.[20]

Title X of the Public Health Services Act: The nation's family planning assistance efforts—whether under Title X or any other program—must provide education and outreach to prevent unintended pregnancies. Congress should authorize and sufficiently fund national family planning programs to ensure that all women and men, regardless of income, have access to family planning and related reproductive health care options. In addition, these efforts should be strengthened to enhance information, education, and outreach capabilities—particularly for men and underserved or hard-to-reach populations.

The principal program providing comprehensive public family planning services to low-income women is Title X of the Public Health Service Act. Title X monies fund contraceptive supplies, information on contraceptive methods, counseling, cancer screening, screening for HIV/AIDS and other sexually transmitted diseases, infertility services, other features of reproductive health care, and information, education, and research activities. Some 4,000 clinics and other agencies nationwide received $193.4 million in fiscal year 1995 and provided services to more than four million clients. More than 60 percent of Title X clients are under 25 years old, 30 percent are adolescent, and 85 percent are low income. Although the numbers seem large, Title X reaches fewer than half of those eligible for the services it provides. In particular, men, teens, substance abusers, and the homeless are populations that under-use Title X services.[21]

Funding for Title X, however, fell by more than 70 percent in real dollars between 1980 and 1992 and has not been re-authorized by Congress since 1984. Because of this, the ability of Title X to provide funds for services to high-risk individuals and hard-to-reach populations has been severely hampered. The family planning services that it does provide are estimated to prevent an average of 1.2 million unintended pregnancies per year and about half that number of abortions a year. It does this at a cost of about $200 per woman for comprehensive family planning services. In comparison, an ordinary, nonsurgical birth without complications cost $6,400 in 1992. Family planning is dramatically cost-effective. For every dollar spent on publicly-funded family planning services of any kind, $4.40 is saved that the federal government would otherwise be obliged by law to spend on medical care, welfare benefits, and other social services.[22]

In addition to Title X, three other federal programs fund contraceptive services and supplies: the Maternal and Child Health Block Grant, Medicaid, and the Social Services Block Grant (all under the U.S. Social Security Act). Funds are targeted specifically for family planning only in Title X; block grants can be used for many different purposes[23]

Congress should fund Title X sufficiently so that funded programs may enhance information, education, and outreach capabilities, particularly for populations not currently reached, such as men and rural residents. Similarly, sufficient funding is needed to ensure that all women and men, regardless of income, have physical and financial access to the full range of contraceptive options and related reproductive health care services.

Medicaid Reform: The Medicaid program also should be reformed to help ensure that recipients who become eligible as a result of pregnancy have access to family planning services for an extended period after birth to encourage birth spacing and to discourage future unintended pregnancies. Medicaid is the largest public funder of family planning services, but because eligibility is tied to welfare eligibility, fewer than half of poor women are covered by Medicaid. In 1986, the federal government expanded Medicaid coverage to women with infants and pregnant women who have incomes which are one-third higher than the poverty level, regardless of whether they meet other welfare requirements. But coverage under this extension does not include family planning services until after childbirth, and then only for 60 days. Medicaid in its current form is not an effective source of services for preventing first pregnancies among these women, nor for ensuring that future pregnancies are planned ones.

Congress should reform Medicaid requirements to ensure that Medicaid recipients, like all Americans, have access to the full range of safe, voluntary reproductive health care in a confidential manner. In addition, Medicaid reform should allow women who qualify as a result of pregnancy to receive family planning benefits for up to five years after birth, in contrast to the current 60-day limit. Medicaid does not fund abortion except under very restricted circumstances.[24]

Private Health Insurance: Private health insurance coverage of comprehensive reproductive health services is another essential means of preventing unintended pregnancies. The private health care industry can reform health insurance coverage to ensure that all recipients are afforded choices among the broadest range of safe, voluntary reproductive health services.

As noted above, the rate of unintended pregnancies is higher among poor and low-income women, but women from all social and economic backgrounds experience unintended pregnancies. Therefore, private insurance coverage for reproductive health services also needs to be considered in examining the effectiveness of services to women for the prevention of unintended pregnancies. Almost two-thirds of women of reproductive age in the United States do not rely on publicly provided family planning because they have insurance provided through employment. But private insurance does not uniformly offer adequate coverage for family planning services.

100

An important strategy for reducing the number of unintended pregnancies and births in the United States is to expand access to contraception and related reproductive health services. Contraception is cost-effective, assists women in having the number of children they want when they want them, prevents abortions, and works toward the goal of having every child born in the United States be a wanted child. Up to 85 percent of insurance policies and health maintenance organizations cover sterilization and abortion, but fewer than half of the typical plans cover the five major reversible contraceptive methods–IUDs, diaphragms, Norplant, Depo-Provera, and oral contraceptives. Only 15 percent of plans cover all five reversible methods. Expanding private insurance to cover the full range of reproductive health services should be explored. The federal government should urge private health insurance companies to cover all family planning methods (surgical and nonsurgical) and related reproductive health care services.[25]

Contraceptive Research: Congress should fund–through federal medical research laboratories, public-private partnerships, and other innovative arrangements–increased research in both basic and applied reproductive health sciences. Consideration also should be given to strategies that address product liability concerns that impede contraceptive research and product development by private industry.

Both private and public support for contraceptive research has declined sharply in the last 25 years. In 1970, 13 major drug companies were involved in the development of new contraceptives worldwide, nine in the United States. Today, four are involved and only one is based in the United States. Support of research by the National Institutes of Health and the U.S. Agency for International Development–the two principal federal sources of funds for contraceptive research–has also waned significantly. Analysts identify political factors and the withdrawal of federal support during the 1980s, as well as standards of legal liability for harm from contraceptives, as the leading causes of the decline.[26]

Congress should fund increased research in basic and applied reproduction health sciences. This should include research into alternative birth control technologies to expand the range of medically safe contraceptives available to women and men. Particular attention should be given to woman-controlled barrier methods, methods that protect against

101

sexually transmitted diseases, post-ovulatory methods, and improved male methods.

New Contraceptive Technologies: The federal government should develop procedures to ensure expedited approval of all medically sound methods of contraception, such as appropriate contraceptives for emergency post-coital use. Organizations and educational institutions responsible for training physicians, nurses, and reproductive health providers should also educate individuals in the use of new contraceptive technologies, including oral contraceptives and other methods for emergency contraception.[27]

Emergency Contraception: Not all opportunities for new contraception require new research. Emergency post-coital contraception–which uses already packaged oral contraceptives in a different combination and intensity from ordinary use–is available now and is used in emergency rooms for rape victims, in universities, and in some family planning clinics.

Of the more than 50 brands of oral contraceptives currently approved in the United States, six are effective for emergency post-coital use. These are not labeled as approved by the Food and Drug Administration for such use, however, and physicians and other medical personnel either do not know about the legality of this use or are not at ease with it. Furthermore, pharmaceutical companies are not permitted to market drugs for uses that are not labeled. Yet, it is estimated that wider use of emergency contraception could reduce unintended pregnancies by 1.7 million and abortions by 800,000 annually.[28]

The Role of Men: Reducing unintended pregnancies in the United States depends on the participation of both men and women. Though a male participates in every pregnancy that occurs, he often plays a far from equal role in making sound family planning and reproductive health choices. This is especially true of young men.

In general, reproductive health services are targeted to women, but outreach needs to include men as well. Men need to be encouraged to play an equal role in safeguarding their own reproductive health and that of their partner and in making sound contraceptive choices. Years of experience with Title X and other subsidized family planning programs show that few men use these services without special outreach, counseling, education, and other efforts to make them feel at ease. Special programs should be developed to reach young men before they become sexually active to help them build the skills and strategies needed for sexual health and responsibility.

The U.S. Department of Health and Human Services should set aside appropriate amounts of Title X Service Delivery Improvement Grant funds for research efforts that will enhance the provision of contraceptives and family planning information and services for men. In addition, the federal government should encourage and fund research and demonstration projects that study how best to provide contraceptives and family planning services for men. Finally, government and the religious community can provide encouragement for men to take greater responsibility in child-rearing and family life.[29]

Professional Education and Curriculum: The American Medical Association and American Association of Medical Colleges should be encouraged to increase their educational programs for medical students at the undergraduate and graduate levels to enhance the training of future health care providers in terms of knowledge, skills, and attitudes for reproductive health, family planning, and all contraceptive methods[30]

Financial Incentives: Many observers of population and fertility dynamics in the United States think of financial incentives as ways to encourage the use of contraception, delayed childbearing, or smaller families. Tax deductions for only two children and linking welfare payments to family size, are proposals that surface from time to time. Several factors suggest that reliance on such financial incentives is not appropriate in a wealthy country with as much unintended fertility as this one. People already want fewer children. Broader access to family planning services and more education about sexuality and contraception seem more appropriate than financial incentives. Additionally, financial incentives related to fertility and family planning have a bad reputation. In poor countries, incentives tend to be offered in isolation from broader reproductive health services. Even small payments (such as clean clothing or travel costs to a clinic) carry the risk of being so large in a poor individual's eyes that they override individual judgment, becoming so attractive that they destroy meaningful choice. In short, they are coercive.

One of the most common suggestions from activists interested in financial incentives is limiting the federal tax deduction for dependents to two children only. It is unlikely that this would affect childbearing by acting as an authentic financial incentive, in part because of the extent of unintended fertility. But such an action could have symbolic value; the federal government would be stating an official, rhetorical preference for small families by adopting such a provision.[31] (Editor's note: The President's Council on Sustainable Development did not take an official position on this matter).

Action: Adolescent Pregnancy Prevention:

Adolescent fertility is also a special case requiring programs designed specifically for young people. The costs of adolescent pregnancy in the United States are incalculable. They are seen in the impaired health of the teen mothers and their infants; in the stunted lives of the families created; and in the lost educational, economic, and social opportunities of the youths affected. Every year, more than one million teens become pregnant–a number that represents 11 percent of all teenaged women and 20 percent of sexually active teenaged women. Half a million of the four million births in the United States annually occur to teenaged mothers. The pregnancy rate among U.S. teens is at least twice as high as in Canada, England and Wales, France, and Sweden, and more than nine times as high as in the Netherlands. This is so despite similar levels of sexual activity. And the birth rates among U.S. teens appear to be rising.[32]

Unintended pregnancies in teenagers–and the unintended births that follow–occur because contraceptives are not used at all and because available contraceptive methods are ineffective. Contraceptive failures are not entirely failures of technology. Contraceptives fail more often among U.S. women who are single, younger, and poor. And Americans experience higher contraceptive failure rates than their European counterparts. Variations such as these suggest that human behavior contributes to contraceptive failure.[33]

Inquiry into why Americans experience higher rates of contraceptive failure and unintended pregnancy than Europeans has found, among other things, that Americans are distinctly of two minds about sex and sexuality. First, Americans are reluctant to discuss these issues as either parents or children and are sometimes ambivalent about having them taught by professional educators. Only 10 percent of American students receive comprehensive sexuality education, for example, although 73 percent of U.S. parents support sexuality education in the schools. Second, media images in advertising, television, and movies are laden with sex and, especially, sex without consequences. It is perhaps not surprising that conversations and knowledge about reproduction and contraception–both required for effective contraception and fully planned pregnancies–are rare, when the media provides so few models for this behavior?[34]

U.S. teens become pregnant for a complex set of reasons, however, and programs to prevent teen pregnancy must take all of them into account. Among the causes most often identified are inadequate health care, lack of access to family planning, lack of knowledge about sexuality, poverty, poor schools, sexual abuse, parental neglect, and lack of hope for the future. While both higher-income and lower-income teenage girls become pregnant, poverty is an important predictor of adolescent pregnancy. Only slight differences exist in levels of sexual activity among adolescents from lower and higher-income families–yet young women from poorer circumstances are less likely to use contraceptives. They are also more likely to become pregnant even if they do use a method and they are more likely to give birth if they become pregnant. Finally, they are also less likely to marry if they give birth?[35]

The younger a girl is when she first engages in sexual activity, the more likely it is that the activity was pressured, if not coerced, often by a significantly older male. Nearly 70 percent of children born to teenaged girls are fathered by men 20 years of age or older. Usually the younger the mother, the greater the gap between her age and that of the father. One study has found that girls 11 to 12 years old were impregnated by men on average 10 years older.[36]

The best strategy for preventing teen pregnancy has always been to urge adolescents to postpone sexual activity. Programs must train teenagers in the negotiating skills required to say no. But programs must also build reasons for saying no–individual self-esteem, alternatives to sexual activity and childbearing, and hope for the future. As important as the promotion of abstinence is to preventing teen pregnancy, it cannot be the only strategy. Approximately one-third of American 15-year-olds have had sexual intercourse at least once. At age 18, the percentages are

56 for girls and 73 for boys. Effective teen pregnancy prevention programs, then, must acknowledge the reality of sexual activity among teens and equip young people to behave responsibly.[37]

Such programs can be school or community-based. They should educate young people in reproductive health, contraception, and sexuality. They should involve males as well as females and they should be built on the successes observed around the country. At the same time, there also needs to be better understanding of the elements of successful teenage pregnancy prevention programs. Through families, social institutions, and community-oriented programs, education should be increased and appropriate services provided for adolescents. Programs can be initiated to encourage parents and other caregivers to fulfill their role as the primary provider of values and information. In addition, access to appropriate services should be provided to adolescents who are sexually active. The federal government should sufficiently fund programs that provide family planing services to adolescents, including programs under Title X.[38]

Educational Environment: Educational providers should be encouraged to improve the educational environment of adolescents through innovative partnerships focusing on improving gender relations and on eliminating violence, sexual harassment, and drugs in schools. In addition, efforts should be undertaken to develop creative programs where teens can continue their education during and after pregnancy.[39]

Parental Involvement: Programs should be initiated to encourage parents to fulfill their role as the primary provider of values and information that promote responsible sexual behavior by young people.[40]

Community-Based Programs: The federal government should continue to fund community-oriented, peer-based, and adult-mentoring programs for young people who are at the highest risk of pregnancy and sexually-transmitted disease and HIV infection. The government should also fund research into the programs that are most effective in preventing adolescent pregnancy. National, community, and religious leaders can foster in all Americans the shared values involved in personal responsibility and the strengthening of the family–the most important unit of society. Government, businesses, and the religious community can encourage innovative community and peer-based counseling efforts for disadvantaged youth and women to encourage these at-risk groups to abstain from early sexual activity and realize their full economic, educational, and social potential.[41]

Educational Programs: All educational curricula and programs, including vocational education, should benefit both boys and girls. Health education should emphasize the role and responsibility of males in family planning. The federal government should augment funding for local school districts to develop comprehensive, age-appropriate sexuality education that stresses abstinence, and age-appropriate, medically accurate information about family planning.[42]

Public Education Messages: The federal government should fund public education efforts to create awareness and provide information on sexual responsibility. This should include the development and marketing of public service announcements developed for a broad audience–adults as well as adolescents. These announcements should cover a broad range of topics including abstinence, contraceptives, unintended pregnancy, sexually-transmitted diseases, the importance of responsible sexual behavior, and the responsibilities of parenthood.[43]

Entertainment and Advertising: The U.S. Department of Health and Human Services should establish a cooperative working group with representatives of all branches of the entertainment and advertising industry to discuss opportunities and strategies for introducing appropriate messages and story lines about responsible sexual behavior.[44]

Initiatives: Adolescent Sexual Behavior:

There are many successful model programs around the U.S. which enhance responsible adolescent sexual behavior. These include the Meharry Medical College *I Have A Future* program in Nashville and the *Harriet Tubman Express* adolescent pregnancy prevention program in Chattanooga. Some adolescent fertility programs have succeeded with small payments to teens for staying *unpregnant*. A scholarship to college can also be a meaningful incentive for some teens to delay childbearing. This approach has been used successfully by the *I Have A Dream* foundation and in the Children's Aid Society program in New York. One of the most successful pregnancy prevention programs in the United States began in 1985 by the Atlanta public schools and the Grady Health System. The program has helped hundreds of Georgia teenagers avoid unwanted pregnancies. Each summer, juniors and seniors from the Atlanta public schools train to become student leaders. Then, for five sessions during eighth-grade health classes, the older teens encourage the younger ones to postpone sex. A Ford Foundation study confirms that students from low-income families who participate in the Atlanta program are less likely to be sexually active than those who do not participate. By the senior year of high school, although participants' abstinence rates drop, their use of birth control practices is significantly higher than among those students that did not participate in the program.[45]

Fighting Poverty

Poverty is an important thread running through the tapestry of unintended pregnancies and births in the United States, both for adult and teenaged women. Poverty and the lack of economic, educational, social, and political opportunities are important influences on early and unintended childbearing. Confidence that one can get a job—as well as other factors that help determine one's sense of hope and self-worth—are powerful determinants in teen decision-making about childbearing. While unintended pregnancies occur at all incomes, poor women—both as teenagers and as adults—experience a higher proportion of unintended pregnancies because of lack of access to services and a lack of opportunity and autonomy of various kinds. Unintended pregnancy often becomes yet another unfortunate consequence of poverty. Women shoulder more than half the burden of poverty in the United States; almost two-thirds of the adult poor are women; and more than half of all poor families are headed by a single mother. Poor women shoulder more than their share of the burden of unintended pregnancies because they have less access to contraceptive services and fewer resources to use in achieving their desired family size.[46]

Beyond poverty, a variety of other conditions can affect childbearing decisions—most notably hope for the future, a sense of self-worth, and the expectation of a job and career. Even in a country as advanced as the United States, there is considerable room for improving the educational, social, economic, and political opportunities for all Americans—particularly for women and minorities. Improving high school completion rates for adolescents at risk of pregnancy; encouraging high school completion even for those young women who bear children; achieving further progress toward ensuring equal opportunities for women in the work-force; and providing women with equal pay for equal work—these all create conditions that enable women to avoid unintended pregnancies, as well as care for the families that they have. The same is true of eliminating institutionalized discrimination against women and expanding their participation in public policy and in holding public office.

Action: Improve Individual Opportunity:

The government and private industry should work in partnership to reduce poverty and provide greater economic, social, and political opportunities for all Americans, particularly women. There must be increased efforts to deal with socio-economic conditions that are closely related to high rates of teen and unintended pregnancy. Government has a role to play in developing laws and regulations to level the playing field in society, encouraging greater equity, and enhancing opportunities for disadvantaged Americans. Private industry can play an important role by voluntarily taking the initiative to break down barriers to women's advancement in the workplace. In addition, by providing jobs, employment training, and economic opportunity, industry can create opportunity for disadvantaged segments of society. Finally, all Americans—as parents, community members, and civic leaders—have roles to play in promoting personal responsibility and common values, which will also support stronger families. Following are representative strategies for realizing these objectives:

Poverty Reduction: All levels of government; philanthropic, charitable, and other non-governmental organizations; and individuals should intensify efforts and work together to reduce poverty in the United States. Family assistance, compensatory education programs, job training, health care, and micro-lending programs, should all be part of on-going poverty reduction efforts.[47]

Eliminate Discrimination in Public Policy: Evidence indicates that, with access to information, services, education, and equitable economic opportunities, women voluntarily have smaller families. Therefore, coercion (for example, forced contraception) or punitive measures (such as conditioning financial assistance on a particular family size) should not be used to influence women's childbearing and contraceptive decisions.[48]

Increase Opportunities for Women: Government and industry should work in partnership to ensure that women are not penalized for child-bearing decisions in terms of their jobs and professional advancement. Special attention should be given to the socioeconomic factors that result in disproportionately high levels of unintended and teen pregnancy among disadvantaged segments of society. These partnerships should work toward ensuring equal pay for comparable work among women and men. Similarly, child care should be made accessible, safe, and affordable enough to enable parents to maintain employment. Lending institutions should also ensure that women have opportunities equal to those of men. Efforts must be made to ensure that women are not disadvantaged by decisions to bear and raise children, in terms of educational, employment, and professional opportunities and advancement. Opportunities for women to participate in political and leadership positions should be expanded at all levels of society, in both public and private life.

Government and industry should expand opportunities for women to participate in the workplace, ensuring pay equity, enhancing the availability of capital for women-owned enterprises, and promoting women into leadership positions in business.[49]

Initiative: New Economics For Women:

Casa Loma is an apartment complex located in one of the poorest sections of downtown Los Angeles and the site of the cornerstone project of *New Economics for Women*, a non-profit development corporation fully owned and operated by women dedicated to improving the lives of poor single parents and their families. Casa Loma has been an incredibly successful public-private partnership because it has facilitated and strengthened opportunities for women to help themselves. The Casa Loma project, which relies on private donations as well as public funds, combines housing with an aggressive agenda of on-site educational, social, and business programs. The U.S. Department of Housing and Urban Development considers Casa Loma a national housing model for the 21st century.[50]

Immigration Policy

Addressing immigration is also an important aspect of the broad question of population stabilization in this country. Immigration accounts for one-third of total U.S. population growth and is a significant factor in the overall effort to stabilize population voluntarily.[51]

The United States is a nation of immigrants and has a strong tradition both of fueling population and economic growth with immigration and of acting as a haven for oppressed and persecuted peoples from all over the world. Large-scale immigration to the United States has occurred in four waves, each–except the current wave–ended by war and followed by a period of reduced immigration. The movement of predominantly British and western European people to the New World to settle what became the United States constituted the first immigration wave, ending with the Revolutionary War. The second wave began in 1820, was dominated by Irish and German migrants, and came to an end with the Civil War. During the third wave, which began in 1880 and ended with World War I, southern and eastern Europeans migrated to the Midwest, and Chinese, Japanese, and other Asians migrated to the West. The fourth wave of large-scale immigration began in 1965 and is still under way–Latin Americans and Asians outnumber Europeans in this most recent migration stream.[52]

In earlier decades, U.S. immigration policy and law were designed to develop vast open spaces and to favor some nations' immigrants over others. More recently, the principles of reunifying immigrant families, whatever their national origin, and of adding needed skills to the workforce have guided immigration policy. The two most recent immigration laws are the Immigration Reform and Control Act of 1986 and the Immigration Act of 1990. The 1986 law–attempting to change the conditions that draw illegal migrants to the United States–addressed illegal or undocumented immigration by creating sanctions against employers who knowingly hire them. The law granted legal resident status to certain illegal immigrants who had been living in the Country for some time and also included various anti-discrimination measures. The 1990 law changed the composition of–and raised the numerical ceiling on–legal immigrants, placing a greater emphasis on work-related migration than previous laws had done. It also established a program to diversify the sources of legal immigration. Both laws have worked to increase the numbers of immigrants.[53]

During fiscal 1994, the Immigration and Naturalization Service, acting under these two laws, admitted 830,000 legal immigrants to the

111

United States. The INS estimates that about 300,000 illegal immigrants also entered the country, intending to remain on a long-term or permanent basis. Seventy percent of legal immigrants settle in six states: California, Texas, Florida, Illinois, New York, and New Jersey. Among illegal immigrants, 85 percent also settle in these six states. Thus, the impacts of immigration, both legal and illegal, are concentrated on a few localities and regions. Through the Immigration Act of 1990, Congress established the U.S. Commission on Immigration Reform to review immigration issues and strategies. The commission has initiated a comprehensive review of current U.S. immigration policy; the review should be complete by the end of 1997.[54]

Action: Develop Immigration Policy:

Little information on the effects of immigration on various aspects of American society and sustainable development is available. There is broad agreement, however, that one of the most undervalued strategies related to immigration involves the promotion of broadly based international policies to address the economic, political, and social conditions that influence an individual's decision to emigrate. It is possible to moderate illegal immigration levels with development, trade, and foreign policies that help to reverse the worldwide poverty, oppression, and environmental degradation that force people from their homes. The United States should develop comprehensive and responsible immigration and foreign policies that reduce illegal immigration and mitigate the factors that encourage immigration.[55]

U.S. Commission on Immigration Reform: It is vital to U.S. population policy that the Commission on Immigration Reform continue its work, and support research to promote the implementation and fair enforcement of responsible immigration policies. Congress and the relevant federal agencies should review and address the appropriateness of recommendations presented by the Commission on Immigration Reform with respect to American traditions of fairness, freedom, and asylum as well as the aim of sustainable development. Priority attention should be given to implement and enforce national policies on illegal and legal immigration policy. The U.S. Commission on Immigration Reform should pursue its work on illegal immigration with due attention to the human rights and general welfare of those affected.[56]

Immigration Research: The federal government should fund research on the environmental and economic effects of migration to the United States and population growth in general to guide immigration and other demographic policies. Research on linkages between demographic change, including immigration factors, and sustainable development should also increase. The technology to collect data for empirical research on U.S. migration and the environment should be improved.[57]

U.S. Foreign Policy: U.S. international trade, environmental, and economic policy should deal comprehensively with the causes of migration to the United States. An effective strategy to prevent unlawful migration should be based on international policies that directly or indirectly address the factors that encourage people to leave their home countries, including lack of employment; poor working conditions; political, social, and religious oppression; and civil conflict. Active measures should be adopted to ensure that U.S. trade and investment policies result in a decrease, not an increase, in rural poverty and landlessness, since these are two factors that directly contribute to emigration.[58]

Development Assistance: The United States should adopt the United Nations' humanitarian aid target of 0.7 percent of Gross National Product each year, targeting these funds at long-term job creation and income-generation activities. The focus should be on assistance for women and men in rural areas who would otherwise migrate to urban areas or other countries.[59]

Population Distribution: Population in the United States is unevenly distributed and always has been. The concentration on the eastern seaboard has been a familiar feature of U.S. population distribution since the original 13 colonies. Additions to the U.S. population are also unevenly distributed. Between 1980 and 1990, the West grew by more than 22 percent; the South by 13 percent; the Northeast by 3.4 percent; and the Midwest by just 1.4 percent. More than half the country's total population growth took place in California, Florida, and Texas. In all, more than 40 percent of the nation's 265 million people live in coastal areas. Population densities exceed 192 people per square kilometer in 20 percent of coastal counties. Densities in the urban cores of some of these areas exceed 3,800 people per square kilometer. Government studies indicate that a 15 percent increase in coastal population over the next two decades is

113

likely, with growth again concentrated in California, Florida, and Texas.[60]

The impacts of domestic migration and rapid growth are felt most concretely at the local level. From small towns in New England and the West, to cities such as Los Angeles and Miami, localities are struggling to manage rapid growth so they can enjoy the economic prosperity that often comes with growth while preserving the character of their communities that they value so highly. Many areas that aggressively sought growth in the past are finding that they cannot sustain it either economically, environmentally, or socially. Uneven population distribution intensifies all of these effects of rapid local growth. The uneven distribution and movement of people also has important national implications. The destruction of coastal areas, the massing of population in areas that would suffer from rising sea levels and severe storms due to climate change, the loss of prime farmland, and concentrated stress on scarce water resources are all issues of national concern.[61]

At the same time, the right to move anywhere is a constitutionally protected right for Americans, and derives from some of the most strongly held beliefs in American culture. Indeed, the freedom of mobility is nothing less than the basis on which the country was founded and built. America is at an early stage in understanding the impacts of uneven population growth and intense population impacts on the local level–and at a similar early stage in the development of policy tools for dealing effectively with these dimensions of the population issue in the U.S.

Efforts should be made to attempt to achieve a geographic distribution of U.S. population which is consistent with the long-term ability of environmental, social, and economic systems to support those populations. This requires policies which respect the right of individuals to live and work in the community of their choice. It also requires that private industry and government at all levels take into account the symbiotic relationship of economic development strategies and population distribution and movements.

The President and Congress should authorize and appoint a national commission to develop a national strategy to address changes in national population distribution that have negative impacts on sustainable development. The commission should be comprised of federal, state, and local

114

government officials, members of private industry, and members of non-governmental organizations. It should be appointed to develop a comprehensive national strategy for mitigating the adverse impacts of settlement patterns within the United States. Topics of inquiry should include, but not be limited to, transportation, tax, development, and land use policies.[62]

The stabilization of the growing U.S. population is a vital component of achieving a sustainable America. Continued population growth puts increasing pressure on all other efforts to lessen the environmental burdens which the American economy places on the natural world. By lessening the number of unintended pregnancies–through education, better health care, and the reduction of poverty–America can begin to move in the direction of a stable and sustainable population. By assisting other countries in these same efforts, America can also lessen the impact of increased immigration on its own shores.

Chapter 5

Sustainable Natural Resources

America is blessed with an abundance of natural resources which provide the foundation for its powerful and vibrant economy and serve as the source of aesthetic inspiration and spiritual sustenance for many. America's continued prosperity directly depends on its ability to protect this natural heritage and to learn to use it in ways that do not diminish it.

Stewardship is at the core of this obligation. The concept of stewardship calls for everyone in society to assume responsibility for protecting the integrity of natural resources and their underlying ecosystems and, in so doing, safeguarding the interests of future generations. Without personal and collective commitment, without an ethic based on the acceptance of responsibility, efforts to sustain natural resources and environmental quality cannot succeed. With them, the bountiful yet fragile foundation of natural resources can be protected and replenished to sustain the needs of today and of the future. ·

Stewardship will become more challenging, however, as human population continues to expand and people's needs and expectations put greater pressure on the environment. As the population increases, so too will demands for fertile soil, clean and abundant water, healthy air, diverse wildlife, food, fuel, and fiber. And as the stresses on society intensify, so too will the need felt by individuals and families to turn to the natural landscape for beauty, solitude, and personal renewal. If present trends continue, however, more people will face a future with less natural resources available for them.

Recent years have presented Americans with numerous examples of conflicts between human needs and the ability of natural resources to meet them. Some stem from the use of or harm to resources which were once perceived as inexhaustible. Other conflicts stem from past development decisions which were made when information was too sketchy to anticipate their full consequences. The depletion of once-abundant ocean fish stocks, the decline of Pacific salmon runs, the loss of old-growth forests, and struggles over the uses of freshwater supplies are clear reminders of the need today for greater stewardship of natural resources for the future. Less than half of America's original wetlands remain. In the last two centuries, the country has lost 90 percent of its northwestern old-growth forests, 99 percent of its tallgrass prairie, and hundreds of species of native plants and animals.[1]

Renewable resources–together with such nonrenewable resources as oil and gas, metals, industrial minerals, and building materials–contribute to the foundation of the economic and social development of the country. Conversion of these resources for human benefit has sometimes resulted in costly and unforeseen environmental consequences, many of which are only recently being fully recognized.

Public lands–including national forests and grasslands, national parks, national wildlife refuges, and rangelands–comprise a significant portion of the landscape. By statute, federal agencies are to administer these lands for the benefit of all Americans, including those who live near public lands or whose economic well-being depends on the goods and services these lands produce. Public lands are managed for multiple purposes; at times these purposes can conflict. They offer extensive recreational opportunities and support millions of acres of cattle and sheep grazing. They produce billions of board feet of timber and are the source of extensive energy and mineral resources. Public lands supply water to many metropolitan areas and often represent the last remaining reserve for unique ecosystems and biological resources. Studies by the U.S. Department of the Interior's Bureau of Land Management have shown that the cumulative effects of past activities on public lands have led to serious environmental problems. These lands suffer from degraded aquatic and riparian systems. Public rangeland has become less productive. Many

117

plant, animal, and fish habitats have become fragmented and there is an overall decline in forest health. Future stewardship of these public lands is critical to the economic and environmental well-being of many regions of the United States, and has important implications for the country as a whole as well.[2]

Nonfederal lands comprise 71 percent of the acreage in the United States. Private landowners and state and local governments are responsible for the natural resources on nearly 1.6 billion acres of land. The majority of these nonfederal lands, almost 1.4 billion acres, are privately owned. Thus, the commitment Americans have to conserving the natural heritage for future generations will depend upon the stewardship of their own lands. Many owners of private lands have pursued ideals of stewardship–enhancing the economic and aesthetic values of the land. Private decisions on managing these lands have long determined the quality, vitality, and fate of natural resources and will continue to do so. The ecological integrity of the nation's natural systems will continue to depend on private choices.[3]

Privately owned lands, however, are most often delineated by boundaries that differ from the geographic boundaries of the natural system of which they are a part. In some cases, therefore, individual or private decisions can have negative ramifications. For example, private decisions are often driven by strong economic incentives that result in severe ecological or aesthetic consequences to both the natural system and to communities outside landowner boundaries. The keys to overcoming this problem are to strengthen stewardship commitments through public policies and individual actions that reflect the principles of sustainable development. There must also be sustained support for collaborative processes that can enable landowners to enhance the value, productivity, and ecological integrity of their lands.

Although much remains to be done, the United States has made major strides in achieving a healthier environment and better protection of its natural resources. For example, by 1994, 14 million acres across the United States were protected through regional, state, and local land trusts. These private and voluntary efforts have produced a 49 percent increase in conservation acreage since 1990. Citizens, environmental organizations, and government at all levels are working together to save precious natural resources while safeguarding jobs and local traditions.[4]

Actions to protect the bayous of southern Louisiana, Mono Lake in the Sierra Nevada Mountains, and striped bass in the Chesapeake Bay are but a few examples of collaborative approaches to natural resources stewardship. Soil conservation is another case in point. Faced with increasing soil losses due to erosion, Congress enacted the Conservation Reserve Program in 1985, which authorizes contracts with farmers to convert highly erodible cropland to less intense forms of production such as trees and permanent grasses. Since then, 36.4 million acres, or 9 percent of cropland has been retired from crop production; on this land, soil erosion has dropped by 93 percent. Stewardship of the ocean's resources is also critical to the nation's public trust responsibility. Oceans provide jobs, recreation, and transportation to coastal communities–home to nearly half of the country's population. The sustainable use of these marine ecosystems, as well as the species that inhabit them, is crucial to the future of these regions and the nation at large.[5]

Ensuring that an environmental stewardship ethic is a guiding principle of natural resources management requires a lifelong commitment from individuals, communities, corporations, and the nation–today and for generations to come. How can society best develop and maintain a commitment to stewardship? The answer is multifaceted, but it starts with understanding the dynamics at work in the environment and the connection between environmental protection, economic prosperity, and social equity and well-being. It depends on the processes by which individuals, institutions, and government at all levels can work together toward protecting and restoring the country's inherited natural resource base. Education, information, and communication are all important for developing a stewardship ethic. Also important is the widespread understanding that people, bonded by a shared purpose, can work together to make sustainable development a reality. The following policy recommendations and actions offer ways in which stewardship can help move the nation toward sustainable development.

Collaborative Natural Resource Management

The collaborative decision-making processes described in Chapter 10 can be particularly useful in the responsible stewardship of natural resources. Collaborative approaches can apply both to public and private resources when the decisions made on their use have broad implications for the whole community. The conflicts over natural resources increasingly are exceeding the capacity of institutions, processes, and mechanisms to resolve them. Adversarial administrative, legal, and political processes are common venues for challenges to the many interests in natural resources. These processes typically stress points of conflict, in the process dividing communities and neighbors. Litigation tends to be acrimonious and costly, often resulting in solutions that do not adequately address the interests of one or more key parties. What is usually missing from the process is a mechanism to enable the many parties to work together to identify common goals, values, and areas of interest through vigorous and open public discussion.

Many types of groups are discovering and demonstrating that collaborative approaches offer useful tools for identifying common goals and resolving conflicts. Experience is showing that they can serve as reliable means for addressing different interests; putting near-term problems in the context of long-term needs; and integrating economic, environmental, and social considerations. Cooperative approaches allow parties to move beyond the limits of narrow jurisdictions to adopt innovative solutions and reflect community interests as well as the interests of citizens elsewhere. Collaborative approaches can give impetus to all parties to make use of the best available science in their decision-making processes, monitor natural resource trends, and exercise collective responsibility for natural ecosystems.

Basing collaborative approaches on natural systems encourages people to identify with a particular place and take responsibility for it. Frequently, people do not feel connected to a place or locale and so do not feel responsible for taking care of it. Decisions typically get made in fragmented ways, and the connection between individual lives and the health of an ecosystem can seem remote. Yet human activities are very much connected to the ecological integrity of a natural system—such as a watershed. Considering human impacts within a framework based on a defining natural system can highlight cause-and-effect relationships. It can also help identify long-term implications which lead to solutions that integrate economic, environmental, and equity goals. For example, construction practices that keep harmful sediments from accumulating in rivers and lakes help protect the quality of water for drinking and swimming purposes. Careful planning of a community's development along a lake or river can enhance property values, increase merchants' sales, add to people's appreciation of the natural environment, and protect wildlife habitat. The possibilities for recognizing and responding to these kinds of inter-relationships abound.

Government plays a critical role in conserving, protecting, and restoring natural resources by setting and maintaining a foundation of strong environmental laws and regulations. Enforcement is an important component, particularly for pollution control. No single government agency or collection of unconnected agencies is sufficient. No set of statutes or regulations–however comprehensive and detailed–can take the place of the commitment by individuals and communities to protect natural resources and ecological integrity. Individuals, communities, and institutions need to work individually and collectively to ensure the stewardship of natural systems.

Finding an acceptable integration of local, regional, and national interests is not without difficulty. Issues involving public lands and marine resources, for instance, require that a broad, national perspective be maintained. However, collectively, the various interests directly involved in a particular natural resource issue may be able to contribute to more informed and reasoned choices for resolving issues. At the same time, many people who live at a distance from a particular natural resource system can have strong and legitimate interests in the outcome of its multiple uses. To ensure that all interests are represented, all parties need to be involved in the decision-making process–including federal, state, and local governments; private institutions; businesses; national and other non-governmental organizations; and private citizens.

The characteristics of successful collaborative approaches are emerging. Among them are the use of a framework based on a natural system such as a watershed or bioregion, voluntary multiparty discussions, a process which is open to the public, the incorporation of existing law, and the use of the best available science. Government agencies at all levels have a pivotal role to play in encouraging interested parties to search for common goals, resolve conflicts, apply the best available science, inventory and monitor natural resources status and trends, and exercise collective responsibility for overall natural resources conditions.

Action: Use Collaborative Approaches:

The nation should use voluntary, multiparty, collaborative approaches to protect, restore, and monitor natural resources and to resolve natural resources conflicts. The President should issue an executive order directing federal agencies under the Government Performance and Results Act to promote collaborative approaches toward managing and restoring natural resources. Governors can issue similar directives to encourage state agencies to participate in and promote collaborative approaches. Public and private leaders, community institutions, nongovernmental organizations, and individual citizens can take collective responsibility for practicing environmental stewardship through voluntary, multiparty, collaborative approaches.[6]

The federal government should play a more active role in building consensus on difficult issues and identifying actions that would allow parties to work together toward common goals. Both Congress and the Executive branch should evaluate the extent to which the Federal Advisory Committee Act poses a barrier to successful multiparty processes, and they should amend regulations to help accomplish this.[7]

Ecosystem Natural Resources Management

America's history of natural resources management began just before the turn of the last century. Since then, a complex array of state and federal natural resources management laws and implementing agencies has been created, each attempting to balance new tensions over the use and conservation of a particular resource. Around each resource–whether forests, water, fisheries, wildlife, or recreation areas–distinct policies, institutions, constituents, and professions have evolved. Because the health and productivity of these resources and the communities that depend on them are often linked, policies and practices in one resource area have frequently had negative and unintended consequences in another. In addition, science and experience have shown the importance of ecological processes such as nutrient cycling, fire, and hydrologic cycles–some of which operate over broad geographic areas–in determining the condition of a natural resource in a particular place. For example, forest management policies in the Rocky Mountain region were developed before the importance of fire as a factor in forest health was recognized. Because the role of ecosystem processes was not considered, today there are difficult and costly management decisions to be made to restore the vitality of the region's forest ecosystems and the local economies that depend on them.[8]

Concerned about the cumulative impact of numerous local management actions, many scientists and resource managers now believe that biodiversity, water quality, and other natural resources can only be protected through cooperative efforts across large landscapes–landscapes that often cross ownership boundaries. At the same time, conflicting demands for all resources are forcing public agencies to explore new planning and policy mechanisms that would involve broader public participation in order to minimize conflicts. Since 1992, federal agencies, including the U.S. Forest Service, the U.S. Bureau of Land Management, the U.S. Fish and Wildlife Service, the U.S. National Park Service, and the U.S. EPA, have established ecosystem management policies to guide their decisions for achieving various goals, including those set by law.[9]

Independently, a number of efforts have been undertaken to combine the use of ecosystem approaches with greater public participation. They have used such mechanisms as regional planning or advisory groups to integrate natural resources management decisions. Conservation groups; local governments; private landowners; and forest products, energy, and utility firms are now involved in dozens of cooperative efforts to use ecosystem approaches for natural resources management around the country. More open communication and closer collaboration can enable those using ecosystem approaches to anticipate potential problems and conflicts, and identify potential solutions.[10]

Still, the effective and widespread application of collaborative ecosystem approaches faces a number of challenges. First, the approaches are new and experimental. Of the nearly 150 examples of ecosystem approaches to natural resources management in the United States, nearly all have been initiated since 1990. Because the lessons of these early initiatives are just beginning to emerge, public agencies, landowners, and various interest groups can learn from these efforts. Second, ecosystem approaches offer the most promise for public and private lands that are managed for multiple uses–such as forestry, fisheries, grazing, and recreation. It is in these areas that cooperative efforts to maintain important ecosystem processes will offer the greatest benefits for long-term resource productivity and biodiversity conservation.[11]

Ecosystem approaches have been recognized by parties with differing perspectives as the best means to move forward in a new era in which scientific information, communication, and management cooperation will be essential in making widely accepted decisions that will perpetuate America's natural resources. The following recommendations provide a basis for making ecosystem approaches to natural resources management more effective.

Action: Sustain Ecosystem Integrity:

America should work to enhance, restore, and sustain the health, productivity, and biodiversity of terrestrial and aquatic ecosystems through cooperative efforts that use the best ecological, social, and economic information to manage natural resources. Federal and state agencies should identify and address areas in which interagency cooperation is needed for sustaining ecosystems, natural resources productivity, and biodiversity; and they should allocate funds to ensure successful cooperation. Since many agencies operate under laws passed decades ago, they should help revise legal and policy frameworks to address the needs of maintaining ecosystem processes and the resources that depend on them.

Conservation groups, private landowners, and local governments should identify actions and conditions that will advance their objectives. Their participation in ecosystem approaches to natural resources management are vital to success. Government agencies at all levels should help cooperative local efforts begin to use ecosystem approaches to natural resources management by providing access to information, technical assistance and funding, and by removing any policy and administrative obstacles to successful ecosystem approaches.

Federal and state agencies, in collaboration with localities, should develop indicators which can be used to monitor the status of ecosystems and natural resources productivity. They should encourage consensus goals and shared responsibilities for restoring damaged ecosystems. Government agencies, conservation groups, and the private sector should expand the use of ecosystem approaches by using collaborative partnerships, developing compatible information databases, and carrying out appropriate incentives for responsible stewardship.[12]

124

Emphasizing Incentives/Eliminating Disincentives

Another important step for encouraging natural resources stewardship of public and private lands and waters is to review and, where necessary, overhaul the wide range of incentives and disincentives which affect such stewardship. The need for review is particularly important in light of funding cuts in government natural resources programs. The challenge is to identify new market-based approaches that promote stewardship and participatory planning and to eliminate those subsidized programs that encourage the unsustainable use of federally owned resources such as minerals, forage, and timber.

While public lands play an important role in achieving the national goal of sustainability, private lands are also critical. Sixty-four percent of the lands in the continental United States are privately owned. Moreover, of the 728 species listed as endangered or threatened under the Endangered Species Act, 50 percent are found on federal lands, while the other 50 percent are found on a combination of nonfederal lands, including state and locally owned lands and private lands. To date, existing laws and regulations by themselves have not been entirely satisfactory in achieving positive results.[13]

In the case of timber lands, encouraging improved stewardship of private industrial and nonindustrial forest lands offers an opportunity to enhance profitability and accrue long-term ecological benefits. Encouragement could come in the form of increased technical or financial assistance, or both. Nonindustrial private forest landowners own 287.6 million acres or 59 percent of the nation's 490 million private forested acres. The forest industry owns another 70 million acres or 14 percent. Although most forest lands are managed for multiple use, private forest lands are often managed with a stronger emphasis on timber production than are public forest lands. Private lands are also capable of producing more wood at a lower cost per unit than public timber lands. Because of these factors, private forest land figures significantly in market-based approaches to promoting natural resources stewardship. A review of potential incentives for timber production on private forest lands might lead to opportunities to meet society's demand for forest products while providing jobs and environmental quality in a more economically efficient way.[14]

As discussed in Chapters 2 and 3, correctly designed market incentives used within an appropriate regulatory framework can provide the most efficient set of tools to redirect pressures that are leading to the degradation of the country's natural resource base. Public policies that undermine stewardship and encourage excessive exploitation of resources include public expenditures that lead to ecologically harmful projects and tax policies that promote resource degradation. Public policies and private activities aimed at conservation can use a combination of economic self-interest, voluntary action, and, when necessary, regulatory controls to promote sustainability. By integrating public policy with market-driven economic incentives, appropriate regulations can encourage private property owners and public lands users to make socially desirable and economically beneficial decisions that promote resource conservation.

Action: Incentives For Resource Conservation:

America should create and promote incentives to stimulate and support the appropriate involvement of corporations, property owners, resource users, and government at all levels in the individual and collective pursuit of the conservation of natural resources. Commercial users of public resources should pay the full cost associated with the depletion or use of those resources–reflecting both market and nonmarket values. For example, decisions on providing access for timber and grazing uses on public lands should take into account not only financial costs but also the total net impacts on ecological systems (positive as well as negative), including any effects on water quality and biological diversity.

Federal, state, local, and tribal officials, in making decisions on public infrastructure projects, should weigh the economic benefits of the project against the full costs–incorporating both market and nonmarket costs, such as the net impacts on the ecological system. Existing projects should be re-engineered to the extent possible to restore ecological functions and habitat using cost-benefit analyses, again including both market and nonmarket values.

Legislative bodies at the federal, state, local, and tribal levels should extend tax credits and deductions to promote actions taken by property owners to enhance the long-term conservation value of their property beyond compliance with existing regulations. However, landowners who take conservation action beyond mere compliance with regulations–such

126

as establishing habitat for endangered species–should not face penalties for returning to the regulated standard.

State, local, and tribal governments should identify habitats of particular ecological concern and establish impact fees or mitigation requirements to shift effects to regions of lower concern. State and federal governments should establish, through general taxes or user fees on public resources, a trust fund to be used in purchasing particularly ecologically sensitive or valuable habitats.

The federal government should develop a matching fund program to encourage federal, state, local, and tribal investment in sustainable programs and projects. The federal government should establish a revolving fund to enable local communities to undertake the planning required to develop incentive-based resource conservation programs.[15]

Such changes also lead to specific areas which will improve the implementation of sustainable development. The challenge here is to reform natural resource policy in three distinct areas:

Subsidies: Many subsidies encourage consumption-based rather than conservation-based behavior by obscuring the true costs of decisions. Examples of such subsidies include subsidized overgrazing of public lands which leads to the destruction of habitat and reduced productivity. Similarly, cheap hydropower and subsidized diversion of water for irrigation jeopardizes the continued existence of Columbia River salmon and other endangered species. Additionally, price supports for sugar production lead to habitat loss and increasing pollution of Florida waterways![16]

Expenditures: Public expenditures on economic infrastructures such as roads, dams, schools, and industrial parks can encourage investment and induce development in areas that might not otherwise be attractive for development. Such developments are often environmentally destructive. This is the case, for instance, when such developments encourage sprawl that requires costly new infrastructure. Agriculture that requires costly subsidized electricity is another example of government spending which may not always be efficient and sustainable![17]

Taxation: Tax codes and policies, if properly designed, can promote sustainability and resource conservation by creating incentives and disincentives to promote sustainability. These tools do not eliminate costs of sustainability and conservation, but rather transfer costs from the private to the public sector. Tax incentives include property tax reductions for those who commit to managing their property for threatened or endangered species. Other incentives are the allowance of tax credits for expenses incurred in improving degraded habitat or creating new habitat for target species. Preferential capital gains treatment of returns from sustainably managed timber operations can be used to encourage this type of land use. Other capital gains incentives could include tax deferral on land transfers that facilitate or continue to provide for conservation. Another incentive could be tax deductions for income which is derived from lands that are managed fully and perpetually for threatened or endangered species. Inheritance tax reform can promote conservation by ensuring that large tracts of habitat do not have to be liquidated, broken apart, or devoted to more economically intensive use as a consequence of inheritance taxes (or their avoidance). Non-tax incentives include the use of transferrable development rights and land swaps and the use of conservation credits as a mechanism to create a market for environmentally protective actions.[18]

In sum, executive and legislative bodies at the federal, state, local, and tribal levels responsible for tax, economic, and other policies that influence natural resources should remove disincentives that undermine stewardship and establish incentives for sustainable resources management and protection.

Stewardship of Natural Resources

Concern for the environment and the growing gap between the rich and the poor at home and abroad are leading many Americans to give new and serious attention to humanity's moral responsibility to care for the planet, its people, and the generations that will follow. In a recent poll, ninety percent of Americans agreed that "an underlying cause of environmental problems is that we focus too much on getting what we want now and not enough on future generations."[19]

Religious communities have for centuries examined what is today called sustainability—terming it *stewardship*. In many religious teachings, stewardship derives from the perception that creation is a gift that includes the responsibility to care for it. Also, certain American intellectual traditions, not part of a formal religion, have examined the same territory in determining the nature of the *good life*. These traditions include civic republicanism, the thinking of Ralph Waldo Emerson, and John Dewey's progressivism.[20]

Most Americans associate themselves with a religious community. Recent polls reveal that more than 90 percent express a religious preference, two-thirds are members of a church or synagogue, 40 percent of adults attend services in any given week, and more than half say that religion is "very important in their lives."[21]

The vast majority of America's religious communities embrace an understanding of the stewardship tradition. A North American Coalition on Religion and Ecology poll of 30 Christian denominations found that 93 percent support the notion of stewardship of the Earth. Eastern and Native American religious traditions are rich with respect for the Earth. Various U.S. ecumenical and interfaith organizations have had an interest in environmental concerns for some decades. The National Council of Churches established an Environmental Stewardship Action Team in 1969. During the 1970s and 1980s, congregations all over the country concerned themselves with grassroots issues such as energy efficiency and recycling, while theologians examining the doctrine of creation and the concept of stewardship created a large body of scholarly literature. The World Council of Churches worked throughout the 1980s on a program entitled, *Justice, Peace, and the Integrity of Creation*. The *National Religious Partnership for the Environment* was launched in 1993 at the White House, bringing together major Catholic, Jewish, and Protestant institutions. Faith communities were a major presence at both the 1992 Earth Summit in Rio de Janeiro and the 1994 Cairo Conference on Population and Development.[22]

Much reflection on the concept of stewardship centers around four interacting moral concerns. The first is a commitment to sustainability—the same kind of sustainability discussed in this book, or a belief that current practices resulting in deforestation, groundwater depletion, mining, pollution, and other assaults on the health of the natural world must be corrected. The Native American concern for the seventh future generation has become a widely embraced example of the commitment to sustainability. The second moral concern is represented in a commitment to live in solidarity with the poor. Religious communities are making connections between social injustice and environmental degradation and are drawing attention to environmental justice and the need to fight poverty at home and abroad. The third and related concern is a commitment to sufficiency. Religious communities emphasize that all people have a moral right to certain basic human needs, and that a satisfying life is discovered more in the sharing of wealth than in its accumulation. Finally, many religious communities insist that all people must have the ability to participate in the decisions that affect their lives.

This rejuvenated reflection on the ancient stewardship tradition has given rise to a critical examination of materialism in American culture. A recent poll taken by Princeton University's Center for the Study of American Religion found that 74 percent of working Americans believe that materialism is a serious social problem in the United States. And yet, apparently without ambivalence, Americans live the most material-intensive lives of anyone in the world.[23]

This contradiction is an indication of how difficult it is to live out an ethic of stewardship and achieve sustainability—to resolve the contradictions between moral beliefs and the messages and incentives sent by the larger society. Religious communities have nurtured the concept of stewardship over the centuries and have much to share with those who are struggling to arrive at models for sustainable living today

Further elaboration of an explicit ethic of stewardship—care for all creation, for all time—would enrich understanding of sustainable ways of living, would provide grounds for choosing the most moral among the many alternative ways of living sustainably, and would inspire commitment to sustainable ways of life.[24]

Action: Incentives for Stewardship:

Religious and cultural organizations, consumer groups, environmental groups, and others should investigate the nature, role, and application of a stewardship ethic and highlight its importance in all their public education materials and programs. In conjunction with representatives of labor, business, academia, and philanthropy, these groups should be bold in sparking a new national discussion about the *good life*, affirming the many aspects of our economy and culture that are already inherently satisfying while pointing to the need for greater balance in the pursuit of material and non-material needs.[25]

Sustainable Management of Forests

Forests cover about one-third of the country—more than 737 million acres. They provide a great diversity of economic, ecological, recreational, cultural, and spiritual benefits. Important steps—including both public and private action—have been taken to put the United States on an effective course for achieving sustainable forestry management. There is a rich fabric of laws, institutions, and activities under way at the federal, state, local, and tribal levels to guide the management of the nation's forests.[26]

In 1992, during the United Nations Conference on Environment and Development in Rio de Janeiro, the United States announced its commitment to carry out ecosystem management on all federal forest lands. And, at the Second Conference on the Protection of Forests in 1993 in Helsinki, the United States declared its commitment to the goal of achieving sustainable management of all U.S. forests by the year 2000. A variety of international and domestic efforts are emerging that are intended to promote and expand sustainable forest management. These efforts include work by the U.S. Forest Service and other federal agencies, the Forest Stewardship Council, the Canada-U.S. Association of Rainforest Alliances through the *Smartwood Network*, the *Stewardship Incentive Program*, and the Society of American Foresters through its *Long-Term Health and Productivity Initiative*. These efforts offer a variety of approaches, including technical assistance, education, financial incentives, monitoring, and certification. Also contributing to promoting and expanding sustainable forest management are U.S. efforts in international negotiations.[27]

Private initiatives include the American Forest and Paper Association's adoption in 1994 of the *Sustainable Forestry Initiative*. This is a significant development. The association's membership is comprised of more than 400 forest and paper companies and related trade associations. Its members account for approximately 84 percent of the paper production, 50 percent of the solid wood production, and 90 percent of the industrial forest land in the United States. The initiative lays out principles and measures of performance for sustainable forestry management on industrial lands and nonindustrial private lands that supply timber to industry. One of the recent key events in forestry was the 1996 Seventh

131

American Forest Congress. It was convened by a broad range of participants–including environmental, industry, government, and academic leaders–to develop a shared vision; a set of principles; and recommendations for forest policy, research, and sustainable management of America's forests into the next century.[28]

Action: Achieve Sustainable Forest Management:

America should establish a structured process involving a representative group of parties to facilitate public and private efforts to achieve the national goal of sustainable management of forests by the year 2000. The President should direct the U.S. Department of Agriculture, the U.S. Department of the Interior, and other relevant agencies to build upon, support, and promote ongoing efforts to achieve sustainable forest management. These efforts should address such areas as national and international initiatives, terms of reference, criteria for defining sustainable forest management, and indicators to measure progress toward their achievement, and the use of resulting information in policy formulation. The agencies should explore various means for accomplishing this.[29]

Initiative: Sustainable Forested Wetlands:

The Nature Conservancy and Georgia-Pacific have embarked on an unprecedented collaborative effort to manage forested wetlands along the lower Roanoke river in North Carolina. The area is inhabited by a rich diversity of wildlife, including deer, wild turkey, black bear, bald eagles, bobcats, and over 210 bird species. In 1994, The Nature Conservancy and Georgia-Pacific agreed to implement a plan to manage the area's forests in a sustainable manner. Under this plan, Georgia-Pacific will own the land, but all of the management activities, including timber harvesting on the seven tracts along the river, will be agreed upon by a joint ecosystem management committee. Representatives from the U.S. Fish and Wildlife Service and scientists from North Carolina State University are participating in the joint management team. Georgia-Pacific has agreed to relinquish its harvesting rights on 21,000 acres of land that are of special ecosystem concern. It will continue to harvest timber on other tracks along the river, but it will follow methods agreed upon by the joint management team. The project represents a significant step toward the sustainable management of forested wetlands.[30]

Replenishing and Protecting Fisheries

Stewardship offers a conceptual framework for integrating the use of marine resources with environmental safeguards. With stewardship, future generations can enjoy a rich diversity of freshwater and marine life. The need is evident. Entire communities and the nation as a whole have experienced significant economic and social damage due to the precipitous decline–and sometimes complete collapse–in fisheries. Habitat degradation combined with overfishing can create what has been called commercial extinction in once-abundant fish stocks.

From Georges Bank off the New England coast to the Gulf of Mexico to the Columbia River, the decline is evident. For example, on the West coast, 214 salmon runs are considered at risk, two of which are endangered due to commercial exploitation and habitat degradation. Habitat degradation, hydropower generation (which hinders salmon migration and diminishes water quality), hatchery practices, and overharvesting are the primary causes of decreases in stocks of fish. The dramatic decline in freshwater, marine, and estuarine fisheries underscores the need for stewardship based on a system of effective laws, regulations, and programs.[1]

Applying sound, comprehensive scientific information to the development of national fishery policies can reduce or eliminate much of the uncertainty that is impeding the protection of freshwater and marine fisheries today. Implementation of science-based fishery management plans will help resolve the problems facing some fisheries, such as overfishing and the loss of spawning and nursery habitat, including fragile freshwater and coastal habitats. But improved management and correction of overfishing alone will not be enough to turn around the sharp decline in fish stocks. Protection and restoration of aquatic ecosystems and proper care of watersheds and riparian habitats are also critically important. New policies need to be initiated and existing ones continued and enhanced to eliminate, mitigate, and prevent activities that degrade fishery habitats.

Action: Restore Fisheries:

America must restore habitat and eliminate overfishing to rebuild and sustain depleted wild stocks of fish in U.S. waters. The U.S. Department of Commerce–in conjunction with the National Marine Fisheries Service; the Regional Fisheries Management Councils; and other relevant federal agencies, state fisheries management agencies, and tribes–should develop fishery management plans that remove the human causes of fish population decline. These plans should include the elimination of habitat degradation activities and the removal of incentives that encourage such activity. These plans should adopt the *precautionary principle* in decision-making—that in the face of scientific uncertainty, society should always err on the side of resource conservation.

These plans should address a wide range of issues affecting fisheries, including a reduction in fishing fleets; an improvement in the precision of the science which is used for decision-making; an expansion of quantitative assessments of the social and economic effects associated with specific fisheries; an examination of all of the public and private actions which diminish or harm fisheries; reductions of *bycatch* (sea life incidental to the catch of targeted species); improvements in cooperation and coordination between fisheries and land management agencies, private industry, hydropower agencies, and other parties; and the development of better programs to prevent the accidental introduction of exotic species into the nation's waters.

The federal government, working with regional councils, states, and other parties, should establish an allocation system for threatened U.S. fisheries as a possible fishing management tool. The system would set a limit on the number of fishermen eligible to work in threatened fisheries. In these cases, the parties could explore a trading program that would enable fishermen to buy and sell the limited fishing rights. This action would create a cost-effective program for limiting fishing and thereby reduce pressure on endangered fish stocks. In determining whether to adopt a system of tradable fishing rights, the economic impact on the existing fishing industry must be considered.[32]

National Natural Resources Information

Information on the current condition of natural resources and related trends is vital to measuring national and site-specific progress toward sustainability. There are already numerous sources of natural resources data which are collected by many different government agencies, communities, tribes, private landowners, and others. Much of the information, however, is not readily accessible to public and private policy-makers, managers, or interested citizens because it exists in different formats at different locations. This situation impairs the ability to monitor and assess the long-term effects of management actions and to evaluate sustainability. This problem is particularly acute in the case of baseline data.

It is essential to make data more accessible, to make better use of the data now available, and to move toward compatibility of data from numerous sources. While actions to protect and restore ecosystems need to occur as more complete data are gathered, a comprehensive inventory and assessment of the nation's renewable and nonrenewable natural resources and biodiversity are equally essential. These data can help provide a sound and scientific basis for guiding public and private natural resource decisions.

The long-term goal for strengthening national natural resources information is to bring about better strategic and operational decisions at all levels of government and in private industry based on reliable, high-quality information that integrates economic, environmental, and social considerations.[33]

Action: Improve Natural Resources Information:

America must strengthen the available information on natural resources by integrating and building on existing international, federal, state, and tribal natural resources and biodiversity inventories, assessments, and databases; and by developing and using compatible standards, methods, and protocols. Federal and state natural resources agencies should convene planning sessions among all parties to agree on data and information uses, standards, and methodologies for collecting data and conducting assessments of the nation's biodiversity and natural resources stocks, and the formats for reporting such data and information.

Federal and state natural resources agencies and private institutions can intensify efforts to collect and inventory data—involving contractors, volunteers, and others in the process—and applying agreed-upon collection and reporting standards and methodologies. Federal and state natural resources agencies should also establish accessible and useful data repositories.

All those involved in collecting and reporting natural resources inventories can coordinate their efforts to develop indicators of sustainability and indices which show the status of efforts to achieve the sustainable use of resources. Private natural resources managers can monitor their management practices on a voluntary basis. Independent third-party verification of biodiversity assessments and sustainable practices may also prove valuable. Finally, the federal government should support data collection and analysis efforts for migrating species that breed in the United States but winter in other countries.[34]

Initiatives: Natural Resource Information:

Many initiatives are aimed at improving compatibility and accessibility of natural resources data, including information that is comparable in the computer-based analysis methods used. For example, interagency, region-wide ecosystem assessments are being conducted in the Pacific Northwest, the upper Columbia River Basin, the Sierra Nevada region of California, and the southern Appalachians. These efforts should be continued and expanded to include other regions across America.

Federal and state agencies and tribes can play an important leadership role by collaborating in the development of methods and protocols for data collection, analysis, display, and access. It is useful to build on past experience, such as the national natural resources surveys conducted for the past 20 years by the U.S. Department of Agriculture's Natural Resources Conservation Service and Forest Service, and by the U.S. Fish and Wildlife Service.[35]

The national natural resources surveys and region-wide ecosystem assessments focus primarily on generic resource categories. In addition, there is the national network of *Natural Heritage Programs* which provides more detailed information on the distribution and abundance of plant and animal species and types of ecosystems. This network of state databases is the product of 20 years of partnership efforts involving state government agencies and The Nature Conservancy. The resulting *Heritage Network* offers a comprehensive source of data on biological diversity and is a useful complement to other resource databases.[36]

Partnerships for Conservation

In areas that lie between densely populated urban land and protected wildlands, the interaction between people and their environment is critically linked to the protection of biological diversity and environmental quality for future generations. Owners of private property in these semi-natural areas are important participants in preserving biodiversity and creating sustainable economies. Future economic and ecological prosperity will depend to a significant degree on the ability to recognize and support the role that private landowners–in partnership with public and private conservation organizations–can play in promoting natural resources stewardship. Additionally, effective biodiversity conservation can help prevent species from declining to the point of endangerment and being listed under the Endangered Species Act.

Private voluntary partnerships can complement efforts under the existing system of laws that safeguard the environment. The effects of these efforts can extend to public and private protected lands, including conservation areas and preserves that provide an important measure of biodiversity protection across the country. The ability of future generations to make a living in these areas will be influenced by the extent to which private owners' efforts to conserve the landscape receive recognition and support.

Voluntary partnerships for conservation will benefit by drawing on three principles: (1) sharing the lessons already learned about conservation on private lands, (2) recognizing the successful efforts of those who have taken steps on their own property to demonstrate natural resources stewardship, and (3) creating incentives that assist landowners in developing conservation strategies. Conservation easements, land exchanges, and the transfer of development rights are types of mechanisms that can recognize the economic concerns of landowners and the common goal of conservation. Use of these tools as a part of voluntary partnerships can help ensure that ecologically sensitive lands receive a measure of protection, complementing the nation's system of public and private protected areas, conservation areas, and preserves.[37]

Action: Foster Biodiversity Conservation:

All parties should act to create voluntary partnerships among private landowners at the local and regional levels to foster environmentally responsible management and protection of biological diversity, with government agencies providing incentives, support, and information. The federal government should provide incentive grants to landowners who act to protect and manage habitat for native species. Federal, state, and local tax laws, including estate and inheritance tax laws, should encourage private landowners to protect biodiversity by managing lands for conservation, improving degraded habitat, or donating land into protected status.

State, regional, and local authorities can provide incentives to private landowners by targeting the use of bonds to finance the purchase–or protection through easements–of lands with significant natural value that are most threatened by incompatible uses. These funds should be used to capitalize trusts for protected areas, quasi-governmental conservancies, or other land funds wherever possible. State and local land trusts and conservancies can develop covenants among cooperating owners to maintain the long-term health and integrity of ecosystems. State and local land trusts and conservancies can enlist the cooperation of landowners in sustainable management patterns. Finally, voluntary regional or watershed landowner councils can be formed to promote information sharing and cooperation. The federal government should recognize and encourage these efforts by creating partnerships with non-profit organizations.[38]

The prosperity of America is directly related to the wealth of natural resources which it contains. Only through careful stewardship can the fruits of these resources be passed on for the benefit of future generations. Every part of society–industry, agriculture, government, academia, non-profit organizations, and individuals–must become involved in the effort to conserve and protects our abundant natural resources. Working together, creating innovative methods, developing new ideas, and building a framework of trust, America can offer the world an example of true cooperation and progress in the protection of the environment.

Chapter 6

Sustainable Agriculture

U.S. agriculture must become sustainable if the national goal of sustainable development is to be achieved. Sustainable agriculture is agriculture that combines modern technological innovation with proven resource conservation. Sustainable agriculture is food and fiber production practices that protect environmental quality and maintain and enhance profitability. Sustainable agriculture is designed to preserve rural communities and to produce a safe and adequate supply of food for all members of the current and future generations. Environmental quality, natural resource conservation, profitability, preservation of farming communities, productivity, and human health are all interrelated aspects of sustainable agriculture.

Agriculture is held in special regard by many Americans, because farmers, unlike other groups of producers, have played an integral role in the nation's development since its earliest days. Agriculture, of course, is important beyond its role as part of the American heritage. The food and fiber produced by U.S. agriculture has contributed very significantly to the nation's economic growth. Because of agriculture's importance to the U.S. economy—as well as the special reverence in which family farms are held—its continued vitality is essential for the nation's future. Agriculture is so familiar a part of the American landscape, and its products so abundant in the United States, that Americans tend to take the importance of its sustainability for granted. Whether agriculture will continue to meet the needs of present and future generations is not certain, however. It already faces several significant challenges.

Between 1950 and the early 1990s, the real (inflation-adjusted) prices of farm commodities dropped, while crop and animal production nearly doubled. But the production of food and fiber has had negative impacts on the environment, including losses of plant and animal habitat and—as a consequence of runoff from farmers' fields—reductions in water quality. The costs of sediment damage have been particularly significant. A study conducted by the U.S. Department of Agriculture in 1989 estimated the annual costs of this damage to be between \$4-5 billion in the mid-1980s. If these environmental costs were deducted from national farm income, the economic performance of the agriculture would not appear as favorable as it now does. One major challenge for U.S. agriculture, therefore, is to decrease its environmental costs in ways that do not compromise its productivity and profitability.[1]

Stewardship of prime farmlands is a fundamental component of sustainable agriculture. America's prime farmlands are highly productive and are of strategic importance to the nation as a whole as well as to individual regions. A number of pressures, both internal to agriculture and external to it, threaten the quality of the natural resources base upon which domestic production of food, feed, fuel, and fiber depend. Although total cropland in the United States has stayed nearly constant since 1945 at 460 million acres, the loss of farmland to urban and other nonfarm uses is a major local and state issue. Much of the nation's best farmland is adjacent to major metropolitan areas and is being converted to nonagricultural uses.[2]

Management of farms and rangeland is also a key part of sustainable agriculture. Mismanagement can create a loss of productivity through such processes as erosion, salinization, over-fertilization and the misuse or accidental release of pesticides and fertilizers. Agricultural land use is also a significant contributor to the impaired water quality of America's rivers, lakes, and estuaries. Other consequences of agricultural land use include risks to human health, loss of wildlife habitat, and declining biodiversity. Because of these factors, stewardship of productive cropland and grazing land as a natural resources base is critical to the nation's future.[3]

Another major challenge for agriculture is to expand its markets so as to continue its growth and create greater wealth. To some extent, this expansion will depend on the design and development of foods with enhanced nutritional value as well as on the creation of new uses for agricultural products. But expansion also will depend heavily on global markets that are free from the influence of trade-distorting policies.

Agricultural research has played a major role in U.S. agriculture's increased productivity and profitability. To meet demands for environmental protection and enhance its global competitiveness, U.S. agriculture will continue to need long-term, multifaceted, and interdisciplinary research. The challenge will be to focus on public and private research, education, and technology development which leads to integrating profitable agricultural enterprises with the stewardship of natural resources.

American agriculture is in transition. The number of farms declined by almost 31 percent, from 2.9 million in 1970 to 2 million in 1994, as the average size of farms increased about 28 percent in the same period. During the 1978-92 period, the number of families in farming decreased about 15 percent, and total farm employment dropped 19 percent. New strategies are needed to address the changing situation. In the past, federal and state governments have designed many resource conservation programs from the top down, with inadequate local involvement. Community priorities are often not heard or understood. To continue moving toward sustainable agriculture, local communities need to participate. Beyond participation, another challenge is to revitalize the nation's rural farming communities. In recent years, the infrastructure of many of these communities has weakened considerably. Investments in this infrastructure are needed to rebuild rural communities. At the same time, efforts must continue to insure that agricultural commodities produced by rural enterprises are grown and harvested in ways that protect and enhance the environment.[4]

In practice, sustainable agriculture can ensure a readily available, affordable, and continuing supply of high-quality food and fiber for all of American society. It can also provide the commodities necessary to fulfill a range of national objectives, including international trade and national commitments for humanitarian food aid. Sustainable agriculture can contribute to increasing efficiency and profitability on farms and to making rural communities vital and economically prosperous. Finally, the techniques of sustainable agriculture can protect human health and the environment by increasing the emphasis on pollution prevention and conservation of biodiversity through integrated farming systems.[5]

Agricultural Management

The management of agricultural activities must be directed to protect air, soil, and water quality, and to conserve wildlife habitat and biodiversity. This will increase agriculture's long-term productivity and profitability as well as enhance human health and well-being. The nation should harmonize the pollution prevention and natural resource conservation policies of various federal, state, and local agencies to minimize conflicts among the policies that undermine environmental protection. Efforts should be made to link technical and financial assistance to farmers and ranchers to their voluntary implementation of farm and ranch-specific plans for integrating pollution prevention and natural resource conservation into their agricultural production. America must renew and refine its land retirement programs to improve their cost-effectiveness, increase their conservation of natural resources, and enhance their ability to prevent agriculturally related pollution.

Of the 1.9 billion acres of U.S. land, excluding Alaska, approximately 907 million acres are croplands, pastures, or rangelands. The management of these agricultural lands can affect the quality of ecosystems and the condition of natural resources over a significant portion of the U.S. land base. For this reason, farmers and ranchers should be encouraged to control sediment carried in runoff from farms and ranches, use environmentally sound pest and nutrient management techniques, reduce consumption of nonrenewable energy, and take other actions that preserve the health of ecosystems and conserve natural resources.[6]

Action: Improve Management:

Because some federal, state, and local policies and programs relating to agriculture conflict with one another, they may actually undermine efforts to attain national and local environmental objectives and sustainable development goals, as well as inefficiently use public resources. To eliminate this conflict, all levels of government should review these policies and programs and work together to coordinate them. In doing so, they should invite non-governmental organizations, such as university research institutions and agribusinesses, to help identify policies that potentially hinder farmers and ranchers from protecting natural resources and preventing pollution. Successful collaboration will depend on the forging of strong partnerships between the U.S. Department of Agriculture (USDA), the U.S. Department of Interior, the U.S. EPA, the U.S. Army Corps of Engineers, state agriculture and environmental protection agencies, farm groups, universities, agribusinesses, producers' organizations, and other entities.[7]

Using USDA Resources Wisely: The USDA, in particular, should take several actions to promote environmentally sound agricultural practices. In addition to assessing whether its policies encourage sustainable agriculture and revising or eliminating those policies that do not, it should direct additional technical and financial resources to meeting natural resource and environmental protection goals, strengthen its soil and wetlands conservation efforts, and link participation in its farm programs to farmers' voluntary implementation of *integrated* farming systems (that is, systems that integrate pollution prevention and natural resource conservation into agricultural production). The USDA should also develop projects to demonstrate integrated farming systems on both small and large-scale farms and direct its research efforts toward promoting environmental protection and the conservation of natural resources.[8]

Soil Conservation: Controlling erosion not only sustains long-term productivity of the land, but also reduces the amount of soil, pesticides, fertilizers, and other substances that can move into the nation's waters. By 1992, American farmers had reduced soil erosion on cropland by over 1 billion tons per year from 1982 levels, according to the USDAs 1992 National Resources Inventory. This is enough topsoil saved in one year to fill a convoy of dump trucks 95 abreast stretching from Los Angeles to New York. Soil erosion savings have come about through the Conservation Reserve Program (700 million tons), conservation technical assistance (300 million tons), and conservation compliance (100 million tons).[9]

The government has an important role to play in resource conservation efforts relating to *land retirement* programs–through which agricultural lands are managed for environmental benefits by contracts or the purchase of easements–with federal, state, or local funds. These programs generate economic and environmental benefits for farmers and society as a whole. The economic benefits include reducing crop surpluses and federal budgetary outlays for crop subsidies. The environmental benefits of land retirement programs derive primarily from the restoration of wetlands and grasslands and include increased recreational opportunities, improved water quality, and the provision of habitat for wild plant and animal species. The *Conservation Reserve Program*, an existing land retirement program with enrollment at 36.4 million acres, has been credited with generating approximately $8.6 billion in wildlife-related benefits alone. Land retirement programs should target environmentally sensitive, marginal croplands–including wildlife corridors and wetlands–so that these lands can be set aside or managed primarily to preserve their environmental values.[10]

Federal and state actions related to integrated farming systems should be consistent, with a view toward renewing and refining targeted land retirement programs to improve cost-effectiveness. Efforts need to be made to enhance pollution prevention, wildlife, and conservation benefits. Legislatively, work must be done to build on the conservation requirements of the 1985 and 1990 farm bills and the Farmland Protection Policy Act. Finally, there should be greater support for initiatives for environmentally friendly pest management techniques with the goal of encouraging agricultural producers–with assistance from public and private partners–to implement integrated pest management.[11]

State Technical Committees: In the past, federal and state governments have designed many resource conservation programs from the top down, with inadequate local involvement. As a result, community priorities often are not heard or understood. To take these priorities into account in the implementation of conservation programs, the USDA has established state technical committees. These committees–which include federal, state, and local agency representatives–provide an opportunity for parties to establish environmental protection and natural resource conservation goals and criteria for meeting them, as well as an opportunity to develop guidelines for the cost-sharing of payments. The USDA should encourage local environmental, consumer, agricultural, and other groups to contribute input to state committees' implementation of conservation and environmental programs.[12]

Coordination of Government Programs: Government should clarify and revise policies and programs in potential conflict with each other and with the objectives of sustainable agriculture and should closely

144

coordinate and consolidate related programs. For example, this could include consolidating certain conservation programs under the USDAs Natural Resources Conservation Service, integrating USDA technical and financial resources with natural resources objectives, and strengthening soil and wetlands conservation programs.[13]

Integrated Agricultural Approaches: Agricultural sustainability can be enhanced by the application of an integrated whole-farm/whole-ranch systems approach which addresses the related social, economic, and environmental effects of agriculture and recognizes the interrelationships among management practices. The systems approach includes management of various factors, such as nutrients, pests, irrigation, and soil, on a site-specific basis. This approach involves steps to develop, demonstrate, and evaluate whole-farm and whole-ranch systems on a wider scale. The public and private sectors should encourage farmers to adopt this approach on a voluntary basis.

There must also be increased efforts to manage animal waste to avoid pollution of ground and surface water. Efforts should continue to reduce agricultural damage to local air and water quality and the global environment. Violations of drinking water, surface water, and soil quality standards by agricultural practices must decrease. Finally, agriculture should be assisted in its efforts to reduce consumption of nonrenewable energy.[14]

Action: Increase Farmer's Flexibility:

Efforts should be directed at increasing the flexibility for farmers who participate in commodity programs to make their own production decisions in response to market prices. This increased flexibility will allow farmers to implement profitable production practices and systems that conserve natural resources, enhance environmental quality, and optimize resource use.[15]

Reform of Price Supports: Commodity programs–through which the federal government supports prices for some crops–can distort market signals and prevent farmers from making the most efficient use of agricultural inputs and the natural resource base. As a result, the programs impose economic costs on farmers and environmental costs on the rest of the American public. One restriction of commodities programs illustrates how these costs arise. *Base acreage* requirements–which specify the minimum number of acres that must be planted in one of the price-supported crops–encourage intensive monoculture. Therefore, the requirements discourage farmers from diversifying their crops in response to market demand. This prevents farmers from optimizing their use of resources, which would promote environmental stewardship.[16]

If commodity programs gave participants greater flexibility in their production decisions, farmers would be better able to manage their crops in ways that increase both profitability and environmental protection. Past experience indicates that farmers will take advantage of opportunities to do so. In 1990, Congress passed legislation that allowed farmers who had signed up for a particular commodity program–for example, the wheat program–to plant some of their land in a crop other than that specified by the program. In response, farmers reduced the number of acres under monoculture and diversified their crops. By 1994, approximately 42 percent of the land on which farmers were allowed to grow whatever they chose was planted in crops other than those specified by the commodity program in which the farmers were enrolled. Congress should continue to enhance the flexibility of commodity programs to allow farmers to manage their lands in ways that will increase both profitability and environmental protection. The programs should allow farmers to diversify their production and optimize their use of resources–including land, water, fertilizers, pesticides, energy, labor, and equipment–in environmentally beneficial ways.[17]

Action: Expand Agricultural Markets:

America should pursue efforts to expand agriculture markets in order to increase demand for agricultural products. The nation should also support continued negotiations on international agreements that encourage more open global markets. The goal should be to increase U.S. farmers' international market share of commodities that are produced in an environmentally friendly manner.[18]

New Markets: If farmers' revenues increase, they will have greater resources to invest in their farms, ranches, and communities, and in environmental protection and natural resource conservation. The keys to increasing revenues are controlling production costs and expanding agricultural markets. Farmers are already highly motivated to control their production costs, but they could use the assistance of the federal government in expanding agricultural markets. Working with private industry, the federal government should explore the feasibility of revolving loans, repayable grants, or matching grants to conduct market research on and promote the expanded use of agricultural commodities in existing domestic markets. Efforts should also be intensified to find new uses for these commodities and to encourage the creation of businesses that utilize agricultural commodities as raw materials in new products. An effort should also be directed to increase the number of environmentally-sound agricultural industries and entrepreneurs.

The federal government also has a role to play in opening up global agricultural markets to U.S. farmers. As the global population grows and as demand for higher-quality diets increases in developing countries, American farmers must be in a position to compete for this additional food-supply business. The government can help them by supporting continued negotiations on international agreements that discourage trade-distoring policies.[19]

Action: Reform Natural Resource Pricing:

America must continue to move the pricing of its public natural resources and their use toward market pricing, recognizing that there may be circumstances when price supports are warranted for the public good. Getting the prices of resources right is a fundamental tenet of sound resource management, yet policies that result in subsidies for the use of natural resources can provide decision-makers and resource managers with misleading information regarding the value of those natural resources. Leases for the use of public natural resources–such as water, grazing lands, and forest lands–and sales of such resources, both of which sometimes amount to subsidies, illustrate one of the consequences of this wrong information. In drawing up contracts and calculating prices for these leases and sales, the government often neglects to include the full costs of making these public resources available to private parties. The government also often fails to consider the market prices of the resources involved. As a result, the government fails to recover the true costs of resource use from the user.

Policies that result in subsidies for the use of natural resources can undermine sustainability because they can incorrectly signal that supplies of the resources are larger than is actually the case and because they do

147

not reflect the public's rising demand for environmental values as per capita income increases. As a result, such subsidies often have supported the over-consumption or low-value uses of natural resources.

To prevent natural resource policies from undermining sustainability, the government should identify and revise those subsidies that encourage the use of renewable resources at a rate greater than is sustainable over the long term. In addition, in drawing up new contracts for the lease or sale of public natural resources, the government should consider the market prices of the resources and the full costs of making the resources available to private industry. Finally, the government should recognize the rising demand for environmental values by encouraging long-term investments in the conservation of public natural resources.[20]

Action: Protect Prime Farmlands Production:

America should keep prime farmlands in agricultural production by implementing (at the appropriate levels of government) rational land-use policies. Such policies include easement, zoning, taxation, financial incentive, and transportation and land development directives that reduce the encroachment of urban sprawl on prime farmlands and otherwise seek to preserve the prime land base of U.S. agriculture. Highly productive farmlands are an important part of the natural resource base upon which the production of food, feed, fuel, and fiber depend. Stewardship of these prime farmlands, which include both croplands and grazing lands, is critically important to the country's economic, environmental, and social health and well-being. Yet several pressures, both internal and external to agriculture, threaten prime agricultural lands with conversion to non-agricultural uses.

One of these pressures is urban sprawl. More than half of U.S. agricultural production, measured in dollars at the farm gate, comes from counties where the expanding urban fringe threatens prime farmland. Moreover, 30 percent of the nation's agricultural production comes from so-called Metropolitan Statistical Areas, where the human population exceeds 197.7 million, and 26 percent comes from adjacent counties with a population density of at least 25 people per square mile. Another pressure derives from the fundamental disconnection between the best use of land resources and the best use of certain lands for agricultural production. As a result, prime cropland is sometimes converted to housing and other non-agricultural uses, leaving less productive land to support future agricultural production. To prevent the loss of prime agricultural lands to nonagricultural uses, states and localities should identify their most strategic agricultural lands and make these lands the objects of farmland protection programs.[21]

Action: Improve Rural Community Infrastructure:

The nation must help rural communities capitalize on the economic benefits of sustainable agriculture by giving priority in rural business development and marketing programs to investments in enterprises associated with the products of sustainable agriculture. In addition, investments in rural communities' infrastructure must be increased.

The economic viability of many rural counties and that of farms and ranches are closely tied. Mainstreet businesses in rural communities depend on the spending power of nearby farms and ranches. In turn, these operations often depend on the services of local agricultural-input suppliers and local agricultural processing, distribution, and marketing enterprises. Therefore, investments that support enterprises associated with the products of sustainable agricultural systems will help farms and ranches as well as rural communities to capitalize on the economic benefits of these systems.

Investments that directly support sustainable agriculture are not, by themselves, sufficient to curtail the exodus of residents from rural communities. To be healthy, rural communities must have at their base a solid infrastructure to support economic development. Therefore, federal and state rural business development programs and marketing programs should make investments in infrastructure that will help revitalize many rural communities—for example, investments in upgrades of bridges and roads and in the modernization of medical, communication, and capital-lending systems.[22]

Action: Maintain Food Safety And Quality:

In order to assure a safe, high-quality, and affordable supply of food and fiber in a manner that protects and conserves natural resources, America must strive for continued improvements in the safety and quality of U.S. food products. The nation should also pursue international harmonization of food standards while maintaining the right of the

United States to pursue its own high standards for food safety and quality.

U.S. food products have long been among the safest and highest-quality food products in the world. Technologies that are being developed to reduce microbial contamination and to better monitor, sometimes on a continuous basis, the threat of microbial and bacterial contamination should enhance prospects for maintaining the safety of food products. Other technologies are improving food quality by making possible the development or design of food products that are more closely suited to the dietary needs of domestic and foreign consumers. These technologies could, in the future, lower the fat content of meats and increase the nutritional protein content of grains and the vitamin content of fruits and vegetables.

But food safety and quality does not hinge on technological advances alone; it depends significantly on government oversight of the U.S. food complex. To ensure continued improvement in food safety and quality, the USDA should assess grading and testing standards, monitoring mechanisms, and safety standards for their effectiveness in protecting public health. It also should expand programs that educate consumers about safe food-handling practices and strengthen programs that ensure the safety of food for children and other vulnerable subgroups of the population. Efforts should be made to increase opportunities for a more varied and healthy diet—especially for low-income families. Finally, the USDA should encourage the development and use of quick field tests for food safety and quality that can be used to assess compliance with microbial contamination and chemical residue tolerances.

Efforts to enhance food safety cannot be limited to the U.S. food system because the system operates in a global market where the safety standards of some countries are lower than in the United States. Given this reality, the federal government should reinvigorate existing efforts to strengthen food safety programs in foreign food-exporting countries. In addition, as food standards worldwide are harmonized, they should be based on a scientific process that is transparent, and open to public scrutiny.[23]

Action: Increase Agricultural Research Incentives:

Agricultural research has been responsible for substantial efficiency gains in agricultural production. Major advances in agricultural science and technology have helped farmers double and even triple and quadruple the per-acre yields of some crops since the mid-1930s. They also have assisted farmers in increasing the productivity of farm animals. For example, at the beginning of this century, a milk cow produced approximately 4,000 pounds of milk each year, whereas today it can produce more than 15,000 pounds over the same period. Looking ahead to the future, the need is for research that helps farmers and ranchers to be good environmental stewards while they are increasing their productivity. In short, sustainable U.S. agriculture will require research that focuses on integrating productivity, profitability, and environmental stewardship.[24]

The federal government should increase investment in sustainable agricultural research, technical support, and demonstrations of conservation techniques and sustainable farming systems. Successful promotion and adoption of sustainable agriculture practices depends on technological innovation and dissemination. Agricultural research should be refocused toward integrated farming systems. The nation should move to develop institutional incentives and funding arrangements to promote research that shows how to integrate agricultural productivity and profitability with environmental stewardship. This effort will require more interdisciplinary research.

Of course, research serves little purpose unless it reaches the hands of those in a position to use it. Efforts should be increased to convey the latest research findings to local farmers and to educate them about the most promising new technologies and management strategies for achieving efficiency. Educational programs to transfer knowledge of existing and developing technologies can be improved. Effective transfer systems include mechanisms to teach and demonstrate these technologies at the local level. Institutions can provide incentives to reward those who develop such research and educational programs. Moreover, when administrators of grant programs are deciding which projects merit such commitments, they should give priority to projects that include on-farm demonstrations of promising new technologies and management strategies for enhancing the sustainability of agriculture.

Specifically, the USDA should substantially increase its funding of research, including on-farm studies of sustainable production systems. It should also expand its cooperative research with academic institutions and non-governmental organizations on perennial polyculture systems modeled on natural ecosystems. All non-USDA programs that provide federal funding for agricultural research and extension programs should begin assessing proposals for their relevance to sustainable agriculture. The USDA should also develop a plan to overcome any barriers to multi-disciplinary research. Criteria to ensure that agricultural research proposals simultaneously address the issues of profitability, productivity, and environmental protection should also be developed by the USDA. There should be efforts to insure that all applied research has technology transfer and demonstration components and that all research grants administered by USDA are allocated on a competitive merit basis. In addition, it is important to continue to support the efforts of U.S. agencies and international institutions that are promoting sustainable agriculture in developing countries. Finally, consumers, conservation groups, and other public interests should be more involved in USDA decisions about which research to fund.

While both publicly funded and privately funded research have greatly enhanced the performance of agricultural producers in the past, two tendencies may diminish the potential contribution of research to the sustainability of U.S. agriculture in the future. First, agricultural research is often narrowly focused. Second, publicly funded research is conducted within the limits of brief budget cycles. Agricultural research tends to focus on individual aspects of agricultural production—for example, pest control, soil management techniques, or development of new crop varieties—rather than on whole production systems, including the ecological systems that are the settings for farming and ranching operations. Moreover, agricultural research tends to emphasize the insights of single disciplines rather than combining the expertise of multiple disciplines, including biology, chemistry, ecology, and economics. This narrow focus—which has evolved in response to institutional pressures for specialization—impedes the acquisition of knowledge that would enhance the sustainability of U.S. agriculture, particularly where environmental costs and values are concerned. To remedy this problem, the USDA (in cooperation with the U.S. EPA and the U.S. Department of the Interior)

152

should take the lead in developing a plan to focus agricultural research on multiple aspects of agricultural production from the perspective of multiple disciplines. In doing so, it should seek input from universities, scientific societies, agribusinesses, grower organizations, and other organizations. Agricultural research programs also often operate on an annual budget cycle, requiring researchers to submit grant applications each year to continue projects. Because projects often require more than one year's work, they may lose funding before they are completed. To remedy this situation, the USDA should revise grant programs to make provisions for financial commitments of terms longer than one year.[25]

Action: Protect Intellectual Property Rights:

The United States should pursue international harmonization of intellectual property rights in order to provide incentives for the development of new agricultural technologies. America should support the objectives of the International Convention on Biological Diversity in order to conserve genetic resources and protect intellectual property rights.

Given the food and fiber demands projected for the 21st century, development of ever more advanced technologies for increasing agricultural productivity is critical. But this productivity must not jeopardize biologically diverse ecosystems. In the long term, the sustainability of U.S. agriculture depends on both new agricultural technologies and efforts to conserve biodiversity and genetic resources globally. Intellectual property rights are key to the development of these technologies and the success of these efforts.

Recent trade agreements–notably NAFTA (North American Free Trade Agreement) and those agreements reached during the Uruguay Round of GATT (General Agreement on Tariffs and Trade)–have imposed new guidelines for the protection of intellectual property rights. As these guidelines are implemented and adopted by additional countries, the U.S. government should work to ensure that they maximize benefits for genetic resource conservation and sustainable agriculture.

In addition, indigenous people's long-standing knowledge of biodiversity resources has helped fuel innovation and development in multi-billion dollar industries, including agriculture. However, they have rarely been compensated for sharing this knowledge. The U.S. government should help to structure and implement the intellectual property

153

provisions of trade agreements and other international treaties in ways that protect the interests of indigenous peoples. The U.S. should also develop a plan for providing incentives for countries to adopt genetic resource conservation provisions and this policy should be reflected in all U.S. agricultural, trade, and foreign policies[26]

American agriculture has provided the world with an abundance of safe and wholesome products. In many regards, the ability of America and the world to flourish and prosper in the future will rely on the continued fortunes of U.S. agriculture. As more people demand more and better food supplies in the coming years, greater pressure than ever will be placed on agriculture to provide for those demands. Only by assuring that the foundations of American agriculture are placed on a permanently sustainable basis can it be assured that those demands will be met. Only by guaranteeing that the American farmer is provided with the information and assistance necessary to make the transition to sustainable agriculture can America feel secure in its continued safe food supply for the foreseeable future.

Chapter 7

Sustainable Environmental Management

To fully implement sustainable development, America must develop an economy which provides for the needs of current and future generations through efficient and environmentally responsible practices. To reach this goal the United States must reform the current system of environmental management. It must build a new and efficient framework for environmental protection which is based on efficient performance, operational flexibility, and strict accountability. The U.S. system of environmental management, built largely since 1970, has dramatically improved the country's ability to protect public health and the natural environment. The air and water are cleaner, exposure to toxic wastes is lower, erosion of prime cropland has been reduced, and some wildlife species are back from the brink of extinction. Much still remains to be done, however, to continue these gains and address new environmental threats.

For the last 25 years, government has relied on command-and-control regulation as its primary tool for environmental management. The federal government issued detailed regulations and often mandated specific methods of compliance. In looking to the future, society needs to adopt a wider range of strategic environmental protection approaches that embrace the basic components of sustainable development: economic prosperity, environmental health, and social justice and well-being. The relationships between these components are clear. Sustained economic growth is dependent on a clean and healthy environment. The ability of the economy to grow, create jobs, and increase overall well-being can suffer if environmental protection strategies deliver low results at a high cost. Resources for other economic and social needs will be diverted if strategies to achieve environmental goals are not designed to achieve results in the most cost-effective manner.

There are a number of tools, approaches, and strategies that–if carefully tailored to different challenges–could result in more environmental protection, less economic cost, and, in some cases, greater opportunity for the poor and disadvantaged. The objective is to create a new framework for integrating economic and environmental goals into the nation's environmental regulatory system in such a way that these tools are applied to the right problem, in the right way, at the right time.

The experience of the last 25 years has yielded valuable lessons for developing a new framework to achieve the objectives of sustainable development. The adversarial nature of the current regulatory system tends to inhibit solutions that become possible when potential adversaries–regulators and industry–cooperate and collaborate. Technology-based regulations can sometimes encourage technological innovation, but they can also stifle it. America has learned that pollution prevention is better than pollution control and the nation's environmental regulatory apparatus should be redesigned to encourage the prevention of pollution before it takes place.

Enhanced flexibility for achieving environmental goals can also spur industry innovation that will lead to better environmental protection at a substantially lower cost–both to individual firms and to society as a whole. However, such flexibility must be absolutely coupled with strong compliance assurance mechanisms, including active and effective enforcement of standards. The American public has strongly rejected proposals to abandon environmental standards. Science-based national standards that protect human health and the environment must be the solid foundation of any effective system of environmental protection. Finally, many state governments have developed their own significant environmental management skills. Indeed, many of the most creative and lasting solutions arise from collaborations involving federal, state, local, and tribal governments in places where environmental problems exist.

Learning to use new approaches to achieve interrelated goals simultaneously will be an evolutionary process. For this new approach to succeed, it will be necessary to build on the strengths and overcome the limitations of the current regulatory system. Success will hinge on the ability to recognize the interrelationships between economic and environmental policies. The following are the broad measures which will need to be developed in order to reform America's environmental management system:

• The United States must reform its current environmental regulatory system to be more cost-effective and flexible in its operation. The U.S. should also establish a new alternative environmental regulatory system that uses participatory decision-making to set verifiable and enforceable performance goals. The new regulatory system should also have greater operating flexibility. While allowing flexibility, the system must also require accountability to ensure that public health and the environment are protected. The new system would eventually replace the current practice of command-and-control regulation, which often creates adversarial relationships and results in costly litigation and delays in meeting environmental goals.

• Additionally, new intergovernmental partnerships need to be developed that can cut through federal, state, and local red-tape and allow for a more efficient approach to environmental management. Federal, state, and tribal governments need to work together in partnership with local communities to develop place-based strategies. These plans should incorporate local and regional considerations and integrate economic development, environmental quality, and social policy-making with broad public involvement. Such partnerships can also build on the most innovative and successful programs available.

All of these changes must be implemented in order to create a new system of environmental management that will be the most efficient and economical possible. At the same time, the new system must retain the high standards which have protected the American environment so well over the past 25 years.[1]

157

A New Environmental Management System

Just as American manufacturing has adopted a goal of zero defects, the nation can aspire to the ideal of a zero-waste society through more efficient use and recycling of natural resources in the economy and more efficient use of public and private financial resources in the regulatory system. The current compliance-based regulatory system focuses on *end-of-the-pipe* emissions–the final output of pollution into the environment. This system has produced many environmental benefits, but often has not provided the flexibility necessary to try alternative, more cost-effective methods. In addition, the current system has created administrative burdens for both government and industry. A new framework must be created that reorients the current system toward one that emphasizes a market-driven, incentive-based approach. It will also be important to develop a positive reinforcement system to encourage the reduction of environmental impacts throughout the lifecycle of products. Under this new framework, government would set ambitious environmental performance goals and give regulated entities both adequate time to meet the goals and the flexibility to determine the most appropriate processes and technologies to use. To develop a new environmental management system will require pursuing change concurrently on two paths: making the existing regulatory system more efficient and effective, and developing an alternative system of environmental management that uses innovative approaches.

Over the years, the value and limits of the current regulatory approach have become clear. Some regulations have encouraged innovation and compliance with environmental laws, resulting in substantial improvements in the protection of public health and the environment. But at other times, regulation has imposed unnecessary–and sometimes costly–administrative and technological burdens on both industry and communities. The current system has also discouraged technological innovations that can reduce costs while achieving environmental benefits greater than those realized by mere technical compliance with regulations. Additionally, the current regulatory scheme has focused attention on cleanup and control remedies rather than on product or process redesign that could prevent pollution in the first place.

Under the current system, federal and state governments have set health-based standards, issued permits for discharges, and monitored and enforced standards set under each environmental statute. In some cases, regulations implementing these standards mandate specific technologies to control pollution. Current laws, regulations, and incentives focus on pollution control and clean-up. Typically, they address emissions into air, water, and land separately, and they often dictate specific technologies for treating specific waste products. The current system controls environmental pollution using a medium-specific approach, for example, regulating the cleanup of discharges into waterways separately from discharges into the air. This medium-specific approach orients decision-makers to end-of-the pipe pollution control and cleanup strategies. Such solutions are often costly and are usually divorced from core business functions. A new environmental management system would focus on prevention, would address environmental impact within a whole facility or within a whole ecosystem, and would encourage better management of materials and energy flowing through production systems.[2]

The current system also focuses on achieving compliance with sometimes complicated and rigid regulatory requirements. An alternative system would maximize environmental performance as a potential means for businesses to save money and gain competitive advantages. Such an approach could produce efficient pollution prevention measures and resource conservation opportunities that may go unrecognized under the current regulatory framework. The new system would be based on maximizing environmental performance in a way that promotes fairness, economic growth, and competitiveness. While the current system principally focuses on minimum compliance with technical standards, the new environmental management system should induce continuous environmental improvement.

Such concerns have contributed to a growing consensus that the existing regulatory system may be greatly improved by moving toward performance-based policies that encourage pollution prevention. Regulations that specify performance standards based on strong protection of health and the environment–but without mandating the means of compliance–give companies and communities flexibility to find the most cost-effective way to achieve environmental goals. In return for this flexibility, companies can pursue technological innovations that will

159

result in superior environmental protection at far lower costs. This flexibility, however, must be coupled with clear accountability and strong and active enforcement to ensure that public health and the environment are safeguarded.

Although moving away from a one-size-fits-all approach should reduce costs to industry, the creation of a new system could increase administrative and policy burdens on federal agencies in the short term. Like clothing, custom-tailored environmental management may cost government more to deliver than the off-the-rack variety.

The new alternative system should be designed to reduce aggregate costs to society, but it will require both industry and government to use new skills and resources, especially at the beginning. Negotiating facility-to-facility agreements is labor-intensive compared to administering permit compliance checklists. Developing facility-specific performance measures to ensure business accountability for negotiated goals is more expensive than enforcing uniform standards. Convening workshops to reach agreeable environmental goals requires additional travel and staff time. The system will also require a farsighted investment outlook on the part of businesses that wish to break out of prescribed solutions and create their own effective solutions. Nonetheless, an improved environmental protection system will reduce the total costs to industry and government over time and will improve the nation's overall economic performance.

Partnerships and collaborative decision-making must be encouraged and must involve all levels of government, businesses, non-governmental organizations, community groups, and the public at large. Initiatives are needed to verify that increased operational flexibility on a facility-wide basis can produce environmental performance superior to the current system while greatly reducing costs. To help ensure accountability, demonstration projects are needed to increase public involvement and access to information. The new system should facilitate voluntary initiatives that encourage businesses and consumers to assume responsibility for their actions. At the same time, the regulatory system must continue to provide a strong safety net of public health and environmental protection by guaranteeing compliance with basic standards.

Movement toward a performance-based system will be aided by public-private partnerships which promote the research, development, and application of cost-effective technologies and practices. Continued, long-term investment in technology will help ensure U.S. competitiveness and leadership in global technology markets. New manufacturing technologies and processes can lower material and energy use while reducing or eliminating waste. Focusing efforts on the development of cleaner and more efficient products for domestic and overseas markets will help base U.S. economic growth on the concept of better–rather than just simply more–products and processes.[3]

Action: Improve the Existing Regulatory System:

The U. S. must accelerate efforts to evaluate existing regulations and to create opportunities for attaining environmental goals at lower economic costs. The U.S. EPA and other regulatory agencies should work to achieve currently mandated environmental standards in a more cost-effective manner by providing greater operational flexibility to regulated entities and to state and local governments.

Other means of improving the current system should include enhanced public participation, administrative streamlining, and identification of opportunities and incentives to exceed regulatory requirements. Better information for all interested parties should be a common feature of these improvements. Changes to the current system could be reviewed by a multi-party panel. The panel could also propose better ways to achieve or exceed current regulatory requirements.

To help achieve this, the administrator of the U.S. EPA, working in partnership with other federal agencies, should have the authority to make decisions that will achieve environmental goals efficiently and effectively. Where administrative authority is insufficient to improve the current system, legislation should be drafted to provide the needed authority.[4]

Reduce the Economic Cost of Regulation: Federal and state environmental regulatory agencies should accelerate efforts to identify and act on opportunities to reduce the economic cost of current environmental regulatory standards. Industry and non-governmental organizations have an important role in this process as catalysts for new ideas and approaches that will streamline and improve the current system. Government

161

agencies should create more flexible, cost-effective approaches to attain the human and ecosystem health goals of existing programs while maintaining their monitoring and verification functions. Regulated entities should still be responsible for demonstrating that they are achieving environmental goals.

In addition to achieving economic savings, improving the efficiency of the existing system would help set the stage for a longer term, more fundamental shift in the way in which human health and environmental quality are protected. The data, analysis, and lessons learned through these innovations can create a more solid base of experience from which to launch a new environmental management system that uses a wider range of policy approaches and tools.[5]

Adopting Performance-based Regulations: Federal and state environmental regulatory agencies should move to create performance-based regulations where feasible and appropriate. Performance-based regulations should be based upon national standards which are designed to protect the health of people and ecosystems and which mandate only the performance standards to be achieved–allowing flexibility and innovation in the methods for compliance.

Federal and state governments should also build on existing programs to design and carry out a system that allows the buying and selling of emissions reductions, while guaranteeing permanent overall reductions in emissions. Such systems should be appropriate to the local environmental problems being addressed. The federal government should also work with industry and non-profit groups to identify cost-effective opportunities to use materials and energy more efficiently.[6]

Improving Regulatory Effectiveness: Federal, state, and local officials can make the regulatory process more effective by communicating regulatory information in plain English and by organizing regulations by industry operation rather than by environmental statutes. They can also aid compliance by avoiding redundancies, inconsistencies, and confusion in their reporting and permitting requirements.[7]

Using Enforcement to Improve Performance: Enforcement is not the end; it is the means to improve environmental performance. Federal and state enforcement efforts can be made more efficient and effective as incentives to better performance by targeting the facilities with the worst

162

problems and familiarizing inspectors with the industry they are inspecting. Enforcement efforts can also be improved by conducting multimedia, multi-program inspections and by exploring innovative ways to level the playing field between states.[8]

Using the Customer Service Approach: Federal and state agencies should adopt a customer service approach when implementing pollution prevention and compliance assistance activities. Despite being the product of multiple levels of government, the assistance and information that business customers receive should be provided in a unified manner?

Implementing Participatory Goal Setting: Companies, regulators, and environmental organizations should work together to define environmental performance goals for industries. Participatory goal setting that results in consistent, accepted scientific standards for environmental performance is a pathway to environmental improvement, and can also be a potent marketing tool for companies.[10]

Improving Communication: Improved communication between suppliers, distributors, manufacturers, and customers encourages environmentally sound products and practices by helping businesses better understand how to minimize the environmental impact of their job specifications and by helping suppliers understand and address the environmental needs of manufacturers.[11]

Action: Adopt an Alternative Regulatory System:

In addition to improvements in the current regulatory system, the U.S. should create a bold, new alternative environmental management system. The three essential principles of the new environmental management system would be: (1) verifiable and enforceable performance goals; (2) operational flexibility; and (3) participatory decision-making in environmental goal setting. Government has a central role and major responsibility in setting environmental protection standards that reflect a broad range of environmental, health, economic, and scientific factors. There are, however, significant economic and environmental benefits in allowing companies to participate in the process and in offering them a greater range of choice and flexibility in determining how to achieve needed levels of protection. But the new, more flexible approach needs to be an optional program. Some firms, because of circumstances and constraints, may prefer to continue under the more traditional regulatory program. Further, a new alternative system of regulation that shifts the burden of fashioning compliance strategies from government to industry will require a strong sense of trust among all parties in the process—a level of trust that has not been part of the nation's past environmental efforts.[12]

Enhancing Flexibility: Federal and state environmental regulatory agencies should give companies greater operational flexibility to determine the most cost-effective means of achieving the goals of superior environmental protection. Regulatory agencies should enter into alternative compliance agreements with facilities, companies, entire industries, and communities. Such agreements should look beyond reductions in a single environmental medium—air, water, or soil—and encourage approaches to environmental management that are facility-wide and site specific. Regulatory agencies must ensure that the interests of affected communities or socio-economic groups are adequately protected. In any new system, government agencies must still maintain monitoring and verification functions, and regulated entities would still have the responsibility to demonstrate that they are achieving the agreed-upon environmental objectives.[13]

Improving Public Participation: Federal and state regulatory agencies and tribal governments should ensure opportunities for broad and meaningful public participation in the development and implementation of new performance standards and regulations. These collaborative processes should afford other levels of government, businesses, non-governmental organizations, and individuals the opportunity to participate in decisions affecting their future. Steps should be taken to ensure that traditionally under-represented groups have ample opportunity for involvement and that all elements have greater access to information on progress in achieving environmental goals.[14]

Developing Demonstration Projects: Demonstration projects would be the first step in implementing the new alternative environmental management system. The U.S. EPA and state agencies should accelerate efforts to conduct a series of demonstration projects to gain experience with policy tools and innovative approaches that could serve as the basis for an alternative environmental management system. A balanced group—with members from government, business, environmental and community groups—should have an integral role in designing, implementing, and evaluating the new system. They should be ready to work with all interested parties to tailor demonstrations that make a credible commitment to going beyond existing standards. For example, longer compliance periods might be considered for demonstrations that are designed to achieve superior protection, but this flexibility could be coupled with interim reporting requirements.

These projects would be selected based on prior environmental performance; ability to implement a new system; and geographic, industrial, and size diversity. Where administrative authority is insufficient to launch the demonstration projects, legislation should be drafted to authorize projects based on the new system.

Lessons from demonstration projects will provide the valuable feedback necessary to determine whether to reconcile the current and new systems or to continue administering two parallel regulatory tracks. Alternatively, demonstrations that focus on the environmental performance of an entire facility rather than on separate air, water, and soil requirements might stipulate that environmental gains for an entire facility must exceed what would have been achieved through source-by-source or medium-specific regulations. These provisions would help ensure that all parties operate in good faith—an essential element of creating trust.

The federal government, working together with industry and non-governmental organizations, should review and evaluate the lessons learned from the demonstration projects. Based on the success of the first round of demonstration projects, a second set of projects should be selected within two years.[15]

Improved National Research and Standards: Implementation of the new environmental management system must be supported by increased national research. This research would provide essential feedback, ensuring that lessons learned through the demonstration projects would reform and improve the operation of the new system. National laboratories and federal research agencies should be directed to conduct the research necessary to help develop, test, and verify the scientific basis of technologies and practices to move toward the ideal of a zero-waste society. This research would help ensure that, over time, the new system would reflect improved scientific information and understanding. Research agencies should identify health risks, monitor trends and environmental conditions, and inform decision-makers of emerging environmental challenges. National laboratories should have the resources they need to help identify opportunities for public-private technology partnerships. They should also be available to evaluate the effectiveness of new technologies and practices in attaining environmental goals at lower costs. The research should also analyze economic, environmental, and social issues on various scales (i.e., local, state, regional, national, and global). These analyses would help define and measure sustainable development and would help assist in the design of future innovations in environmental management. The analysis would also ensure that all efforts associated with the new environmental management system are based on sound science.[16]

Sound environmental research will enable the drafting of more flexible, effective environmental standards that are based on environmental risk and sound science. Such new standards must be focused on environmental performance. They must be written clearly and concisely and they must be drafted with a multi-media and facility-wide focus.

Environmental programs should be created that allow more flexible implementation and operation, with a focus on promoting good environmental performance through flexible permit programs, compliance assistance, and increased delegation to the states. Greater communication and understanding among all parties must be encouraged to build trust by establishing formal mechanisms for ongoing dialogue and public involvement. Tangible rewards should be established for facilities that operate at high environmental performance levels, such as permit review priority, less burdensome monitoring and record-keeping requirements, and public acknowledgment of a facilities' high performance. Finally, the nation should move to establish industry-wide incentives and promote the use of certain tools that encourage facilities to continuously improve their efficiency through the use of marketable pollution credits and the promotion of research and development needed to develop cleaner and more efficient technologies.[17]

Intergovernmental Partnerships

When the current system of environmental management was created some 25 years ago, most state governments did not have the capacity to operate environmental regulatory programs. This is no longer the case.

As the nation's environmental management system has matured, many states have developed strong programs.

Two related reforms are now in order to help shift the focus from the narrow goal of environmental protection to the broader goal of sustainable development. The first reform is to move from a federally focused governmental decision-making structure to a collaborative design that shares responsibility among levels of government. The second reform is to shift the focus from centralized environmental regulation organized around separate programs to protect air, water, and land to a comprehensive place-based approach. It should be designed to integrate economic, environmental, and social policies to meet the needs and aspirations of localities while protecting national interests.

To accomplish these reforms, the new system will need to rely heavily on partnerships between federal, regional, state, local, and tribal levels of government. These partnerships will require unprecedented cooperation and communication within and among levels of government in a geographic area. For example, carrying out a community-designed sustainable development strategy may depend on close collaboration between a local economic development agency, a regional transportation authority, a state housing department, and a federal environmental agency.

This shift in focus to place-based partnerships will require major changes in the roles and responsibilities of federal and state regulatory agencies in communities interested in accepting new local responsibilities. The agencies should help build local decision-making capacities so that communities can begin to develop integrated economic, environmental, and social equity strategies themselves. Rather than simply issuing regulations from afar, these agencies will need to work in communities and provide information and technical assistance.

Along with the devolution of responsibilities to states and localities, however, some traditional responsibilities must be preserved. For example, the federal government must continue to establish consistent national standards to ensure uniform levels of protection across state lines. Greater flexibility is needed–not in the standards themselves, but to encourage greater efficiency in determining the means to attain such standards. In addition, in the development and implementation of place-based strategies, federal agencies must continue to represent and protect national interests that may not be represented by local interests in all cases. Examples include controlling interstate pollution and protecting biodiversity.

Action: Build Federal-State Partnerships:

Federal and state governments must create intergovernmental partnerships to pursue economic prosperity, environmental protection, and social equity in an integrated way. Federal agencies should develop effective partnerships with state governments to administer environmental regulatory programs. These partnerships should eliminate duplicative activities and greatly reduce federal oversight of state programs that have a proven track record.

Savings from eliminating duplication and unnecessary oversight should be dedicated to cover some of the increased government costs associated with regulatory flexibility and place-based partnerships. States should also share in the increased flexibility when using federal grant monies, but such flexibility must be conditioned on performance-based measures of environmental results.[18]

Action: Build Government-Community Partnerships:

Federal and state agencies should enter into partnerships with communities that wish to develop and carry out sustainable development strategies designed to address local circumstances. Federal agencies should work with national associations representing regional, state, local, and tribal governments to create models of guidance that could be issued to government employees to encourage cooperation and communication between and within government agencies in geographic areas where place-based sustainable development strategies are being developed.[19]

Progress Toward Sustainability

Over the past 25 years, the United States has made significant progress in improving environmental quality and in controlling and cleaning up the contamination of its air, water, and land. Much of this progress is due to the enactment of environmental laws and regulations since the early 1970s. The above policy actions are intended to reform U.S. environmental regulation policies to increase the flexibility allowed in achieving environmental standards, improve environmental performance, and reduce costs. A variety of pilot programs are now underway to test this new approach. In addition, a wide range of activities that support sustainable development are underway throughout the federal government. Federal agencies are beginning to adopt integrated approaches and develop new partnerships with other agencies (federal, state, and local), businesses, non-governmental organizations, academic institutions, and communities to make the most of available resources.[20]

Federal Initiatives:

The U.S. EPA has traditionally used strict command-and-control regulatory approaches to protect and improve environmental quality. It is now beginning to focus on allowing greater flexibility in achieving equal or better environmental results. One of several U.S. EPA programs designed to test flexibility is the Excellence and Leadership program, known as *Project XL*. Project XL was designed to respond to industries, communities, and government agencies that had found that the routine application of federal environmental regulations did not always provide the best solutions to environmental problems.

Project XL provides support for pilot projects that can demonstrate that alternative environmental management strategies can achieve better environmental results than required under existing law. It gives environmental leaders more flexibility to test creative, common-sense ways of achieving superior environmental performance at their facilities and in their communities. The U.S. EPA will use the experience and results from all XL pilot projects to improve environmental regulations and management approaches. The benefits could be significant and include greater flexibility to address environmental problems with an increasing use of innovative technologies. The benefits should also foster improved environmental compliance and greater cooperation between the U.S. EPA and industry.[21]

The *Common Sense Initiative* is another U.S. EPA-sponsored effort that is being used to test innovative and flexible solutions to environmental problems and to improve the cost-effectiveness of the existing regulatory system. The project brings representatives of government, industry, environmental organizations, and community groups together to design cleaner, cheaper, and smarter approaches to environmental protection on an industry-by-industry basis. The current focus of this initiative is on six industries: auto manufacturing, computers and electronics, iron and steel, metal finishing, petroleum refining, and printing.[22]

The U.S. Department of Defense and the U.S. EPA have launched a pilot program to demonstrate that alternative environmental management strategies can be used at Defense Department installations to provide a cleaner, healthier environment while reducing costs. Under this program– known as *ENVVEST*–military installations can propose a combination of actions (e.g., pollution prevention and/or end-of-pipe controls) that can achieve greater overall environmental performance with equal or lower costs than the actions required under current regulations. The proposed projects are ranked according to their return on environmental and economic investments, and priority is given to projects that provide the greatest payback over a period of years.[23]

Interagency Working Groups:

Several federal interagency working groups have been established to coordinate efforts between federal agencies to implement sustainable development. They have focused on identifying federal sustainable development programs, education for sustainability, materials and energy flows, and general sustainable development goals.[24]

The Working Group On Sustainable Development has compiled an inventory of the many federal programs that support sustainable development, and it will continue to facilitate the sharing of information among the federal agencies.[25]

The Education for Sustainability Working Group provides a forum for federal agencies to work together in coordinating and implementing education programs that further sustainability concepts and approaches. In December 1996, the Working Group published *Education for Sustainability: An Agenda for Action*. Please see Chapter 9 for further information regarding education for sustainability.[26]

The Working Group on Sustainable Development Indicators has developed a conceptual framework for indicators of sustainable development, and it published an initial selection of important indicators in the spring of 1997. As discussed in Chapter 3, the framework and indicators are intended to reflect the intergenerational nature of sustainable development, as well as the integration of economic, environmental, and social issues.[27]

The Working Group on Materials and Energy Flows is providing a forum for federal agencies to share information on the United States' use of materials and energy. This Working Group also provides a contact point for industry, academia, non-governmental organizations, and state and local governments who are interested in collaborating with federal agencies to further the efficient use of energy and materials. The Working Group is developing a comprehensive inventory of federal databases on materials and energy flows. It published a report in the spring of 1997. It is also developing case studies that will focus on efforts to improve efficiency, increase the recycling of raw materials, and reduce emissions. In addition, a series of non-technical educational articles will be developed to illustrate how consumer choices and consumption patterns affect material flows and waste.[28]

Federal Offices of Sustainable Development:

Several federal agencies have established new offices to further sustainability goals. The *Office of Sustainable Development and Intergovernmental Affairs* of the National Oceanic and Atmospheric Administration, U.S. Department of Commerce, was established in 1993 by the late Secretary of Commerce Ronald H. Brown. The office has two primary functions: (1) to assist communities that have been affected by the collapse of certain fisheries by designing and implementing strategies to rebuild the fisheries and foster the communities' long-term economic prosperity and (2) to further the development of government-wide sustainability approaches and policies. Please see Chapter 5 for additional information regarding the restoration of fisheries.[29]

The *Center of Excellence for Sustainable Communities* is a demonstration project operated by the Denver Regional Support Office of the U.S. Department of Energy's Office of Energy Efficiency and Renewable Energy. The Center's mission is to provide all types of communities–cities villages, towns, neighborhoods, national parks, industrial parks, and others–with information and assistance in designing and implementing sustainable development strategies. The Center is uniquely suited to providing communities with information about energy efficiency and renewable energy programs that fit their specific needs, and it can help them identify the public and private sources of technical and financial assistance needed to implement their programs. Please see Chapter 10 for more information on sustainable communities.[30]

Finally, the *Council on Sustainable Development* of the U.S. Department of Agriculture serves as a forum for fostering and integrating sustainable development efforts across that Department. In the coming months, the Council will be working to review and examine the feasibility of implementing recommendations on sustainable agriculture. Please see Chapter 6 for more information on sustainable agriculture.[31]

The development of a new system of environmental management in America must be based on a common goal of improving the overall efficiency of how we deal with our nation's impact on the Earth. By instituting the proposed innovative changes, America can move steadily forward in this effort. To accomplish the complex changes required will be much more difficult and time-consuming than simply leaving the current system in place. However, the long-term benefits of adopting the new performance and efficiency-based system will more than offset the short-term effort to embrace the changes. The joint goals of sustainable development—environmental protection, economic progress, and social equity—direct America—as a nation—to begin to take the long view, the view from our children's and grandchildren's perspective. That view, indeed, is the essence of sustainable development.

Chapter 8

Sustainable Energy and Transportation

Although technology and policy have made great progress in the effort to reduce human impact on the natural world, scientists and policymakers are only now beginning to understand the scale of the fundamental global changes which modern technology, a growing population, and a highly competitive and globally interconnected economy are causing. In all of human history, no period of time can begin to match the sheer magnitude of the changes which are currently occurring in the global environment. Economic activity is both the cause of and solution to many of the world's environmental and social problems. On one hand, economic activity can generate substantial waste and pollution and contribute to environmental deterioration and critical health risks. Nonetheless, a robust and prosperous economy is also essential to creating jobs and producing the material goods necessary to support a growing population. Economic activity provides people with the opportunity to meet their physical needs and fulfill their individual aspirations. It also generates the wealth necessary to make important investments in cleaner technologies and better practices to protect public health and the natural world. At the very core of both modern economic activity and environmental problems are energy and transportation.

173

Energy and transportation services create immense economic and social benefits for most Americans. Correspondingly, decisions made by governments, businesses, and individuals regarding energy and transportation use have profoundly important impacts on society. These choices influence the U.S. and global environment as well as the prices of virtually all basic goods and services. Energy and transportation decisions affect national security and the international competitiveness of employers.

The decisions made today will have long-term impacts in these and many other areas. There is greater opportunity for improvements in energy and transportation efficiency in the United States than in any other industrialized nation. The United States has 5 percent of the world's population but accounts for approximately 25 percent of global energy use on an annual basis. The amount of energy used to create one dollar of goods or services in the U.S. it the highest in the world–approximately 36 percent greater than in Germany and 79 percent greater than in Japan. America's use of petroleum is seven times greater than the world's per capita average. In 1994, the United States used 19.9 million barrels of oil per day, while the entire rest of the industrialized world collectively used 23.8 million barrels per day.[1]

Over the course of the last 25 years, the United States has made great progress improving its energy and transportation systems. However, if America is to be placed on a sustainable course, bold new strategies must be developed to make even greater progress in the next 25 years. Realistically, American economic performance must continue to provide the goods and services which fuel the national, and indeed, the world economy. However, as earlier chapters have shown, the pursuit of economic progress need not necessarily result in pollution and the waste of natural resources. In no other parts of the U.S. economy is there a greater need for the elimination of waste and the pursuit of efficiency than in the U.S. energy and transportation industries.

Changes in technology and economic behavior offer an effective way to reduce the environmental and social burden of energy use and transportation. Policies can be designed to limit the various negative impacts of energy and transportation use, but at the same time, they must operate within the context of competitive markets. Providers of energy and transportation services must be given incentives to continuously improve their

174

environmental performance and reap economic rewards for doing so while, at the same time, providing affordable services for all Americans. Consumers of these services must also have a wide range of choices and incentives that will lead them to efficient patterns of energy use. The goal must be to maximize the overall social benefits of energy and transportation in an affordable and environmentally sound manner. The national focus should be on removing the economic and regulatory barriers that prevent America from moving in these directions.

However, it is also important to recognize the global context of energy and transportation issues in crafting strategies for the future. People in developing countries are desperately seeking to escape from poverty and poor health. They want the same kind of economic prosperity which is enjoyed in the United States and other developed nations–the life styles that they increasingly see depicted in movies and television. However, if people in developing countries follow U.S. patterns of development–if they consume similar amounts of resources, and generate as much pollution–the effect will be to eclipse much of the progress which has been made in reducing global environmental problems. At the same time, developing nations must have the same opportunities for advancement that the industrial world has had. Solutions and innovations developed for challenges in the United States can be adapted to conditions in developing countries to help them achieve their economic, environmental, and social aspirations.

The U. S. must pursue economic, environmental, and social policies that encourage global competitiveness. But continued economic growth need not come in the form of further pollution and waste. Economic growth can result from efficiency and the prevention of waste. America must improve the economic and environmental performance of the U.S. energy system while ensuring that all Americans have access to affordable energy. At the same time, the U.S. must strive to improve the economic and environmental performance of the U.S. transportation system while increasing all Americans' access to affordable, convenient transportation.

A number of the recommendations in this book suggest the removal of economic and regulatory barriers that prevent progress toward achieving sustainable development in American energy use. For example, the increased regulatory flexibility envisioned under a performance-based environmental management system would encourage energy efficiency as a method of pollution prevention. For many industries, introduction of innovative technologies that prevent pollution and lower compliance costs will decrease energy consumption. The industries in the United States that produce the most pollution and incur the highest clean-up costs also consume the most energy. U.S. expenditures for pollution control and abatement totaled roughly $25 billion in 1992. Of this total, the chemical, petroleum refining, pulp and paper, and primary metals industries account for about 70 percent. These same four industries accounted for nearly two thirds of domestic industrial energy consumption. Successful research and development aimed at pollution prevention and waste minimization would significantly reduce pollution clean-up costs in these industries as well as their consumption of energy and raw materials. To achieve this, federal technology partnerships can be catalysts for innovation in energy and transportation and can also create important economic incentives. A number of other recommendations that would help foster progress in the energy industry–such as shifting tax policies, reforming subsidies, and making greater use of market incentives–have been discussed earlier in this book.[2]

All of these policies must be designed to work toward certain overall strategic goals in U.S. energy use. There should be strong efforts to reduce the amount of energy which is consumed per dollar of U.S. economic activity. While achieving this goal, there should also be major efforts to increase the share of renewable energy used in the U.S. energy supply. At the same time, there should be extensive efforts to increase the average efficiency of electricity generation in the U.S. Finally, America must make a strong national commitment to a reduction in U.S. emissions of greenhouse gases due to human activity. These overall goals will help develop a sustainable pattern for U.S. energy use.[3]

The U.S. transportation system plays a critical role in the everyday lives of millions of Americans. Transportation choices, land use patterns, community design, and pollution are inherently linked. Transportation also affects national and economic security as it increasingly accounts for the largest share of oil consumed in the United States–two-thirds in 1994. The national goal must be to improve the economic and environmental performance of the U.S. transportation system while increasing all Americans' access to jobs, markets, services, and recreation.[4]

This book outlines many steps that can be taken by government, communities, businesses, and residents to address the challenge of a sustainable transportation system. Many of the recommendations regarding transportation are dealt with in Chapter 10, in the discussion of sustainable communities.

America must improve its general community design in order to better contain its sprawling cities and suburbs. It must expand the range of transportation options to include greater use of mass transit and other alternatives to personal cars. America must make more efficient use of its land to locate homes, places of work, schools, businesses, shops, and transportation in harmony with public spaces. Additionally, the U.S. should significantly reform its tax and subsidy policies to improve the economic and environmental performance of transportation. Market incentives can also be used to achieve environmental objectives in transportation. America should also strive to achieve better transportation technology and encourage public-private collaboration to spur industry innovation.

One of the goals in the area of transportation must be to decrease traffic congestion in metropolitan areas. Further, America should work to increase its economic and national security by reducing its dependence on oil imports. America must work diligently to decrease the rates of transportation emissions of greenhouse gases and other pollutants—including carbon monoxide, lead, nitrogen oxides, small particulate matter, sulfur dioxide, and volatile organic compounds. To help achieve this goal, there must be a major effort to stabilize the number of vehicle miles traveled per person while increasing the share of trips made using alternative types of transportation.[5]

U.S. Energy Policy

In the United States, energy is used in three different areas in about equal amounts—for transportation, for residential and commercial buildings, and for industrial production. Energy in the form of electricity is consumed in buildings (65 percent), industry (about 34 percent), and transportation (less than one percent of the electricity sold in the United States). This electricity is produced from a diverse range of fuels, with coal supplying the largest share—55 percent. Fossil fuel and renewable energy is consumed directly in transportation (24 percent), industries (26 percent), and buildings (18 percent). Renewable energy sources include wind, solar electric (photovoltaic), solar thermal, geothermal, and biomass (wood waste, refuse, agricultural products). Together, renewable energy sources provide a little over 7 percent of the total energy needs of America, with hydroelectric power supplying half of this amount.[6]

Energy and Environmental Changes

Pollution can be an important indicator of how efficiently energy resources are used. Various emissions from energy use are related to different environmental concerns–such as local air quality and acid rain. Carbon dioxide emissions are of particular concern because of their important role in changes that are occurring in the chemical composition of the atmosphere. These changes are occurring at an accelerating rate with consequences that are difficult to predict with certainty or precision. Moreover, the changes that are occurring in the global climate cannot be quickly nor easily reversed once their consequences have been fully understood.

The Earth is kept at a life-supporting temperature by a blanket of gases that trap some of the energy the earth radiates. Water vapor, carbon dioxide, methane, and nitrous oxide are the principal gases that create this natural greenhouse effect. With the industrialization of the past 150 years, atmospheric concentrations of greenhouse gases have increased and new greenhouse gases have been added to the atmosphere. The most important greenhouse gas that is influenced by human activity is carbon dioxide. The buildup of carbon dioxide in the Earth's atmosphere results primarily from burning fossil fuels and deforestation. Concentrations of carbon dioxide in the atmosphere have increased by about 30 percent over preindustrial levels.[7]

The buildup of greenhouse gases in the atmosphere is expected to lead to an enhanced greenhouse effect, popularly referred to as global warming. Because of the enormous complexity of the Earth's climate system, it is not possible to predict with certainty the exact expected temperature rise or other effects of global warming. The Earth has warmed by about 1° F since preindustrial times. In 1995, the international scientific community, as represented by the *Intergovernmental Panel on Climate Change*, concluded that the balance of evidence suggests that emissions of greenhouse gases have caused a discernible human influence on the global climate. The World Meteorological Association and the United Nations convened this group of 2000 scientists and technical experts from 130 countries to study human impact on the Earth's climate. The Panel predicts a warming of the Earth of 0.8° C to 3.5° C in the next century. The resulting effects of this warming and climate change are much less clear. Generally though, it is predicted that there will be a rise in sea levels, increased drought or floods in some areas, and the possibility of more extreme weather events in various places worldwide.[8]

U.S. emissions of carbon dioxide currently account for approximately 25 percent of global emissions. In the future, however, carbon dioxide emissions from developing countries will increase rapidly as their economies develop. If current trends continue emissions from developing nations will surpass those from the industrialized world in several decades. Nonetheless, for decades to come, it is the industrial nations–led by the United States–which will be responsible for most of the carbon dioxide in the atmosphere resulting from human activities.[9]

The United States cannot solve the potential problem of climate change alone. However, unless the industrialized nations demonstrate that a different development path is possible and beneficial, the rest of the world will be reluctant to join in efforts to resolve the problem. Solutions and innovations which are developed for the United States can be adapted to conditions and cultures in developing countries to help them achieve their aspirations for an improved quality of life. The overall approach of greater energy efficiency and cleaner energy technology will help lessen the atmospheric impact of energy use both at home and abroad.

Action: Increase U.S. Energy Use Efficiency:

Despite the progress that has been made in the past 25 years, many existing patterns of energy production and consumption continue to deplete natural resources, degrade ecosystems, and create significant amounts of solid waste, water pollution, and atmospheric pollution. Energy efficiency and waste generation are linked. Pollution and waste are inherently inefficient. The use of more efficient industrial processes will increase productivity and result in less waste and pollution. Increasing the efficiency of energy use will have benefits in all three dimensions of sustainability. It will reduce energy costs to consumers and industry. Reduced energy costs for business will allow them to become more

179

competitive internationally and thus benefit the economy. Increased energy efficiency will also lead to lower environmental compliance costs by lowering overall pollution.

Increased energy efficiency translates into fewer environmental impacts from pollution and waste. The energy intensity of the U.S. economy is a fundamental measure of sustainability. The standard measure of national energy intensity is the amount of energy consumed per dollar of Gross Domestic Product (GDP) which is produced. The goal should be to reduce the average amount of energy consumed per dollar of economic activity from 1990 levels by 30 percent by 2010, and 50 percent by 2025.[10]

For the period from 1990 to 2010, current forecasts predict about a 16 percent decline in energy use per dollar of GDP. This is based on a predicted rise in overall energy use through 2010 of about 27 percent and a rise in U.S. GDP of about 53 percent. Thus, to reach the recommended goal it would be necessary to reduce energy use per dollar of GDP an additional 14 percent below the forecast level.[11]

This reduction is technically feasible and could be economically beneficial if energy and transportation policies, including research and development, are structured properly. More widespread adoption of existing energy-efficient technology could reduce energy demand by as much as 45 percent. If renewable energy use is increased, this will also reduce the energy to GDP ratio. If the efficiency of fossil fuel electric generation is increased and if new environmental technologies continue to reduce many of the pollutants associated with conventional energy supplies, the overall environmental impact of this level of consumption could also be significantly less than today's levels.[12]

A recent study indicates that by meeting the 2010 energy use reduction target of 30 percent, the U.S. could reduce its annual electricity generation by 27 percent and decrease the need for construction of new power plants by over 50 percent. In addition U.S. electricity customers would enjoy an 18 percent overall reduction in their electricity bill (a savings of $50 billion). Finally, emissions of carbon dioxide and nitrogen oxides would be reduced by 33 percent and 12 percent, respectively.[13]

Electric Utility Efficiency Incentives: To achieve a sustainable future in the generation and consumption of power, energy efficiency must become a national objective. Much of the economic growth of the past 20 years has been powered not so much by building new power plants than by redesigning energy consuming industrial processes and rethinking how products are made and used. Utility companies have made large investments in energy conservation in order to defer the building of new utility plants. These include, for example, weatherizing homes and buildings, using power when demand is low, and upgrading the efficiency of equipment, such as appliances, lighting, and industrial motors. Consumers and industry can save energy cost-effectively by using newer technologies and improved practices. Because current patterns of energy production exact a toll on the environment, energy efficiency can directly reduce the environmental effects of energy use.[14]

Electric power has traditionally been bought and sold in monopoly markets that evolved before the benefits of conservation were known. These monopoly markets give incentives to supply more and more energy, instead of incentives to look for smarter ways to use energy. Over the past two decades, however, natural gas and electricity markets have become more competitive and direct governmental influence has waned. This evolution and increased competition has brought significant benefits for consumers and contributed to more efficient energy use. However, many analysts question whether even the best current energy conservation programs can survive the transition to the even more competitive markets which are on the horizon. It is also not clear whether business will respond with innovative approaches to expand current energy conservation programs.

Utilities preparing for competition are striving to cut costs and drive their own prices down. Even those utilities that have shown a willingness in the past to invest in energy conservation programs will only continue to do so voluntarily where the programs clearly enhance their competitive advantage. Although energy efficiency investments are less expensive in the long-term, many utilities fear they will be at a disadvantage in the short term if their competitors do not also provide these incentives. To continue the progress made thus far, energy efficiency programs must continue to be emphasized during the period of transition to more competitive energy markets.

To insure that current energy conservation efforts continue and increase, individual states should be encouraged to provide incentives for energy-efficiency investments until these investments can be maintained by competitive energy markets. A new program should be developed to replace the existing patchwork of utility-sponsored conservation programs with a state-based system which uses a competitive market mechanism to purchase energy savings. Under the state-based energy conservation concept, states would place a small fee on all electricity use. The revenue collected would be placed into an energy efficiency fund which would be awarded to those electricity suppliers that compete for contracts to help residential and commercial consumers reduce their energy bills—and thus their demand for more energy. The competition for projects would largely replace traditional bureaucratic programs with an active market in energy efficiency.[15]

Residential, commercial, and small business customers that do not already engage in extensive energy conservation efforts would benefit from programs of this type. Additionally, many of the least affluent in society have not yet reaped the economic gains from energy efficiency because of lack of financial resources and access to technology. Low income electric users tend to have low levels of participation in energy conservation programs. Federal legislation should require that state programs be designed to assure participation by low income residents.[16]

Energy Efficient Environmental Regulation: Energy efficiency should also be encouraged as a method of pollution prevention in the new environmental management system discussed in Chapter 7. Cost effective energy efficiency investments can lead to economic and environmental benefits by reducing energy costs and the environmental impacts of energy production and use. For the majority of industries, introduction of innovative technologies that reduce pollution and lower compliance costs will also decrease energy consumption.[17]

Initiative: Utility Energy Efficiency Program:

Since 1990, Pacific Gas and Electric's (PG&E) customer energy efficiency programs have saved PG&E customers 10,800 gigawatt hours of electricity and 480 million therms of gas usage. These electricity savings have been enough to power 1.3 million homes, while the gas savings have been enough to heat 1.4 million homes for one year. Customers also save money; since 1990, two million PG&E customers have received a nearly $1.5 billion reduction in their bills. These savings stimulate the economy and enhance the competitiveness of business customers. Reduced electricity generation has also resulted in tremendous pollution savings totaling 6.2 million tons of carbon dioxide, 3,560 tons of nitrous oxides, and 2,176 tons of sulfur dioxide since 1990. These pollution savings are comparable to the savings achieved by removing 775,000 automobiles from the California highways for one year. These results were made possible by a collaborative process crafted by regulatory agencies, the environmental community, investor-owned utilities and other major parties. The success of these programs provides continuing financial incentives for the utilities to encourage their customers to use energy efficiently.[18]

Action: Increase U.S. Use of Renewable Energy:

The environmental impacts of fossil fuels are not always fully reflected in its costs–a practice that tends to place cleaner technologies at a competitive disadvantage. Despite this, renewable energy sources are becoming competitive in many parts of the nation. For example, wind turbines are producing commercial power for one million Americans in California and the Midwest, and solar electric cells are competing in niche domestic markets. Renewable energy systems often are very competitive today in international markets, particularly in the developing world where millions of people have no electric power at all![9]

Renewable energy sources typically have fewer environmental impacts than do fossil fuels and have significant domestic and international market potential. Costs have declined significantly for renewable energy technologies over the past 15 years. When reduced costs are combined with generally lower environmental impacts, many renewable energy technologies are now competitive in niche markets in this country. Continued cost reductions will encourage much greater use of renewable energy sources. In turn, the expanded markets will encourage further cost reductions. These trends enhance the affordability of renewable energy in the United States.[20]

In 1990, renewable energy consumption, including hydroelectric power, accounted for 7.4 percent of total U.S. primary energy consumption. Hydroelectric power accounted for half of this total. The overall goal should be to increase the share of renewable energy use in the U.S. to 12 percent by 2010, and to 25 percent by 2025. Forecasts of U.S.

renewable energy consumption, including hydroelectric power, predict that it will only be about 8.5 percent of total U.S. primary energy consumption by 2010. Hydroelectric power will account for 3.0 percent of this amount. Of the remaining 5.5 percent, biomass and other wastes will equal approximately one percent of total U.S. energy consumption. These projections suggest that the target of 12 percent in 2010 and 25 percent in 2025 will require significant policy efforts if they are to be achieved cost-effectively. Various tax and subsidy policy measures discussed in Chapter 2 should be used to increase the share of renewable energy in the United States to meet the recommended goals.[21]

Action: Increase Electric Generation Efficiency:

Technology is both a cause of and part of the solution to many of the barriers on the path to a sustainable future. New technologies that use resources more efficiently and prevent pollution are being developed, but in many cases these new, cleaner technologies are slow to be implemented into everyday use. From the light bulb to the power plant, there are tremendous opportunities to replace old technologies with newer more efficient methods. This can be done while creating new jobs, reducing environmental impacts, and stabilizing long-term electric rates.

The current average efficiency in providing electricity is about 32 percent. In other words, only about one-third of the energy which is consumed in producing electricity is actually utilized by the ultimate electric consumer. Current projections through the year 2010 do not forecast any improvements in this efficiency level. However, using various techniques, the United States can increase the average efficiency of electricity generated from fossil fuels to 40 percent by 2010 and 50 percent by 2025. Improvements in fossil energy technologies should improve the efficiency of electricity supply and reduce its environmental impact. New electricity generation technology is already exceeding the current average. For example, efficiencies in some new natural gas units are over 50 percent. In addition, two coal technologies with similar conversion efficiencies are expected to be in commercial operation by the year 2010. These technologies are advanced integrated gasification combined cycle and pressurized fluidized bed. Even higher overall efficiencies may be possible with wasteheat recovery techniques in some applications—perhaps as high as 65 percent by 2025.[22]

However, construction of new power plants tends to proceed very slowly in the electricity generation industry. Increased energy efficiency by both industry and the public will also further reduce the need to build new electric generation plants. According to industry projections, by the year 2000 roughly 20 percent of the U.S. electricity supply will be generated by plants 40 years of age and older. Typically, these facilities use generation technologies that are far less efficient than those available today. Although plants built before 1960 are much less efficient than the best current technologies, utility companies are not retiring them because they are valuable for use during times of high demand in summer and winter months. Industry projections suggest that few electric utility plants will be retired by 2010. This will leave a significant number of the most inefficient power plants in operation and contributing the most emissions to the environment. To change this scenario, there must be economic incentives for utility companies to replace their existing low-efficiency power plants with the new generation of higher efficiency plants.[23]

Action: Energy Tax Incentives:

Tax code changes, as well as tax reform measures, could be used to remove barriers and create incentives to move toward more efficient energy generation. Tax incentives should be provided for U.S. electric generators to replace the most inefficient plants with investments in energy conservation and a mixture of new, more-efficient fossil fuel and renewable technologies by the year 2010. Incentives should be linked to the efficiency of the new technologies and should lead to retiring or replacing the most inefficient power plants. The rate and scope of the changes in tax policy would need to be adjusted to prevent any unreasonable utility rate increases.[24]

These tax incentives could be provided to utilities and other power plant owners that agree to invest in a combination of conservation, renewable energy resources, and high efficiency fossil resources—those that have at least 50 percent efficiency. One mechanism that would potentially have significant impact would be to base accelerated depreciation tax benefits on the efficiency of new power plants, investments in renewable power, or improvements in the efficiency of electric use. Shorter tax depreciation schedules for the most efficient replacement technologies should accelerate utility industry decisions to retire old plants and rebuild new ones with efficient and renewable technologies.[25]

This type of tax incentive can be viewed as a reinvestment in America. It will help develop an electrical power system for the future that is more efficient, cleaner, and less costly in the long-term, while creating new jobs and a more competitive industry. Investments in energy conservation technologies would have the most economic and environmental benefits by reducing the need for electricity. This program would increase the use of technologies that rely on the abundance of U.S. renewable energy resources. Renewables have fewer environmental impacts than fossil fuels, and they are gradually becoming commercially competitive with traditional power sources. Since fossil fuels will continue to be an important energy source in the future, however, incentives should also encourage greater use of available technologies that burn fossil fuels cleaner and more efficiently. As a result the air, water, and soil pollution associated with energy use should be reduced.[26]

To be effective, the incentives must be limited to investments in conservation, renewables, and high-efficiency fossil fuel technologies. Because the program would be voluntary, the ultimate impact on electricity rates should be minimal, and would depend on the level of tax subsidy and the magnitude of ongoing fuel savings. Long term rates are likely to stabilize as the newer plants reduce the risk of future rate shocks due to fuel prices or regulatory changes stemming from health or environmental concerns. These tax incentives should stimulate demand for efficient and renewable technologies. This, in turn, will accelerate new investments in technology development that will speed commercialization of new technologies. Greater use of cleaner technologies should also result in significant environmental improvement–in the form of reduced air and water emissions. However, this policy will cost money at the federal level, in the form of lost tax revenues. The short-term costs to taxpayers are an important issue that must be considered in determining the scope of the policy and the pace of its implementation.[27]

Action: Improve Technology and Information Transfer:

Government and private industry should continue efforts to inform the public and businesses about energy efficiency initiatives. Utilities have constructed four regional energy centers with little financial support from the federal government. The Department of Energy has provided grants to establish or enhance 10 regional energy centers. This effort should be expanded to construct 25 such centers by 2000. Federal agencies should also encourage state governments to require energy efficiency information in their educational curricula, provide more information via the Internet, and expand energy efficiency labeling to include more products.[28]

Energy Efficiency Standards: States and certain federal agencies already have responsibility under legislation to periodically upgrade and effectively implement building efficiency standards. Programs to develop energy efficiency standards could be expanded in several areas. Standards for new buildings could be made more stringent and be more effectively implemented. Additionally, standards for most residential appliances, heating, cooling, water heating units, fluorescent lighting, reflector lamps, and most electric motors have been established by statute. These standards should be updated and expanded. The Department of Energy has proposed standards for televisions and should also establish standards for other categories, such as office equipment. The energy, environmental, and economic benefits that may result from expanded and more stringent efficiency standards for buildings or equipment could be significant, as much as $10 billion.[29]

Federal Technology Partnerships: Federal research and development technology partnerships can serve as catalysts for innovation, and can also provide important economic incentives. Opportunities exist for private industry to enter into technology partnerships with the federal government in many areas. Licensing is available for technology transfer from U.S. federal laboratories for private industry demonstration and commercialization. Over 700 laboratories and facilities in the federal system are home to many unique scientific capabilities which can be accessed using a variety of cooperative mechanisms, including personnel exchanges, cooperative research and development agreements, and reimbursable work. Use of such cooperative research offers both industry and government partners the opportunity to effectively use scarce resources.[30]

Federal Research on Renewable Energy: The available funding for federal research and development programs for electric generation technology should continue to be shifted toward renewable resource and high efficiency fossil fuel technologies. Current programs are currently focused on several areas of fossil fuel electric generating systems. These initiatives should continue. However, in a sustainable economy, renewable electric generation technologies are preferred over those that are not renewable. Historically, renewable electric generation technologies have received less federal research funding as compared to other generation technologies. Although the Department of Energy has increased funding for renewable technologies by 66 percent–to $228 million in fiscal year 1995–funding for nuclear, coal, and other technologies still receive 75 percent of the available funding. Accordingly, federal research and development funding should begin to focus to a larger extent on renewable technologies.[31]

To that end, a *Renewable Technology Commercialization Program*, modeled along the lines of the *Clean Coal Technology Program*, should be implemented. The clean coal effort has been a very successful market-driven program that uses federal resources and private industry funding to accelerate the commercialization of clean coal technologies.

There are also important fossil fuel technology development programs in progress. These include the *Advanced Clean/Efficient Power Systems Program*, which supports power systems that achieve minimal environmental impact, high efficiencies, and reliability of supply; *Advanced Research and Technical Development Activities*, which supports research for super-clean, high efficiency coal power systems; the *Advanced Turbine Systems Program*, which seeks to increase the efficiency of gas turbines; and the *Fuel Cells Initiative*, for the commercialization of highly efficient, environmentally superior power systems fired by a variety of fuels.[32]

New Markets for Renewable Energy: Renewable energy technologies may bring electricity to regions of the lesser developed countries that have no electrical infrastructure at a much lower cost than building the traditional infrastructure of power plant electric generation. The major obstacle to selling U.S. renewable energy products and projects in the lesser developed countries is the lack of financing sources compared to those available to conventional fossil fuel energy projects. This recommendation would provide a pool of funds to allow U.S. companies to take advantage of the emerging power markets that are now being exploited by European competitors with financing from their governments. This renewable energy financing fund could be established by using institutions such as the Overseas Private Investment Corporation or the Export-Import Bank. This Fund would provide long-term project financing (10-15 years) at world market rates for renewable energy projects

188

that have signed long-term contracts to sell the power to a foreign utility or government. Exporting renewable energy technology helps the U.S. balance of trade and creates domestic jobs that promote global sustainability. It also assists developing countries in the development of energy sources that do not contribute to the build-up of additional greenhouse gases.[33]

Action: Other Energy Policy Options:

The following policy concepts were considered but were neither recommended nor dismissed. They are offered here for further discussion.

There should be further discussion of the creation of a tradable emission reduction incentive for energy efficiency and renewable technologies. The use of biomass energy production on conservation reserve program land is another possible policy. The creation of a renewable power marketing authority is an option that merits further consideration. Preferred access to government technology partnerships, and regulatory flexibility for companies that demonstrate compliance with environmental performance goals are two incentives that may be valid methods for encouraging energy efficiency. The federal government should also explore the development of incentives to assist in the commercialization of renewable energy technologies for commercial and residential application. There should be more work on the development of federal guidelines for evaluating new electric generation and distribution systems on a lifecycle basis (for both fossil fuels and renewables). A further idea that warrants discussion is the establishment of a market for new electric generation that rewards clean power by requiring fuel price risks and the cost of environmental controls to be borne by investors. High-efficiency fossil fuel use, renewable fuel use, and energy-efficiency technologies can be encouraged by establishing Clean Air Act incentives for these measures or through the establishment of regional air quality programs. Another regulatory possibility to improve the environmental impact of energy use is the establishment of strict overall performance goals for all emissions (including carbon dioxide, nitrous oxide, sulfuric oxide, and other toxics). A final important option is the negotiation of an international greenhouse gas treaty that includes an international emissions trading mechanism.[34]

U.S. Transportation Policy

The U.S. transportation system relies almost entirely on oil. Transportation accounts for 64 percent of the oil consumed in the United States. Although the United States is an oil producer, U.S. consumption of petroleum products from politically unstable regions of the world is increasing and is projected to continue to rise. However, an array of alternative domestic fuels is beginning to appear in the marketplace along with vehicles capable of using them. Natural gas, other alternative fuels, and electricity currently power three percent of the nation's vehicles.[35]

Major gains have been made in automobile fuel efficiency in the last 15 years, but these gains have been overwhelmed by market forces and other changes, with the result being that oil consumption is increasing. Oil prices are currently low by historical standards and, thus, the real cost of driving per mile has dropped over the same period. Consequently, Americans are again turning to bigger cars and light trucks, and they are driving more miles than ever. Further, even today's more efficient vehicles only turn an average of 20 percent of the energy they consume into actual motion. All of these factors lead to increased oil imports and continued air pollution problems in metropolitan areas.[36]

The latter part of the 20th century has been characterized by increased concentration of the U.S. population in metropolitan areas. The number of Americans living in metropolitan areas increased 65 percent from 1970 to 1992, a result of net migration of people to metropolitan areas as well as overall population growth. Despite the improvements in vehicle efficiency of the past 20 years, transportation in many metropolitan areas is characterized by increasing commutes for work, rising traffic congestion, and continued air quality problems. All of these factors lower the urban quality of life and have contributed to a nationwide flight from high-density central cities to suburban metropolitan areas. As populations and economic development relocate to lower-density areas where homes, schools, stores, and jobs are more spread out, more people need to travel farther to reach employment and other important destinations. Traffic congestion and the waste of fuel, thus, continues to increase.[37]

America must embark on a national effort to improve the economic and environmental performance of the U.S. transportation system. To achieve this, there must be efforts to steadily reduce U.S. dependence on oil imports. As discussed further in Chapter 10, efforts must also be made to steadily decrease suburban sprawl. Traffic congestion must be reduced significantly. Finally, there must be real efforts to reduce greenhouse gas emissions from transportation sources in the United States. To achieve this goal, it will be necessary, by 2010, to stabilize average vehicle miles traveled per capita at 1990 levels while enhancing the desirability of alternatives to single occupancy driving.[38]

Action: Reduce Dependence on Oil Imports:

Reducing petroleum imports will strengthen U.S. economic and national security. Petroleum imports are rising and currently account for 44 percent of U.S. oil consumption—a quarter of it from nations in the politically unstable Persian Gulf region. Because of reduced domestic exploration, dwindling reserves, falling production, and the relatively high cost of U.S. production, oil imports have grown from 37 percent of domestic consumption in 1987 to 44 percent in 1994. Motor vehicles account for approximately two-thirds of all domestic oil consumption and are therefore the major force behind this rising demand. In the short-term imports help the economy—through lower prices for fuels, reduced inflation, and overall economic growth. However, the immediate benefits of imported petroleum come with longer term economic and national security costs as well.[39]

According to the Department of Commerce, substantial reliance on petroleum imports threatens to impair national security. Although U.S. energy security has improved in recent years with the breakup of the Soviet Union and the apparent disarray within the Organization of Petroleum Exporting Countries, political and economic problems in the Persian Gulf region make disruptions in oil supply a real possibility. Economic and national security risks can be expected to increase as U.S. oil imports continue to grow because of declining domestic production and increased economic growth. The U.S. Department of Energy projects that oil imports will increase to 51.5 percent of domestic consumption by 2000 and that the United States and its allies will become increasingly dependent on Persian Gulf oil, which will account for 55 percent of world exports by 2000. All of the following methods to reduce overall transportation energy needs will reduce national oil consumption. This, in turn, will diminish the need for dependence on foreign oil imports.[40]

Action: Reduce Traffic Congestion:

Traffic congestion in urban and suburban areas is a growing problem facing many regions of the United States. Congestion puts a high economic burden on society–through accidents, wasted time, excessive fuel consumption, and additional pollution per mile traveled. Reducing the growth in vehicle miles traveled per capita and increasing alternatives to cars (discussed later in this chapter) will have a significant impact on congestion.[41]

Between 1983 and 1990, the number of daily vehicle trips per household grew and the average length of these trips increased. Cities with the greatest population density had the most congestion and the greatest increases in congestion. Congestion is estimated to cost over $100 billion per year. Forecasts are that congestion will get worse. By 1999, at least half of all vehicle miles traveled are expected to occur in bumper-to-bumper traffic (compared to 31 percent in 1989) and almost 80 percent of urban interstate travel will be in severely congested traffic (compared to 53 percent in 1989).[42]

The causes of congestion are complex and interrelated and include metropolitan areas population growth, migration to suburban areas, community design that promotes inefficient land use, and transportation systems that do not fully reflect the true costs of travel. Some important strategies to reduce congestion–for example, overall community design– are found Chapter 10. There are other steps, however, that state and local governments can use to reduce traffic congestion.

State and local governments should be enabled and encouraged to develop market-based transportation management strategies that more fully reflect the costs of travel. Specifically, governments can develop methods that more fully reflect the cost of single-driver vehicles using limited road space during peak hours of demand. One approach is toll collection. Congress should enact legislation to remove provisions in current laws prohibiting toll collection on interstate and other federally funded highways. Existing U.S. Department of Transportation *Intelligent Transportation System* funding should be targeted to promote flexible road pricing applications–for example, charging by time of day, vehicle type, number of occupants, and so forth. Time-of-day charges are common in the utility, telephone, airline, public transportation, and entertainment industries to allocate scarce peak capacity to those most willing to pay. Existing federal transportation funds should be used to provide funding bonuses for states and regions that adopt such systems. Specific implementation of road pricing should be under local and state control. Employer commuter programs, toll discounts, exemptions, and/or rebates for low-income commuters who must travel should be encouraged to offset the effects of toll collection on low income commuters.[43]

The U.S. Department of Transportation should encourage states and manufacturers to work together to standardize technology to enable communities interested in using these strategies to adopt common standards for electronic toll and parking pricing technologies. Federal funding bonuses should be available to states or regions that implement road user fees that more fully reflect the actual costs generated by each motor vehicle trip.[44]

A recent study indicated that a nationwide congestion toll system would reduce vehicle miles traveled at peak periods by 11 percent on the busiest highways and generate annual revenues of $44 billion and net savings in travel time exceeding $4 billion. To achieve the equivalent amount of reduced traffic congestion by building new highways would cost approximately $50 billion in otherwise avoidable highway construction.[45]

Telecommuting, or working at home for a corporate employer by using telecommunications technology such as fax machines and the Internet, is another new strategy for reducing overall travel congestion. The number of conventional corporate employees who telecommute rose from 2.4 million in 1990 to 6.6 million in 1994. Estimates are that the figures will climb to 11 million by 2000. If non-employee contract workers are included, the number could rise to 14 million.[46]

Action: Reduce Greenhouse Gas Emissions:

Emissions of greenhouse gases are an important concern and transportation emissions are growing significantly. Due to the combined effects of truck deregulation and increased speed limits, carbon emissions from freight trucks rose by 25 percent per mile from 1980 to 1990. Carbon emissions per mile from light duty vehicles (cars, vans, and sport utility vehicles) were 13 percent higher than full-size trucks in 1990.[47]

A wide range of policies can be used to confront this problem, including increasing the energy efficiency of vehicles, encouraging the use of alternative modes of transportation, increasing vehicle occupancy, or making use of alternative technologies and fuels. There is considerably more opportunity to reduce emissions in the next 15 years through a combination of changing people's behavior and new more energy-efficient vehicle technology. Such policies must become a priority for American transportation.[48]

Initiative: Energy Efficient Cars:

One of the greatest challenges in realizing sustainable development relates to the use of private automobiles. Federal agencies and the U.S. auto industry have now joined forces to conduct the necessary technological research and development to address these challenges. Chrysler Corporation, Ford Motor Company, and General Motors Corporation are involved in the *Partnership for a New Generation of Vehicles* (PNGV). This public-private partnership is focused on developing a car that it is three times more fuel efficient than today's comparable vehicle. PNGV partners expect to narrow the research and development focus by the end of 1997 and to present a concept vehicle by 2000. The goal is to produce prototype vehicles by the year 2004 which can achieve up to 80 miles per gallon, accelerate from 0 to 60 miles per hour in 12 seconds, hold six passengers, meet all safety and emissions requirements, and be purchased for approximately the same cost as today's comparably sized cars.[49]

Among the technologies being evaluated through the PNGV is a fuel processor that can use a variety of fuels–gasoline, ethanol, methanol, and natural gas–to produce hydrogen. The hydrogen can then be used by on-board fuel cells to produce electrical power. If successful and affordable, this technology could make it possible to use existing gasoline stations and could speed the transition to renewable transportation fuels. Fuel cell vehicles are expected to be exceptionally clean, with near zero emissions. The Chrysler Corporation recently announced that it hopes to demonstrate a complete system in a vehicle within two years.[50]

General Motors recently introduced the first modern electric vehicle known as the EV1. This vehicle was developed specifically as an electric vehicle, not as a conversion from a traditional automobile. The EV1 incorporates innovative changes in design, processing, and materials that result in a completely new class of vehicle with improved energy efficiency and environmental performance. The EV1 is now available at Saturn retailers in Arizona and Southern California; and a commercial sibling–the Chevrolet S-10 electric pickup truck–is available to government and commercial clients nationwide.[51]

Action: Stabilize Vehicle Miles Traveled per Capita:

One effective way to lower overall greenhouse gas emissions is to stabilize the annual miles traveled per person in trucks and cars. The average miles traveled per capita in personal cars and trucks rose 25 percent between 1980 and 1991. The average vehicle occupancy during all trips in 1990 was 1.6 persons, with commuting trips averaging 1.1 person per vehicle. The number of passengers carried by the mass transit industry remained approximately the same during this period, with small declines in bus transit and small increases in rail transit. Forecasts predict a further increase of about 25 percent in vehicle miles traveled per capita between 1990 and 2010.[52]

Stabilizing the amount of vehicle miles traveled per person will require significant changes in land use, transportation infrastructure, mass transit, and commuting patterns. Recent federal statutes such as the Intermodal Surface Transportation Efficiency Act and the Clean Air Act Amendments of 1990–as well as state efforts–have begun to focus on reducing the growth in transportation demand. Attempts to stabilize vehicle miles per person include methods to increase the number of passengers in each vehicle, such as through the use of toll collection. Other efforts should be undertaken to increase the use public transportation (busses, trains, or planes). There must also be major national efforts to encourage walking and bicycling as alternatives to using cars and trucks.[53]

Action: Increase Use of Alternatives to Cars:

In 1990, 87 percent of all personal trips were made by private vehicles, seven percent by walking, two percent by school buses, two percent by public transportation, one percent by bicycles, and the rest (two percent) by trains, planes, taxis, and other means. In 1990, 62 percent of all trips were five miles or less. Many of these short trips could be completed by walking or bicycling.[54]

Currently 5 percent of adults report walking or bicycling as their primary means of transportation. Given adequate facilities, 13 percent would state that they would prefer to meet their transportation needs by walking or bicycling. A recent poll showed that 23 percent of U.S. adults would sometimes commute to work by bicycle if safe bicycle lanes or paths were available. Fifty percent of adults said they would walk more if there were safe paths or walkways. The United States must make a concerted effort to meet this unmet need for safe alternatives to car and truck transportation. Doing so will substantially improve total travel efficiency and reduce the overall volume of travel.[55]

Initiative: Intermodal Surface Transportation Efficiency Act:

Transportation relates to many elements of sustainable development—from providing all citizens with equal access to economic and social opportunities, to land use and air quality. In implementing the Intermodal Surface Transportation Efficiency Act (ISTEA), the U.S. Department of Transportation helps communities improve transportation services, while integrating economic development, land use, and social concerns into local planning processes. Under this program, state and local officials have received unprecedented flexibility in using the federal funds they receive to meet the unique needs of their communities. For example, over $3 billion normally allocated to traditional highway uses has been transferred to local high-priority transit projects. Investments in bicycle/pedestrian facilities went up 1000 percent. ISTEA has also strengthened regional partnerships—involving federal, state, and local governments; metropolitan planning organizations; and private industry. Such partnerships have become a model for solving cross-jurisdictional problems such as sprawl, congestion, and air pollution. The Act has helped communities provide improved connections between different modes of transportation and in fiscal year 1995, over $6 billion was invested in mass transit—the most ever invested in a single year. Through ISTEA, communities throughout the United States are adopting integrated approaches to transportation and air quality issues.[56]

Action: Other Transportation Policy Options:

The following policy concepts were also considered but neither adopted nor dismissed. They are listed here to spur additional discussion.

Efforts could be made to utilize government travel procurement policy to establish markets and promote development and production of low emission vehicles. Government procurement contracts could be awarded to producers of vehicles employing new energy-efficient and environmentally-sound technologies. Efforts could also be made to remove regulatory barriers to the development of new types of transit services. Market pricing of fuel could reflect its true environmental costs, possibly through the use of higher gasoline taxes. Vehicle registration fees could be based on personal motor vehicle miles travelled and/or the amount of pollutants emitted. Finally, there should be further discussion of the use of corporate average fuel economy requirements (CAFE standards).[57]

The greatest opportunities to make a significant impact on the sustainability of the American economy are in the areas of energy and transportation. However, it is in these very same areas that the efforts to implement both behavioral and policy changes will meet with the strongest resistance. Modern American society is based in large part on both cheap energy and cars. A major effort must be made to educate both the public and industry of the ramifications of maintaining the status quo in energy and transportation policy. A clear understanding of the benefits of moving society in a sustainable direction must be developed among every element of society. For a sustainable America to become a reality will take the participation of everyone–from contented commuters to auto industry executives, from coal miners to bicyclists. It is possible to create a society in which energy efficiency and clean, affordable transportation are more than a distant vision. With a national commitment and appropriate policies, America can begin to show the world how to begin to take the path to achieve such a society.

Chapter 9

Education for Sustainability

From individual consumers to international corporations, from youths to seniors, households to communities—America is taking its first tentative steps toward becoming a sustainable society. The consumer who selects a recycled paper product at the supermarket or who rejects a product because it is over-packaged is taking positive action. The corporation that redesigns its manufacturing process to save energy and raw material has taken an equally positive step. The young person who devotes hours of after-school or weekend time to volunteer in his or her community is also participating. However, despite the encouraging trend toward sustainable living, many Americans do not understand the concept of sustainable development.

Most Americans have little, if any, understanding of such pervasive environmental issues as biodiversity and global warming. A 1992 national opinion survey indicated that only one percent of respondents consider endangered species to be a serious environmental problem, and only one in five respondents had even heard of the problem of loss of biological diversity. Additionally, many people confuse the issue of global warming with depletion of the ozone layer. A 1994 study revealed that even well-educated citizens wrongly believe climate change can cause increased cases of skin cancer and are convinced that their personal response should be to give up aerosol sprays. Not only are these respondents confusing global warming with depletion of the ozone layer, they also seem to be unaware that ozone-depleting chemicals have been federally banned from aerosols for over 20 years.[1]

If widely reported concepts such as global warming remain unfamiliar to so many Americans, it is not surprising that sustainability–a complex and multidimensional concept–is totally unknown to many citizens, including many policy makers, business leaders, educators, and community leaders.

Many approaches can be used to raise public awareness of sustainability. But education–lifelong education both within and outside the nation's formal schooling system–is the primary tool for creating a common understanding of this concept. This education may occur in formal schooling or in such non-formal venues as the media, adult education programs, museum exhibits, conferences and workshops, and nature center programs. The objective of sustainability education must be to ensure that awareness, knowledge, and understanding of sustainability become part of mainstream thinking, both nationally and internationally. Awareness and concern about environmental, economic, and equity issues must become firmly rooted in the public consciousness. Americans must develop an in-depth understanding of the short and long-term implications of decisions and choices. To produce that understanding, students and adults need to know how natural systems work. They also need an understanding of the interdependence of economic, social, political, and ecological conditions–locally, regionally, nationally, and internationally. This is an enormous educational task–one of the greatest that has ever confronted the national educational system.

Education for sustainability can give people the tools, skills, and experience they need to understand sustainable development. It will create a more highly skilled and globally competitive workforce and develop a more informed, active, and responsible citizenry. Advances in computer technologies and other information and communication technologies will help in this effort by broadening awareness of sustainability and helping bridge cultures and continents in ways never before possible. Achieving this objective will require using a multitude of educational formats–town meetings, conferences and workshops, task forces and commissions, and community and group sessions. Other venues should include electronic mechanisms such as the Internet, radio and television talk shows, feature articles, op-ed articles, and letters to the editor in newspapers, magazines, and newsletters. Practical citizenship skills must be applied to organize groups to act on issues related to sustainability. Conflict resolution techniques can be used to find ways to negotiate divergent interests. An understanding of the economic incentives that drive decision making can help people develop a sense of how they can change behavior.

Educators at all levels must reach beyond school walls to involve parents, industry, communities, and government in the education process. Colleges and universities must work with other schools and communities to deliver information, identify questions for research, and provide direct services to help solve community problems. Communities must take a stronger interest in educating their citizens for sustainability, recognizing that current and future generations will need to be well-educated in order to bring about a sustainable future.

Learning about sustainability cannot and should not be confined to formal settings such as schools, universities, and colleges. Education for sustainability should thrive in all types of classrooms, exposing students to local, state, national, and international issues through hands-on experiential learning—such as wading through streams to do water quality testing, volunteering in the community, or participating in school-to-work programs. Non-formal education settings, such as museums, zoos, extension programs, libraries, parks, and mass media, provide significant opportunities to complement and build on classroom learning.

Educating for sustainability must emphasize connections between all subject areas, as well as geographic and cultural relationships. Rather than weaken the rigor of individual disciplines, education for sustainability offers an opportunity to strengthen them by demonstrating vital interrelationships. Education for sustainability involves consideration of diverse perspectives, including those of ethnic groups, businesses, citizens, workers, and governments. While delving into many disciplines, education for sustainability also helps students apply what they learn to their daily lives. Part of sustainability education is learning citizenship skills and understanding that citizens have the power to shape their lives and their communities. Continual efforts should be made to institute programs about sustainability in a variety of arenas, including the workplace and community centers and through the media. A citizenry that is knowledgeable about the benefits of sustainable living will have the capacity to create and maintain lasting change.

Among some educators there is a debate about the relationship between environmental education and education for sustainability. Some say that education for sustainability is a subset of environmental education: others say vice versa. Regardless of which vision of education one holds, it is important to seek out and engage professionals from many related areas such as population education, economics, human rights, religion, and other social sciences. While each discipline has been exploring its own singular contribution to sustainable development, it is time to bring together thinkers from all of these related fields to explore the potential synergy that can be unleashed by creative interdisciplinary thinking.

Although a number of individuals, schools, businesses, government entities, and communities across the nation have taken the first steps toward sustainability, much more can be done to nurture a sustainable society. Three major recommendations are presented in this chapter. First, there must be changes in the formal education system to help all students (from kindergarten through higher education), educators, and education administrators learn about the environment, the economy, and social equity. Second, there must be increased non-formal access to information on sustainability as it relates to every citizen's personal, work, and community life. Finally, America must begin to institute policy changes at the federal, state, and local levels to develop and expand access to information technologies in all educational settings; and to encourage understanding about how local issues fit into state, national, and international contexts. Together with numerous specific educational actions, these three recommendations form a comprehensive educational strategy to help lead the nation to a more sustainable future?

Formal Education Reform

Formal classroom education plays a primary role in shaping the minds of our nation's youth—the next generation of leaders, activists, managers, parents, and government officials. As America participates in an increasingly interdependent world, educators must find ways to prepare students to meet the challenges created by rapidly changing global conditions. In particular, education for sustainability must counteract the long tradition of splintering knowledge into smaller and smaller pieces. Education for sustainability is not an add-on curriculum. It is not a new course subject like math or science. Instead, it involves an understanding of how each subject relates to environmental, economic, and social issues. Confronting the challenges of a new century will require a purposeful refocusing of the nation's education system into a more hands-on, interdisciplinary learning experience. Principles of sustainability can be used as a catalyst for innovation and restructuring of educational institutions, curricula, and teacher training efforts.

To achieve this will require defining the essential skills that are needed for understanding sustainability and emphasizing interdisciplinary learning. It will also require expanding pre-service and in-service professional training for teachers and having educational institutions serve as models for sustainability in their communities.[3]

Action: Defining Essential Skills:

Educators should identify the essential skills and knowledge that all students should have at specified grades for a basic understanding of the interrelationships between environmental, economic, and social equity issues. Building knowledge of the interdependence between these issues will help citizens understand and participate in the decisions that affect their lives. This reorientation to an integrated, interdisciplinary approach will succeed only if standards are established to ensure that sustainability education achieves high levels of quality and performance. Standards have been set for disciplines such as math, science, and geography. Additionally, educators have long recognized the need for a set of standards for environmental education. Organizations and businesses that fund environmental education projects also have called for a set of widely accepted materials standards that could be used in curriculum selection. To date, 19 states have adopted legislation mandating environmental education and 33 have enacted formal guidelines. Without a peer-reviewed framework of essential standards, however, implementation and evaluation of programs will be difficult. Education for sustainability requires that curriculum connections be made across all the standards. It also requires that environmental, economic, and social issues be a part of each discipline. Various organizations have focused on developing a set of consensus standards for environmental education.[4]

Sustainable Education Standards: Educators–working in partnership with communities, and businesses–can define the skills and knowledge students will need in order to understand how various human actions affect environmental, economic, and social issues. Defining standards for a core of basic knowledge about sustainability will accelerate the infusion of these concepts throughout the nation's educational system. The standards also can serve as a resource for media strategies and other non-formal education about sustainability.

In 1990, the National Science Teachers Association adopted a set of general *Criteria for Excellence in Environmental Education.* More recently, the North American Association for Environmental Education has been collaborating with the World Resources Institute and members of the President's Council on Sustainable Development to develop a set of learning standards for environmental education that can be used at the state level, by school districts, or by individual schools as guidelines for curriculum benchmarks at various grade levels. These standards cover such areas as the importance of ecological and socio-political knowledge, appreciation of the interdependence of all life forms, concern for human impacts, problem-solving skills, knowledge of citizen action strategies, and respect for different perspectives and values.[5]

Many states have already begun to address the changes needed to ensure that an informed citizenry has the awareness, understanding, behavior and skills necessary for a sustainable future. In New Jersey, legislation was passed in 1996 to create a permanent Environmental Education Commission to implement a *Plan of Action* which addresses the basic principles of sustainability. New Jersey hopes to educate its citizens through many venues and, in particular, by establishing a New Jersey Environmental Education Network, a New Jersey Global Forum, and an annual Environmental Education/Earth Week celebration. This Plan of Action has been acclaimed by leaders in the field of environmental education as a template for state level sustainable development.[6]

Action: Emphasizing Interdisciplinary Learning:

Equipping today's students for tomorrow's decisions means that educators must promote long-term thinking and interdisciplinary learning. This shift will require new methods of teaching as well as new curriculum content. It will require that educators work with communities,

203

businesses, and organizations to develop materials that expose students to local, national, and global issues. It means ensuring that issues and ideas from a variety of cultures and disciplines are represented in the class-room. Building a knowledge of the interdependence between economic prosperity, environmental protection, and social equity will help students become responsible citizens. It will also help them understand and participate in the decisions that affect their lives. Through *Goals 2000*, the U.S. Department of Education is supporting such state and local restructuring efforts.[7]

School administrators, and other educators should continue to support education reform—emphasizing interdisciplinary approaches and experiential hands-on learning at all levels. If the nation's elementary, secondary, and higher education schools are to infuse sustainability concepts into their curricula and offer separate courses in issues related to sustainability, universities and colleges must take the lead in reorienting education's approach away from compartmentalization and toward the integration of disciplines. More courses that support interdisciplinary approaches need to be offered and existing courses need to be refocused to include sustainability topics.[8]

Initiatives: Sustainability Curriculum:

The Kellogg School at Northwestern University sponsors an elective course that involves a spring-break trip to Costa Rica to research such initiatives as the ecotourism industry and paper production from the waste products of banana processing. The Crouse School of Management at Syracuse University has a mandatory course focusing on what business students need to know about the environment and sustainability; it also offers courses on land development law and environmental law as part of the business school curriculum. Widener University offers a Sustainability and the Law course which has three themes: the role of law in achieving sustainability, sustainability as a basis for evaluating laws, and the potential effectiveness of different types of legal instruments in achieving sustainability.[9]

The *Columbian International Center* graduate studies program of the American Institute for Urban and Regional Affairs in Washington, D.C., is accredited to offer the first master's and scholar-practitioner doctorate degrees in sustainable development. Both degrees are in accordance with requirements established by the World Council on Sustainable Development. These programs are interdisciplinary; incorporate a global awareness of social, economic, technological, and environmental change; and foster the integration of theory, research and professional practice. The degree programs provide an international off-campus curriculum for practicing professionals.[10]

The Georgia Institute of Technology's *Center for Sustainable Technology* was created in collaboration with the World Engineering Partnership for Sustainable Development. This partnership was itself established in 1992 to unify the global engineering community to implement sustainable development initiatives. Recently, the center was awarded a grant to develop an educational program in sustainable development and technology that cuts across all engineering disciplines.[11]

In 1996, The SUNY College of Environmental Science and Forestry launched the *Randolph G. Pack Environmental Institute* to promote the philosophy of sustainable development. The Institute focuses on such topics as democratic processes, environmental decision making, public participation, environmental equity, and sustainable development.[12]

The University of Louisville's *Institute for the Environment and Sustainable Development* was established to promote multidisciplinary analysis and research on the needs, causes, and consequences of development. It seeks to expand knowledge on the environment and economic development while providing an effective interface between scientific inquiry and the policy-making process.[13]

In 1994, the University of Oregon chartered its *Institute for a Sustainable Environment*, which is particularly interested in encouraging cross-disciplinary environmental research, education, and public service. The Institute is also focused on working with the community on sustainability projects. Recent collaborations include Oregon Benchmarks, Quality of Life Indicators for Coos County, and a sustainable forestry plan for 64,000 acres of forest land belonging to the Caquelle Native American Tribe.[14]

The *Center for Sustainable Communities* is one of three centers at the University of Washington's Cascadia Community and Environment Institute. The center is a central source of information for many areas of sustainability from environmental design to sustainable building practices to community planning.[15]

The *Tahoe Center for a Sustainable Future* is working in collaboration with a variety of partners—including the University of California at Davis and the Sierra Nevada College—to develop a sustainable development curriculum for the Tahoe-Truckee Region. The overall mission is to develop a model process for environmental education teachers and K-12 students that will focus on promoting a healthy environment.[16]

To ensure that the momentum to develop programs on sustainability continues, universities need to work with federal, state, and local agencies to shift funding priorities toward interdisciplinary research. At present, fewer than two percent of federal funding to universities supports research related to environmental subjects, including the human causes of environmental change. Too often, interdisciplinary research is regarded as "soft" science which does not advance a faculty member's professional standing, fulfill publication requirements, or earn tenure. The nation's higher education system must focus on the need for information and research on sustainability and eliminate such barriers.

Elementary and secondary schools also need to work with other schools and communities to develop curriculum, deliver information, identify questions for research, and provide direct services to help solve community problems. Many elementary and secondary schools are already making progress in this area. For example, the *Community High School Environmental Research and Field Studies Academy* in Jupiter, Florida, incorporates sustainability concepts into classroom subjects, school activities, and community service projects. This gives students an opportunity to share in decisions related to creating a more sustainable future for their school and community.[17]

Initiatives: Community Service Education:

Although some educators believe that schools should impart only knowledge and skills—and not foster changes in attitudes or actions—other educators contend that participation in real-world activities is an integral component of education. Courses in citizenship, for example, sometimes involve the development of action plans to resolve real-world environmental problems and the opportunity to implement those plans. Community service can be a powerful educational tool. Taking young people out of the classroom has a long, successful tradition in environmental education. The *Global Rivers Environmental Education Network* (GREEN) initiative is an educational program with a strong focus on real-world problems and community service. This program is helping students take community action by providing the tools necessary to learn about the environmental, economic, and social conditions in their communities, as well as the global community.[18]

Since 1957, the *Student Conservation Association* has encouraged more than 30,000 student volunteers to perform conservation work in national parks, national forests, national wildlife refuges, and other public lands.[19]

The World Resources Institute's *Environmental Education Project* has completed a series of teachers' guides with comprehensive course work focusing on the global environment. Separate units include sustainable development; watershed pollution; oceans and coasts; energy, atmosphere, and climate; biodiversity; natural resource economics; population, poverty, and land degradation; and citizen action.[20]

Action: Expanding Professional Development:

Educators are the best means for infusing sustainability into formal learning–but only if these educators have had relevant high-quality professional development before and during their tenure in the classroom. Professional development can bridge the gap between what educators know now and what they will need to know to prepare the nation's youth for changes resulting from the global transition to sustainability. Professional training for sustainability poses a number of challenges. Because it is a relatively new concept for teachers as well as students, education for sustainability needs to be incorporated into teacher pre-service and in-service education programs. Teachers in all subject areas will have to acquire some knowledge and understanding of the principles of sustainability. Adequate pre-service training will depend on institutions of higher education adding appropriate courses. In-service professional development presents the formidable challenge of retraining the 2.8 million teachers in the nation's public and private K-12 schools. Adequate funding through legislation or grants is essential for expanding pre-service and in-service training in sustainability. To ensure adequate financial support, partnerships among state departments of education, institutions of higher education, professional societies, and school districts are critical. Funding for developing, demonstrating and disseminating exemplary programs–especially for professors who educate pre-service teachers–could strongly influence the future of sustainability in the United States.

Few high school students graduate with the ability to analyze and assess global environmental problems. A 1995 study found that global topics such as population change, ocean pollution, and land use–some of the most pressing problems facing society–were among the least common subjects addressed in environmental education classes and teacher training programs. Although many teachers would like to include global environmental studies in their courses, they are discouraged by a variety of barriers including the need for new information, the need for new ways to integrate information and materials into learning situations, and the necessity for making global issues relevant to students. In addition, teachers worry about overwhelming students–either with the somber nature of the topics or as an addition to an already overcrowded school year. Most teacher training courses and curriculum materials offer little help. Training courses tend to focus on local and regional issues. Most materials are appropriate for elementary and middle schools, but not sufficiently challenging for high school use.[21]

Overcoming these obstacles is the goal of a recent partnership formed between the World Resources Institute and the Global Network of Environmental Education Centers. By combining their respective strengths–teacher training and the production of top-quality curriculum materials–they hope to bolster the professional development of environmental educators nationwide and stimulate the infusion of global environmental studies into U.S. secondary schools. The plan is to develop model teacher training courses using curriculum materials that link global environment and sustainable development issues with similar concerns.[22]

Federal Support: Two federal agencies, the U.S. Department of Education and the U.S. EPA, have established programs that support professional development for teachers. The Department of Education, through its *Eisenhower Professional Development Program*, provides grant assistance to state and local education agencies, institutions of higher education, and non-profit organizations to ensure that teachers and other staff and administrators have access to high-quality professional development. The U.S. EPA helps fund training for educators on how to increase

208

environmental literacy. Under the 1990 Environmental Education Act, the U.S. EPA has created *the Environmental Education and Training Project* to fund educators who need additional training in order to provide education to underserved populations of adult learners.[23]

Requiring Environmental Education: Of the states that mandate environmental education, only two–Maryland and Wisconsin–also require pre-service training to prepare teachers for implementing that mandate. Besides including environmental education objectives in its pre-service teacher certification programs, Wisconsin also has a large in-service program in environmental education. Both of these Wisconsin-based programs have elicited strong support from students, teachers, and school administrators. These innovations need to be emulated by other states.[24]

Environmental Literacy: The Tufts University *Environmental Literacy Institute* provides environmental literacy training to secondary school teachers and university faculty, helping them weave environmental themes into their courses. The institute exposes participants to current educational theory, teaching strategies, assessment techniques, and information retrieval methods. The Institute's *Global Partners Program* promotes interdisciplinary research, information exchange, and international partnerships. Faculty members from schools around the country–in fields ranging from medicine to the arts–attended institute workshops.[25]

Middle Schools Sustainable Education: A U.S. EPA grant is supporting a two-week summer training institute for middle school teachers by the *Columbia Education Center* in Portland, Oregon. The center also will expand its program to establish environmental education demonstration sites at public and private schools in five states.[26]

Biodiversity Training: *The Science Improvement Through Environmental Studies Program* uses an investigative and problem-solving approach to study the ecological and social principles of biodiversity. Following summer training, qualified teachers are certified as state-level peer leaders to provide in-service programs for their colleagues.[27]

Action: Models of Sustainability:

Schools, colleges, and universities should promote curriculum and community awareness about sustainable development and should follow sustainable practices in school and on campus. Educational institutions–from K-12 schools through colleges and universities–can and should

209

serve as models for sustainability. As such, schools at all levels can be potent forces in educating the communities they serve while reducing their own operating costs and increasing their own efficiency. For students, participating in a school's conservation efforts is a valuable form of hands-on experiential learning.

The operations of universities and colleges should be restructured so that they serve as models for sustainability. The university is a microcosm of the larger community, and the manner in which it carries out its daily activities is an important demonstration of ways to achieve environmentally responsible living. Students can be made aware of the impact that their attending school has on the natural environment and the community, and they can be actively engaged in the practice of sustainable living. By using the campus as a laboratory, students can learn to analyze complex multidisciplinary problems, develop real solutions, and focus on their own behavior—skills that are critical for the realities of the 21st century. By engaging in environmentally sustainable practices in its operations, purchasing, and investments, higher education can help reinforce desired values and behaviors in all members of the academic community. The annual buying and investment power of the nation's institutions of higher learning—$120 billion in purchasing; $75 billion in endowment—makes them important players in creating market demand for environmentally sustainable goods and services.[28]

Initiative: School Sustainable Practices:

Not only can institutions develop curricula that integrate sustainability concepts, they can also incorporate these concepts into a wide range of activities, including research projects, career counseling, administrative procedures, procurement practices, academic curricula, and other university services. Increasing awareness is a key responsibility of schools. Schools educate the leaders, managers, and visionaries of tomorrow. Institutions of higher education can exert a strong influence on society by turning out literate citizens who have witnessed first hand the benefits of sustainability. Universities and schools nationwide should develop plans to make sustainability a central focus of their operations. Through their own experiences in becoming more sustainable, universities and schools can serve as catalysts for encouraging local communities to move toward a sustainable future. Many universities have already adopted this approach.

210

In response to recommendations made at the Campus Earth Summit, Yale University switched from incandescent to fluorescent lighting, with projected savings of $3.5 million over the next 10 Years. The University of Arizona realized savings of more than $12,000 in disposal costs by modifying laboratory procedures to eliminate 3,600 gallons of hazardous waste. The Stony Brook branch of the State University of New York system instituted conservation measures for its heating and air conditioning systems that saved 1.53 million gallons of fuel oil, worth over $1 million. Energy-saving practices at Benedict College of Columbia, South Carolina, initially cost $28,900 but saved more than $91,400 during its first year. The University of California at San Francisco uses co-generation to heat its medical center with recovered steam heat; the initial cost of $247,000 will be amortized quickly through annual savings of $87,000. Brown University installed energy-efficient improvements through its *Brown Is Green* program; Tufts University did the same through its *Tufts Clean!* effort. In 1994, The George Washington University developed a detailed plan to foster and enhance leadership for environmental management and sustainability. The comprehensive plan is available to other interested schools via the *National Environmental Information Resources Center.*[29]

In 1990, the presidents, rectors, and vice chancellors of more than 200 institutions in 40 nations formed a *Secretariat of University Leaders for a Sustainable Future* to promote university leadership for global environmental management and sustainable development. The secretariat supports universal environmental literacy, faculty development, socially and ecologically responsive research, ecologically sound institutional practices that minimize environmental impact, and expanded outreach through partnerships.[30]

Second Nature, a non-profit organization dedicated to education for sustainability, targets its efforts at colleges, universities, and professional schools as the institutions responsible for educating future teachers, policy makers, and managers. Second Nature fosters partnerships and provides guidance on how groups can work together to incorporate sustainability into their day-to-day operations, curriculum, and research priorities. It works with organizations to make them models of sustainability in their communities.[31]

In 1990, the National Wildlife Federation launched the *Campus Ecology* program to help college and university students, staff, and faculty promote environmental education throughout their campuses and make campuses more sustainable. The program has involved over one-third of the institutes of higher learning in the United States. Campus Ecology's mission is to establish environmentally sound practices on college campuses by promoting leadership and action within the campus community.[32]

Primary and secondary schools can also follow suit. Some of the nation's 80,000 primary and secondary schools have already made great strides. In an era of tight funding, the Chicago Public School System, in partnership with the *Center for Neighborhood Technology*, is developing a comprehensive energy and environmental evaluation of public school facilities and transportation systems. The results will be translated into better resource management, new investment strategies, and improved education opportunities for students. The plan is being developed under the U.S. EPAs *Project XLC* (Excellence and Leadership for Communities). Project XLC assists communities in the use of creative approaches to attain greater environmental benefits.[33]

State-of-the-art facilities that include a recycling center, roof garden, greenhouse, composting center, weather station, computerized research library, and million-dollar media center are a few of the innovations at the *High School for Environmental Studies*, a public school in New York City formed to foster environmental education in an urban setting. The school was established in 1991 by a partnership between the Surdna Foundation and the New York Board of Education. A highlight of the school's curricula is its voluntary internship program that places students in an environmentally oriented organization for a full academic year.[34]

The *New York Healthy Schools Network* was created to bring together the perspectives of over 30 health, environment, education, and parent groups. The coalition motivated the State Board of Regents and Education Department to create an "environmental bill of rights" for schools. The bill encourages schools to serve as role models of environmental awareness and states that every child and school employee should have the right to have a safe school that uses its resources effectively.[35]

Guidance materials, brochures, videos, and books like *Blueprint for a Green School*–produced by the Center for Environmental Education–are helping school administrators, teachers, maintenance staff, students, parents, and community leaders create environmentally safe and healthy school buildings. *Blueprint for a Green School* is a guide on how to tackle environmental safety issues and make practical, responsible decisions about the operation of school buildings and classrooms.[36]

Encouraging Non-Formal Education

If sustainability is to become a reality, educational strategies must reach people of all ages, at all phases of their lives. Museums, zoos, libraries, extension programs, the media, the workplace, and community organizations are just a few venues for providing lifelong non-formal learning opportunities. These diverse educational settings can expand awareness and put sustainability concepts in a familiar context. To be most effective in doing so, non-formal educational institutions should expand their relationships with formal educators to identify those areas in which schools are inadequately preparing students and to help fill those gaps and develop appropriate materials.

Several sources of non-formal education deserve special consideration. Because Americans obtain most of their news and information from the print and broadcast media, a key strategy in non-formal education is to foster public awareness of sustainability via television, computers, newspapers, and magazines. Information on sustainability must be communicated through these media in appropriate and accessible formats. Work-based learning is another avenue for equipping adults with the knowledge and skills they need in a fast-changing world. School-to-work opportunities and retraining programs for dislocated workers will become increasingly important as the economy shifts to more efficient enterprises and sustainable practices. Also in light of these shifts and changes, communities will be instrumental in coordinating sustainability concepts and including them as part of community outreach and participation plans.[37]

Action: Encourage Lifelong Learning:

Most adults have received very limited information directly related to sustainability during their formal schooling. Through the U.S. educational system, many students do not develop an understanding of the interconnections between economic, environmental, and equity issues. More than three-fourths of U.S. citizens do not obtain a college degree, and even those who do graduate from college generally lack an understanding of sustainability. For the vast majority of Americans, knowledge of sustainability will have to be obtained during their adult years. Continuing education programs and educational opportunities offered by the media, museums, churches, and civic organizations—such as the 4-H, the YWCA and the YMCA—are needed to fill the gap and equip adults with the knowledge and skills required for committed and effective action.

The challenge for non-formal education is to find ways to reach a voluntary adult audience. Motivations of adult learners range from the opportunity to socialize, mental stimulation, personal growth, and professional advancement. The challenge is to harness some or all of these incentives to stimulate interest in educational experiences related to sustainability.

For some aspects of environmental education, the challenge of attracting adult learners is not a difficult one. Outings offered by environmental organizations such as the Sierra Club, The Nature Conservancy, and the Audubon Society often contain instruction in natural history and attract intensely interested learners. Interpretive programs offered in national parks are drawing participants at a faster rate than park visitation overall. Interest in this area is also indicated by the explosive growth of ecotourist excursions led by naturalists.[38]

Although these programs are growing in popularity, a new challenge is emerging—how can these programs help adult learners link environmental education experiences to their everyday lives? Extension offices and conservation districts offer one avenue for widening participation. In recent years, the U.S. Department of Agriculture's Cooperative Extension Service has boosted its efforts to create an environmentally literate citizenry, targeting a broader audience than their traditional farm clientele. Other avenues are continuing education classes offered by community colleges and school districts. The nation's 1,200 accredited community colleges represent the fastest growing type of educational institution in the United States. Since they are well-connected to local businesses, community colleges are ideally suited to serve as catalysts for sustainability.[39]

Non-formal educational organizations should work closely with educators to identify areas in which schools traditionally have not prepared students adequately. Once these opportunities are identified, non-formal educators can develop materials and work with formal educators to determine possibilities for partnership. In this way, non-formal education can complement classroom teaching.

Initiatives: Non-formal Sustainability Education:

Founded in 1972, Earthwatch has become a model for global education for sustainable development. To date, 40,000 citizen volunteers have served in Earthwatch's *EarthCorps* program, which has funded 2,000 expeditions to 120 countries. The program is intergenerational and interdisciplinary in design, and involves citizens from 30 countries each year who protect heritage, biodiversity, public health, and treasured habitats worldwide.[40]

Education for Global Responsibility is a program for educating YWCA members, volunteers, staff, and the community about the causes of global poverty and how it affects people–particularly women. With support from the U.S. Agency for International Development, the YWCA has held international conferences and workshops on women's sustainable economic development. Participants have included local and national leaders from the United States, Africa, Asia, Latin America, and the Caribbean. The purpose is to develop a cadre of consultants on women's sustainable economic development issues who will work to educate others in their communities and networks.[41]

The Presidio Institute, in the San Francisco Bay Area, helps businesses, citizen organizations, and governments promote sustainable economic development. Located at a former military base, the institute is a laboratory to explore policies, practices, and technologies to enhance sustainability worldwide.[42]

To promote the development of their local business ventures, Appalachian communities created the *Community in the Classroom* project. This program takes a community-based participatory approach to educating citizens by integrating education into community development activities. Components of the program include workshops aimed at building knowledge, skills, and leadership abilities of staff and volunteers. A

215

series of special projects have also been developed to focus on particular community needs.[43]

The American Forum for Global Education created the *Sustainability Education Center* to integrate environmental, economic, and social issues in the local community with those in the global community. The center's mission is to develop teacher education and professional development programs as well as programs at the local, national, and international levels that promote lifelong learning about sustainability.[44]

The mission of the *National 4-H Council* is to build partnerships for community youth development that involve youth in solving issues critical to their lives, their families and society. The Council is implementing a hands-on environmental stewardship program which encourages partnerships to be built between young people and trainers.[45]

Located in Utah, *Four Corners School* offers many educational programs on environment, culture, and sustainability in the Southwest. Since 1984, the school has been dedicated to educating people of all ages and backgrounds about the need to preserve the natural and cultural treasures in the Southwest and around the world. The school provides scholarships to teachers so that environmental education may be presented throughout schools, and offers accredited courses that can be transferred for use in undergraduate and graduate educational institutions.[46]

Action: Raising Public Awareness:

Raising public awareness is central to any plan to move the nation toward sustainability. If citizens are to reverse such negative trends as urban sprawl, loss of biodiversity, and decreasing voter turnout, they must understand the issues and have accurate and accessible information. In general, people rely on the mass media for their news. A 1995 poll found that 72 percent of survey respondents obtained most of their news and information from television, 38 percent from newspapers 18 percept from radio, and eight percent from magazines. The fact that Americans rely so heavily on print and broadcast media underscores the importance of supplying information which is accurate, can be easily understood, and readily applied to everyday life. Americans need more information about sustainability—what it is and what they can do to live more sustainably. They also need information and ideas—presented through the popular broadcast and print media—about practical things they can do that have a positive effect on sustainable development. For many people, the desire to change is not the issue; they are ready to change their behavior but need the guidance and mechanisms to do so.[47]

Media campaigns on nationally and regionally relevant issues should be used as a vehicle to raise awareness about sustainability. These campaigns should feature and publicize easily understood benchmarks of sustainable development. People have become familiar with national numeric measures of the economy—such as the gross domestic product, inflation rate and unemployment index—as well as such indicators of environmental quality as the air quality index. As indicators of sustainability are developed, the media should feature these measures as part of their regular coverage. Daily and weekly reports of trends and measures will help increase understanding of costs and benefits, and contribute to public awareness of areas where a change in course is needed. Like economic indicators, sustainable development indicators will provide policy makers and the public with a more accurate view of progress in achieving sustainability goals. These national benchmarks will make it easier for all sectors of society to reach consensus on tough issues related to sustainability. As discussed in Chapter 3, much is being done toward developing relevant indicators and benchmarks.[48]

Initiatives: Media Awareness:

The award-winning *Color Me Green* campaign has produced music videos aired as public service announcements; developed a series of *Ecotips* (individual actions that people can carry out in the community) and *Earth Notes* (which describe current issues, such as what industries are doing to become more environmentally responsible); and a public education program that disseminates a Color Me Green school kit to schools throughout the State of Maine.[49]

The Pittsburgh public broadcasting station, WQED, in conjunction with New Vision Communications and the Jefferson Energy Foundation, is producing a series of one hour programs about the implementation of sustainable development practices in the United States and throughout the Americas. The goal of the series is to introduce viewers to the concept of sustainable development using documentary profiles of compelling case studies. It will use many of the success stories featured in this book, as well as examples based on research by the World Resources Institute.[50]

Action: Expanding Community Vision:

Local and state governments should continue to extend their partnerships with community organizations and other levels of government to support community sustainability planning processes and assessments. People need to embrace their own vision of the advantages of living in a sustainable world before they will be inspired to act and make the necessary behavioral changes. Community residents need to create a collaborative vision of what their community needs to sustain itself into the next century.

Agenda 21, the central agreement of the Earth Summit, charges communities around the world with formulating action plans to move toward a sustainable future. The first step in each municipality's long-range planning for sustainability involves bringing diverse members of the public together to discuss and define sustainability at the local level. From the collective community vision, plans and projects can be developed. The progress on such plans, in turn, should be measured periodically by indicators which gauge the community's success in meeting its goals.[51]

Each community will need an overall plan for becoming sustainable that addresses its unique local economic, environmental, social, or technological demands. Each plan must be regionally specific and must consider interconnections between the community and other locations, both near and far. Education is crucial to this process. An active community outreach and education program must be in place to help people understand and adjust to changes in their community brought on by the transition to sustainability. Formal and non-formal educational efforts as previously mentioned will contribute to the community planning process and follow-up assessments.[52]

Initiatives: Community Sustainable Planning:

In a year-long series of meetings, the town of Noblesville, Indiana, developed goals and set benchmarks to guide the community's future in the areas of land use and social and economic development. The process, coordinated by Indiana University, was modeled after an Oregon statewide initiative but included several aspects unique to Noblesville. These included consideration of social issues through the involvement of a local group representing community social service providers and

218

information on interrelationships between various elements of the community.[53]

The *Plymouth Institute*, in Plymouth, Wisconsin, is a non-profit consortium whose purpose is to define, demonstrate, and communicate values and practices of sustainable living. The 292-acre Institute includes an organic farm, aquaculture system, solar homes, and a 70-acre eco-village that is in the design phase. It also cooperatively administers a comprehensive education and outreach program with several universities and school districts to local, national, and international communities. The Plymouth Institute helped organize *Sustainable Wisconsin*, a statewide initiative to build a public agenda for sustainable development.[54]

The United Way and Community Planning Council of Greenville County, South Carolina, helps produce a community wide *Needs Assessment Planning Study* every three or four years. Using a community process that involves a broad range of citizens, the survey identifies a set of issues related to the social problems faced in the county. Task forces representing broad areas of the community then tackle the issues identified.[55]

Action: Fostering Workforce Training:

Educators are the key to readying the nation for the transition to sustainability. They can shape the workforce in part by focusing increased attention on career preparation, especially for those who do not attend college. But formal, in-school education will not answer all the employment-related needs raised by sustainability. Workers in all vocations—from farmers and computer technicians to plant managers and shop owners—will need to be trained to incorporate sustainability into their jobs. New industries employing sustainable practices will require a flexible and adaptable workforce that is prepared for a world in transition. At the same time, many resource-intensive industries may contract out for services, displacing workers who will need to be retrained for work in sustainable enterprises.

Employers should develop training programs to create a workforce with the skills and abilities needed to adapt to changes brought on by the national and global transition to sustainability. Incentives such as increased wages, greater job security, and increased training opportunities should be offered to employees who find innovative ways for their companies to conserve resources, reduce production costs, and help the company prosper.

Jobs in environmental industries contribute to sustainability and are presently high-growth areas. Demand for trained workers in environmentally related fields such as air quality management, sustainable energy production, hazardous waste management, and resource recovery is projected at an annual growth rate of six percent. More jobs will be needed to design and build water treatment plants, increase the efficiency of power plants, insulate homes, build bike paths, and manage parks and wildlife. Workers will need to be trained for these jobs.

Business and organized labor can play constructive roles in educating workers for sustainability. Companies can help finance formal and non-formal educational programs and can support work-based training in sustainable practices. Labor can help focus attention on the need for this kind of training and the fact that in a sustainable economy all citizens can obtain secure, ongoing means of livelihood with full benefits at livable wages.

Education, however, must go beyond simply training workers. Educational outreach programs are needed to help community leaders and community-based economic development organizations become aware of the need for new strategies to develop a sustainable job base. Communities will need technical assistance to implement similar economic development strategies. Entrepreneurs will need access to financing so they can establish sustainable enterprises, and communities will need funds for programs to train workers in the new industries.

Educating workers and employers for a sustainable world needs to become a national priority, and a national effort to provide workforce training should be launched. In particular, training efforts should target students receiving vocational training at the secondary and post-secondary school levels, new employees and employers, employees and employers who need on-the-job upgrading of skills and training in sustainable practices, and displaced workers who must be retrained so they can find work in new industries.

Work-based learning is critical in equipping adults with the knowledge and skills they will need in a fast-changing world. On-the-job training is important in every economic sector, including service industries. Training and retraining programs must proliferate as the economy shifts to more efficient practices. Some businesses already are taking a proactive approach to training in business schools and should extend that effort. For example, companies are partnering with business schools to create internships and courses in environmental management that will help produce graduates knowledgeable of the environmental implications of business practices. Initiatives in vocational education at the secondary and post-secondary levels should be established so that business will have the skilled workforce it will need to remain competitive in the global economy. Cooperative efforts by business and organized labor in this area would benefit both.

School-to-work opportunities offered through partnerships between industry and education also should be encouraged. Promising models for career preparation range from career academies to *tech-prep* programs. The latter are often referred to as *2+2* programs, because they generally involve two years of high school and two years of post-secondary instruction. A recent study of innovative school-to-work programs recommends that federal policy promote common themes and underlying principles rather than prescribe a specific program model. Localities should have the flexibility to customize their own school-to-work strategy, whether that means restructuring existing vocational programs or adopting another approach such as youth apprenticeships.[56]

Enhancing Sustainability Education

Efforts in four separate areas are required to strengthen efforts in sustainability education. First, governments, parents, teachers, schools, environmental organizations, and business associations should form partnerships to coordinate educational programs which focus on sustainable development. Such coordination should reduce the duplication of efforts and increase availability of resources. Sustainability also requires that learners of all ages be prepared for today's increasingly technological society. Computer-based instruction can foster achievement in technological disciplines and increase employment opportunities. The use of information technologies in and out of the classroom must be expanded and equitable access to technology must be ensured. Next, educating for sustainability requires that learners have an understanding and appreciation of the international forces that affect their lives. Environmental problems such as air pollution and pollution of the oceans are global in scale. At the same time, economic and social forces are becoming increasingly globalized. If today's students are to be ready to make tomorrow's decisions, they must understand the links not only between various subject areas but especially between local and global conditions. Finally, individuals from diverse backgrounds must have equal access to education for sustainability. Equally as important, their differing voices must be heard and their input included in the educational process. As the demographics of America's schools and communities change, it is essential that students learn to function in a multicultural society.[57]

Action: Forming Partnerships:

Federal, state, and local governments should form partnerships with private organizations, businesses, professional societies, educational institutions, and community groups to develop and implement coordinated strategies which support education for sustainability. Such partnerships can serve to create common ground, reduce conflict, and encourage consensus-based decisions. Through partnerships, schools and communities can create high-performance learning environments—both in the classroom and outside—by incorporating information technologies and developing community-based communications programs on sustainable development.

Using limited federal resources to spur private initiatives directed at educational needs should be a high priority. Another priority should be to encourage agencies to make partnership opportunities related to education for sustainability central to their missions. A collaborative effort should also be initiated to develop models that could be used by states to strengthen their education for sustainability programs in a comprehensive way—through legislation, statewide coordination, funding, curriculum guidelines, and professional development. Those states that have not yet formed advisory councils on sustainability education should be encouraged to do so. Each state advisory council should link existing networks of public and private entities within the state to integrate research, education, and extension functions.[58]

Initiatives: Partnerships for Sustainability:

Education can be a link that draws people and organizations into partnerships. Successful sustainability partnerships are evident at the highest levels of government. The *President's Council on Sustainable Development* itself is one example of diverse parties coming together to develop a consensus on how best to meet national goals involving environmental protection, economic progress, and social harmony.[59]

The *National Science and Technology Council*, a cabinet-level Council, under the umbrella of the Office of Science and Technology Policy, works to coordinate science, space, and technology policies across the federal government. It also establishes clear national goals for federal science and technology investments. The 1995 publication, *Bridge to a Sustainable Future*, was their response to the mandate for a long term national strategy and goals for the advancement of environmental technologies. The Council also created the *Working Group on Education About Sustainability*. This group's mission is to coordinate federal policies and programs supporting education for sustainability. It will also facilitate partnerships with state government, businesses, professional societies, educational institutions, and community organizations.[60]

Educational partnerships are more frequently forged at the state rather than the federal level. A consortium of various universities and non-profit organizations led by the North American Association for Environmental Education manages a national environmental training program–*the Environmental Education and Training Partnership*. The Partnership includes existing successful teacher training programs such as *Project Learning Tree, Project WILD*, and *Project WET*. Through these and other programs, the Partnership provided training for approximately 35,000 teachers and environmental education professionals in 1996 alone.[61]

Many states are integrating environmental education programs and curricula into their school systems. Five states–Illinois, Iowa, Kentucky, Louisiana, and Hawaii–are working with the *National Environmental Education Advancement Project* to develop comprehensive plans to strengthen their environmental education programs.[62]

The *U.S. Global Change Research Program* is a public-private partnership and education initiative designed to develop national teaching capability in sustainability education through improved science information concerning global change issues. Organized in state teams, professional educators partner with non-governmental organizations, state

223

government officials, businesses, and educators to design and implement state action plans. The National Science Foundation offered planning grants to seven states in 1995 (Alaska, Arkansas, Florida, Iowa, Maine, Ohio, and Utah); and NASA supported 19 states with implementation grants for statewide action plans (Colorado, Connecticut, Florida, Hawaii, Indiana, Iowa, Kentucky, Louisiana, Maine, Massachusetts, Minnesota, New Hampshire, New Jersey, New York, Oregon, Rhode Island, South Carolina, Wisconsin, and Wyoming).[63]

Action: Expanding Information Networks:

Information technologies are transforming society and it is becoming clear that students and workers who have access to computers have an advantage over others without such access. Technologies such as the Internet, World Wide Web, and interactive CD-ROMs can advance education for sustainability by linking educators, policy makers, students, and parents nationally and internationally. Incorporating these technologies into educational contexts and improving computer-based instruction is becoming increasingly important. However, the application of information technologies in the classroom varies dramatically between locales. One explanation is a lack of telephone lines in classrooms which effectively bars student participation in electronic communications networks. Another barrier is the speed at which technology is changing; many schools simply cannot afford to keep upgrading their equipment every few years. Even if technology is available in a school, educators frequently are not properly trained in its use and do not know how to incorporate it into their teaching.

Despite these problems, the proliferation of information and communications technology in schools is rapidly increasing. By 1994, nearly 65 percent of all schools, and 77 percent of all high schools, had modems and access to telephone lines. Ten years ago, schools had one computer for every 125 children; that ratio is now one computer for every 12 children. The Internet today reaches approximately 40 million people in about 168 countries and its use is rapidly increasing. Technology is rapidly becoming an invaluable tool for supplying access to information about new programs, resources, and materials related to education for sustainability. There is a vital need for the development of the National Information Infrastructure by private industry to increase access to public information and improve access for all. This network will be a seamless web of communications networks, computers, databases, and consumer electronics putting vast amounts of information at users' fingertips. Its continued development will ensure that the best schools, teachers, and courses will be available to all students, regardless of geography, resources, or limitations.[64]

Additionally, educational programs should be encouraged to incorporate data from environmental monitoring tools such as geographic information systems. Teachers and students should be aware of databases maintained by international, national, and state governments as well as by private organizations. Courses should familiarize students with the availability of different types of databases, how they are accessed, and how they can be used to monitor environmental change and guide decisions about the environment.[65]

Initiatives: Information Technology Clearinghouses:

The Island Institute in Rockland, Maine, supplies students in 150 classrooms with innovative environmental education software and satellite imagery of the students' school and town. The program's material is made available under the direction of the Remote Sensing Facility at the Bigelow Laboratory for Ocean Sciences. Sponsors include NASA and Apple Computer, Inc.[66]

Bell Atlantic Foundation is working with teachers to engage students in collaborative learning projects based on sustainable development issues in a new multimedia learning project co-sponsored by *Earthwatch*. Using electronic networks and the World Wide Web, *Earthwatch On-line* is able to support these teachers and their students throughout the school year.[67]

The U.S. EPAs *Multimedia Development Laboratory* provides computer-based learning products on diverse safety, health, environmental and sustainability matters to over 2,600 organizations throughout the U.S. and abroad. Using state-of-the-art technologies, it produces and distributes learning, information, and performance support tools, including interactive CD-ROMs. The Laboratory recently started work with the Urban Consortium's *Environmental Task Force of Public Technology* to develop and deliver computer-based learning, information, and performance support products to local governments and communities to help them achieve their sustainability goals. The U.S. EPA has also established a *Government Information Locator Service* for anyone who needs to locate, access, or acquire environmental information. The service lists more than 200 of the Agency's public information resources, describes the information in those resources, and provides assistance in obtaining the needed information.[68]

The Global Action and Information Network provides current legislative information on almost every environmental issue, as well as background data and analyses, action alerts, organizational resources, and contact information for congressional members, cabinet officials, and federal agencies. It also is developing a computer program, *Vision Into Action*, that helps individuals, businesses, and communities determine the scope of their ecological impact.[69]

EE-Link is an on-line source of information about environmental education. It provides access to teaching resources on the Internet, including articles, databases, grant information, and instructional materials. EE-Link is administered through a partnership with the U.S. EPA, the North American Association for Environmental Education, and the National Consortium for Environmental Education and Training.[70]

Greenwire, an on-line environmental news service, provides a daily briefing on environmental news. Editorial commentary comes from over 100 U.S. and international media sources. The Greenwire database provides 24-hour-a-day access to over 20,000 stories published since 1991.[71]

Global Network of Environment and Technology provides access to information on environmental products and services, marketing opportunities, contracts, U.S. government programs, policy and law, current industry news, and business assistance resources on the environment, technology, and commerce.[72]

The National Institute for the Environment has developed a *National Library for the Environment*. The library provides access to over 300 reports on various environmental issues, a user-friendly on-line encyclopedia of the environment, and detailed information at all technical levels on specific environmental subjects. Reports are reviewed, prepared, and checked for accuracy by the Congressional Research Service, a division of the Library of Congress.[73]

The *Educational Resources Information Center* (ERIC) is a national information system designed to provide users with ready access to an extensive body of literature on education and related issues. A number of subject-specific clearinghouses and services provide research summaries, bibliographies, reference and referral services, computer searches, and document reproduction.[74]

The *National Environmental Information Resources Center* (NEIRC) was designed to provide professionals, students, and the general public with one-stop access" to diverse environmental, educational, and sustainability related information maintained on the World Wide Web of the Internet. Established in 1995 as a public service by The George Washington University and the U.S. EPA, it provides direct linkages to more than 1,000 Internet sites globally. The NEIRC also serves as a repository of information developed for higher education and research institutions through the *Green University Initiative.*[75]

The *National Urban Internet* is an environmental justice initiative, sponsored by Naval District Washington, that has been designed to provide access and training on the Internet to low-income and minority communities in Washington, D.C. The program provides hardware, software, Internet access, and training.[76]

The *Global Learning and Observation to Benefit the Environment* program (GLOBE), was begun by Vice President Al Gore in 1994 and supported by numerous federal agency partners, including the National Science Foundation, the National Oceanic and Atmospheric Administration, the U.S. EPA, the U.S. Department of Education, and NASA. It is designed to link teachers, students, and scientists around the world in a study of the environment. It is a hands-on scientific experiment. Teachers are trained to help students test soil, gauge water temperature, study plant species and clouds, and measure the height and diameter of trees. These data are then reported on the Internet via the World Wide Web for use by students, scientists, and NASA. To date more than 2500 schools in the United States and 35 partner countries have signed up as GLOBE sites.[77]

Action: Fostering Global Understanding:

Educators must help students understand the international factors that affect the nation's transition to a sustainable society. Sustainable development cannot be achieved without global cooperation. Overcoming obstacles to sustainability requires a global understanding of the effects that one country's actions and policies have on the health and well-being of

227

another country. Environmental problems such as air pollution and pollution of the oceans are global in scale. At the same time, economic and social forces are becoming increasingly globalized. Solutions to global problems will require long-term education at regional and international levels. In particular, Agenda 21, the central agreement of the 1992 Earth Summit, stressed the necessity for international cooperation and partnerships in education as the launching pad for future sustainability initiatives. Many countries have embraced the themes of Agenda 21 by exploring how sustainability could be integrated into schools, organizations, businesses, and government at the national and community levels. Spurred by the recommendations in Agenda 21, many governments and groups have begun to develop strategic plans for sustainable development. The popular version of this monumental agreement–*Agenda 21: The Earth Summit Strategy to Save Our Planet*–provides a clear, concise version of the tenets of sustainable development which many governments, communities, schools, businesses, and organizations are using in their strategic planning.[78]

Students and youth groups must participate in the emerging global dialogue on sustainability. New alliances centered around economic, political, and related issues are continually emerging and have a great influence on global progress toward sustainability. These factors are making information and other resources more readily available. Students must know about these options and opportunities as they embark on a journey of discovery and understanding of global systems and what it means to be a responsible citizen of the global community. International issues are discussed further in Chapter 11.

Action: Integrating Multicultural Perspectives:

Formal and non-formal educators must also ensure that education for sustainability invites and involves diverse viewpoints. Everyone–regardless of background and origin–must have the opportunity to participate. This will ensure that education for sustainability is enriched by and relevant to all points of view. The demographic composition of classrooms and communities in the United States is more diverse than at any other time in our nation's history. This transformation challenges educators–both in formal and non-formal settings–to develop relevant teaching materials and curricula which are reflective of the environmental realities in all types of communities. Whether in classrooms, museums, or the media, new inclusive visions are needed to commit an active, multicultural citizenry to a sustainable future.

The goal of integrating multicultural perspectives in the public dialogue on sustainable development has several corollary issues. The teacher population in the nation's classrooms is overwhelmingly female, white, and middle class. The students however, are more racially diverse and many come from non-traditional family structures. For many, English is not their primary language. Teachers need training to address this gap. This training should focus on integrating education for sustainability into culturally diverse settings.

There must also be efforts to ensure that the relevance of the sustainability message is made clear to all groups of this nation's multicultural population. A 1994 survey commissioned by the National Environmental Education and Training Foundation focused on disadvantaged youth. The responses indicated a serious gap in environmental education. The disadvantaged children—who are most likely to be exposed to environmental risks—ranked environmental problems as eighth on a list of 10 societal issues they would like to make better. Youth in general rated the environment as second. One reason for this discrepancy may be that environmental education is either not taught in the schools in lower-income neighborhoods or does not incorporate information about environmental issues that relate to students' everyday concerns. For example, urban youth may not see the importance of saving whales as compared with the more pressing and immediate problems of violence and drugs in their own neighborhood. Urban youth may benefit more from learning about environmental justice issues, waste management, and how environmental hazards affect human health. Regardless of the specific environmental issues taught, however, the overall programs need to be tailored to meet the needs of the specific constituencies they serve. Programs and curricula should be dynamic and able to adjust to changing community, national, and global circumstances. Linking environmental issues with everyday survival issues can expose disadvantaged students to knowledge that can help them take action and make changes that benefit themselves, their families, and communities.[79]

Teachers' familiarity with these issues should begin during pre-service training and continue throughout their tenure. Educator training should stress conflict resolution, intercultural communication, and environmental justice issues while emphasizing an understanding of community-based approaches to environmental education. Multicultural environmental education focuses on students in industrialized areas who are often disproportionately exposed to toxics. Historically, the siting of industrial plants, waste incinerators, landfills, and sewage treatment plants in poor and minority communities has resulted in discriminatory exposure to pollution and hazardous wastes. In recent years, an explosion of interest in urban environmental issues has been consolidated in the environmental justice movement, which links environmental issues with social justice movements, such as civil rights. The focus is on toxic waste dumps, poor air and water quality, and pesticides impact on human health. The movement seeks environmental equity for all people— regardless of race, social class, ethnicity, gender, age, or disability. In addition to pointing out discriminatory siting practices, the movement has condemned the uneven enforcement of environmental laws and remediation efforts.[80]

Initiatives: Environmental Justice:

Since it opened in 1992, the *Southern Center for Environmental Justice* has been inundated with requests for community assistance in responding to accidents, registering formal complaints, accessing information, and understanding technical documents related to the environment. The center's dual mission is to conduct research and policy studies and create partnerships among universities, grassroots organizations, and individuals in a community to assist coordinated actions in fighting for environmental justice.[81]

The Menominee Indian Tribe of Wisconsin, along with other tribes throughout the United States, promote the lessons and concepts of sustainability at an early age and weave them into the levels of education throughout life. At the College of the Menominee, concepts of sustainability are integrated into the curricula and hands-on experiential learning is practiced. In the fall of 1996, the college launched a new degree program in sustainable development, and the *Menominee Sustainable Development Institute* is developing a curriculum for high schools with sustainable communities as the theme.[82]

A U.S. EPA grant is enabling the Davidson School in Elwyn, Pennsylvania, to provide training in environmental education to teachers and university students majoring in special education. The *Curriculum for Environmental Education of the Disabled* will be distributed nationwide through a network of participating organizations and agencies. By targeting disabled secondary school students, this program will reach a traditionally underserved audience.[83]

The Chicago Academy of Sciences' *Project Ecological-Citizenship* is designed for urban multicultural elementary students; it also involves parents and the community. The project's core element is a multidisciplinary ecology program incorporating hands-on explorations of environmental issues affecting inner-city communities. The academy's model program has been used to introduce environmental education in inner-city schools throughout the nation.[84]

Project SEED (Seniors Environmental Education Development) in Fremont, Ohio, is an excellent example of how a community-based organization can communicate with an audience not typically reached through other methods of environmental education. The project educates disadvantaged senior citizens about the health hazards of indoor air pollution and about conservation opportunities within their homes, such as weatherization and water conservation.[85]

Three Circles Center for Multicultural Environmental Education is a non-profit organization that aims to introduce and cultivate multicultural perspectives in environmental education. The center helps create access to environmental education for disadvantaged children across the country through teaching, program design, evaluation, curriculum development, and outdoor field study opportunities. It also helps organizations and educators by publishing a journal and offering presentations and workshops. It has also initiated the Multicultural Technical Assistance Project to support the incorporation of multicultural issues and perspectives into selected San Francisco Bay Area environmental education programs.[86]

Ultimately, our nation's children and grandchildren will be the ones who will see the progress of sustainability. Prosperity, fairness, and a healthy environment are interrelated elements of the human dream for a better future. Sustainable development is a way to pursue that dream. Over the past 50 years, the United States has enjoyed phenomenal success in disseminating the American ideal of democracy, basic human rights, and a decent quality of life. Today, this American dream needs to be expanded to include environmental protection, economic progress, and social equity. Seeking sustainable solutions and taking sustainable action must become an integral part of daily life. The fundamental principles of sustainability should serve to guide not only individuals, but also schools, businesses, communities, the nation as a whole, and societies world-wide. The national quality of life is enriched not so much by things, as by creative accomplishments in every aspect of one's life–jobs, relationships, and civic contributions to communities and society. Organizations that foster the personal growth of citizens and improvements to our communities can produce greater satisfaction and hope, increased productivity, and an enhanced quality of life. Encouraging hope for a sustainable future is dependent upon continually building awareness and knowledge about sustainability matters into the fabric of individuals and institutions. Sharing this information is critical to building a sustainable America.

Chapter 10

Sustainable Communities

Flourishing communities are the foundation of a healthy society. One measure of America's potential for long-term vitality will be the emergence of communities that are attractive, clean, safe, and rich in educational and employment opportunities. The concepts of sustainable development can easily remain remote and theoretical unless they are linked to people's day-to-day lives and seen as relevant to fundamental needs such as jobs, clean air and water, and education. It is often easier to make these connections in the context of communities. It is in communities that people work, play, and feel most connected to society. Problems like congestion, pollution, and crime may seem abstract as national statistics, but they become personal and real at the local level. It is in communities that people profoundly feel the effects of shifts in the national and regional economy. It is within communities that children gain basic education, skills, and training for jobs in the changing marketplace. It is within communities that people can most easily bring diverse interests together, identify and agree on goals for positive change, and organize for responsive action. While the challenges facing the nation are difficult to resolve at any level of government, local communities offer people the greatest opportunity to meet face to face and build a shared commitment to a sustainable future.

233

The scope of a problem determines the level at which it is most appropriately solved. Some issues have global, national, and regional ramifications. Air pollution is one such issue. The air pollutants which create acid rain may originally have been emitted hundreds of miles from where the precipitation ultimately falls. The cooperation of more than one region is required to correct this type of problem. The federal role is important and necessary in areas such as this because national interests may not always be represented in local decisions, and the effects of community choices are felt beyond one municipality.

However, as the United States, and much of the rest of the world, moves toward more decentralized decision-making, the role of local communities will become increasingly more important. The federal government will continue to bear the responsibility for bringing together diverse interests to establish national standards, goals, and priorities. As discussed in Chapter 7, the federal government is moving to provide greater flexibility and expanded roles for states, counties, and local communities to implement policies and programs that address national goals. This new model of intergovernmental partnership will require greater information sharing and an unprecedented degree of coordination among levels of government. Local government will play a key role in this effort, and strong communities will be essential.

America must begin to build stronger, more sustainable communities. There is no single template for a sustainable community. However, cities and towns pursuing sustainable development often have certain characteristics in common. Sustainable communities are cities and towns that prosper because people work together to produce a high quality of life which they want to sustain and constantly improve. In sustainable communities, all people should have access to educational opportunities that prepare them for jobs in a dynamic local economy that is prepared to cope with changes in the national and global economy. Businesses, households, and government should make efficient use of land, energy, and other resources, allowing the area to achieve a high quality of life with minimal waste and environmental damage. Such communities should be healthy and secure, and provide people with clean air to breathe and safe water to drink.

To create sustainable communities, people must work to build a community together. They should be involved in making the decisions that will affect their lives. The decisions that they make should be based on long-term projections that benefit future generations as well as themselves. Successful long-term solutions require partnerships and a process which allows for representatives of a community's diverse population to be involved in the discussions, planning, and decisions that relate to unique local needs. Some problems cannot be solved within the confines of a community and, thus, partnerships with others in the region will be necessary to effectively deal with them.

To create sustainable communities, people must use a participatory approach to begin making conscious decisions about design. The concepts of efficiency and liveability should guide these decisions. Development patterns should be created that promote accessibility, decrease sprawl, and reduce energy costs. The use of environmentally superior technologies for transportation, industry, buildings, and agriculture should be encouraged. These technologies will boost productivity and lower business costs while dramatically reducing pollution and waste.

To create sustainable communities, partnerships must be developed which involve business, government, labor, and employees to promote economic development and jobs. Participants should cooperatively plan and carry out development strategies that create diversified local economies built on unique local advantages and environmentally superior technologies. These efforts can strengthen the local economy, buffering it from the effects of national and international economic trends that result in job losses in a community. Such partnerships must also invest in education and training to make community members more productive, raise their earning power, and help strengthen and attract business.

Much of what is needed to create more sustainable communities is within reach if people and their community institutions join forces. Many communities are beginning to use sustainable development as a framework for thinking about their future. The big institutions in society– including federal and state governments, businesses, universities, and national organizations–can and should provide support for local community efforts. And in some cases, these institutions need to eliminate the barriers that they have sometimes inadvertently erected which diminish the ability of communities to pursue sustainable development.

Communities throughout the country are beginning to use innovative approaches to reinvigorate public involvement. By building upon their leadership and innovation, other communities can marshal and reorient government resources and create new standards in finding solutions to community problems.

Building Communities Together

One of the best ways to strengthen communities is to ensure that people have greater power over and responsibility for the decisions that shape their communities. A fundamental component of implementing sustainable development locally is having people come together to identify a community's needs and then work toward collaborative solutions. Accomplishing this requires both political leadership and citizen involvement. Creating mechanisms for individual communities to work together cooperatively is also necessary to deal with problems that cross political jurisdictions.

The capacity of democratic institutions to solve problems and create a better future depends on the knowledge and involvement of citizens. For society to fully benefit from an engaged citizenry requires a community-based, decision-making process that encourages integrated thinking and broad-based action. Integrated thinking is required so that economic, environmental, and social problems are recognized as being interrelated, and actions to address all of these problems are coordinated. Because these problems are interconnected in daily life, approaching them one at a time does not work. In fact, such a strategy is often counterproductive, leading to short-term fixes and long-term difficulties. The integration of local decision-making offers a way to improve the economy, the environment, and social equity in communities.

Broad-based action is needed because local government alone cannot accomplish long-term solutions to community problems. Nor can individuals, businesses, community groups, or state and federal agencies do so by working in isolation. Lasting solutions are best identified when people from throughout a community—as individuals, elected officials, members of the business community, environmental groups, or civic organizations—are brought together in a spirit of cooperation to identify solutions to community problems.

This work is difficult, and there are many barriers to its success. The time and energy of many families are already drained by juggling the demands of the workplace and the home. Cynicism toward government is high, and all too frequently, participation in civic life is declining. It must be the ultimate goal of government and civic organizations to bring more people into the process of community decision-making.

There are fundamental steps to a community-driven strategic planning process. A critical first step is to assemble a broad cross section of the community to participate in an open, public process. Through a series of meetings and events, the community can develop a vision for its future. It then should conduct an inventory and assessment of its economic, natural, and human resources. Specific economic, environmental, and social goals should be determined that build on the community's vision, resources, and needs. Next, the community must set priorities for its goals, identify specific actions, and establish indicators or benchmarks to measure progress toward the goals. If successful, the strategic planning process will result in a clear sense of direction and timing. It should clearly specify the actions and responsibilities to be undertaken by business, residents, government, and community groups.

Fundamental to the long-term success of community-driven solutions is the opportunity for all residents to participate—specifically those people who have been historically underrepresented in decision-making. While citizen participation is primarily an individual decision, government, businesses, and community organizations can encourage people to become more involved by working to remove any barriers to participation. By developing a strategic plan that involves all of the diverse elements of the community and generates the necessary leadership to bring about specific actions, communities can take positive steps to create a better future for their residents.

Cooperation among communities in a metropolitan area is also necessary. There has been a trend toward increased concentration of the U.S. population in metropolitan areas. This trend is linked both to population growth and people's migratory patterns. The number of Americans living in metropolitan areas rose from 140 million in 1970 to more than 203 million in 1992. This pattern affects such concerns as congestion, urban pollution, and the high demand for public space and services. Together these trends lower the quality of life in cities and contribute to the exodus

237

from central cities that is occurring in many parts of America. By working together, communities can tackle these issues that affect an entire region. This collaborative approach is not only an opportunity, it is a necessity. Without regional approaches to solve many critical problems that affect communities—such as economic development, transportation, land use, sprawl, and water quality—little long-term progress can be made!

By creating incentives to encourage communities to work together, state and federal governments can improve the decision-making process and promote long-term, holistic solutions to regional problems. Stronger links between people, communities, and the decisions that affect them can revitalize grassroots democracy and thereby strengthen communities, regions, and the nation.

Action: Community-driven Strategic Planning:

There should be a concentrated effort to create a community-driven, strategic planning process across America that brings people together to identify key issues, develop a vision, set goals and benchmarks, and determine actions to improve their communities. All levels of government, the business community, and private organizations should work together to heighten cooperative decision-making at the local level. They can do this by providing information and financial and technical assistance to communities that wish to engage in a collaborative, community-wide process to integrate economic prosperity, environmental health, and opportunity in their decisions and actions[2]

Public Participation: All levels of government should also ensure that they provide substantial opportunities for public participation in all phases of their planning and decision-making to allow all of those affected to have a voice in the outcome. This should include the creation and expansion of methods for increased public participation in legislation, ordinances, and community advisory boards. Special steps should be taken to ensure that historically underrepresented groups are involved. All levels of government, especially local government, should identify barriers to greater citizen involvement in decision-making—such as lack of child care or transportation—and develop strategies to overcome them. Employers should give employees flexibility and incentives to increase the time they and their families can devote to community activities[3]

Community Coalitions: Community-based coalitions can create educational media campaigns to encourage citizen participation in government. Such coalitions should also disseminate high-quality information on community issues, and promote public discussions that identify solutions to problems. Coalitions should be as broad as possible, including industry and business, schools, newspapers, television and radio stations, community groups, environmental organizations, labor, and local government. Community-based coalitions can work together to draft an economic development strategy to fill basic needs and take advantage of new trends as part of the strategic planning process. Community-based coalitions should also develop and carry out programs to increase voter registration and participation, working with national voter registration projects where possible.[4]

Environmental Risk Profiles: Federal and state agencies should help local communities that wish to use profiles of potential environmental risks as a tool to identify and set priorities for solving environmental problems. The agencies should provide information on and facilitate access to other communities that have successfully used this type of tool[5]

Action: Collaborative Regional Planning:

Major efforts should be made to encourage communities in a region to work together to deal with issues that transcend jurisdictional and other boundaries. States, counties, and communities should cooperate to create a system of regional accounts that measure the costs and benefits of local land use, development, and economic trends on a region's economy, environment, distribution of benefits, and quality of life. States and regions can consider the use of indicators or benchmarks to look at a broad range of social, environmental, and economic measures. The federal government should work with state and local governments to ensure that federal statistical resources are available and used appropriately to support state and local governments in measuring benefits and costs[6]

Incentives for Regional Cooperation: Federal and state governments should encourage cooperation between communities by providing incentives for regional collaboration on issues that transcend political jurisdictions and boundaries—such as transportation, affordable housing, economic development, air and water quality, and land use. In encouraging such cooperation, they should look to the example of the federal

Empowerment Zone-Enterprise Community Program, which requires communities to draft funding proposals using a collaborative strategic planning process. This kind of cooperation should be encouraged between communities within a region to advance common objectives. Federal and state agencies responsible for environmental protection, economic development, land use, and transportation policies should work with one or more geographic areas to establish planning and development activities. These agencies should create incentives to encourage regional planning and development, such as waivers of state matches for transportation planning funds and more favorable federal and state tax treatment for site cleanup costs.[7]

Local and county governments can pool resources from local property taxes to increase equity in public services and improve the quality of local education. This will help to break the increasing regional mismatch between social needs and tax resources. Such funds can also be used to reduce local incentives for sprawl and end competition for the tax base within a metropolitan area. Local and county actions to accomplish this should receive federal and state incentives.[8]

Designing Sustainable Communities

The focus of society's investments should be to create places where people want to live–including the schools, roads, services, and other amenities which are provided. The way that a community is built is a critical factor in shaping the quality of life, accessibility, environmental burden, and unique character of a community. The ways in which homes are designed and constructed, commercial buildings erected, roads and sewers laid, whole neighborhoods and communities planned and built are all fundamental to creating a community that is sustainable. Design and architecture also play an important role in facilitating or discouraging human interaction. Communities that are built with sidewalks, town squares, houses with front porches, parks, and other public meeting places encourage people to interact.

Although well-designed communities and buildings may differ in style, scale, or location, they all tend to be durable, fit well into their natural setting, and efficient in their purposes. Because many design issues–such as transportation, land use, and growth management–transcend political boundaries, sustainable community design also calls for coordinated regional strategies. The principles of sustainable design are reflected in the physical infrastructure of a community by the choices people make. These principles include efficiency, durability and also a strong respect for the human side of design—aesthetics, history, and culture.

Sustainable building design and community planning should make efficient use of existing infrastructure, energy, water, materials, and land. Not only does such use save money, it also safeguards public health and the environment and conserves natural resources. Building codes can shape how much energy, water, and materials a building consumes in its construction and operation. Zoning ordinances frequently influence decisions on the construction, design, and siting of buildings and developments. Efficient land use can protect vulnerable environmental areas that provide important benefits to society. For example, coastal areas, watersheds, and floodplains are able to absorb the forces unleashed by nature, and preserved wetlands can filter water far more cheaply than expensive water treatment facilities. In contrast, development in these type areas exposes people and their investments to unnecessary risks and natural hazards.[9]

Location efficiency is another important component of sustainable design. Zoning ordinances that allow for mixed-use development—such as having a store, apartment building, and school on the same block—can give people easy access to a range of facilities and the ability to walk to obtain goods and services. This can result in decreased reliance on motorized vehicles, thereby reducing congestion and air pollution.

Sustainable community design is also based on an understanding of the powerful effect of the way a community is built on aesthetics and the sense of history and culture. Historic buildings give society an important sense of tradition and education about the past. Preservation of existing structures also offers a way to reuse and recycle materials and their related infrastructure. By rehabilitating older buildings, communities can save energy and materials and establish a sense of continuity.

Some localities have used zoning and other ordinances to foster historical connections. For example, the bay windows contributing to the beauty and character of Boston's Back Bay were the result of a zoning code that allowed one-third of each building to extend to the street.

Charleston, South Carolina, and Savannah, Georgia, among many other historic areas, have protected their architectural heritage and enhanced their property values by using design control measures and by making historic preservation a priority.[10]

Some communities are working together to create regional strategies for transportation, land use, and economic growth. For example, in the Portland, Oregon, metropolitan area, communities are working together to plan for the explosive population growth the area has experienced since the 1980s. By using coordinated decision-making and establishing an urban growth boundary–which will confine future growth–these communities are conserving open space and prime farmland to preserve the quality of life that has attracted so many people to Portland in the first place. They are also using community impact analyses to inform themselves about proposed development during the planning phase when adjustments can be made more easily.[11]

Design that is coordinated among communities can help address issues related to growth. While some growth is necessary, it is the nature of that growth that makes the difference. *Sprawl* typically is development situated without regard to the overall design of a community or region. It often results in types of development–such as rambling, cookie-cutter subdivisions and strip malls–that perpetuate homogeneity, make inefficient use of land, and rely almost exclusively on automobiles for transportation. Sprawl development provides immediate and direct benefits to the people who move there, but many of the costs of sprawl are long term and are borne by society at large. This is a *tragedy of the commons* in which individuals acting logically in their own self-interest harm a common resource. Sprawl is caused by a combination of incentives established by governmental policies and individual decisions made in response to a complex array of factors. This combination results in urban decline and is made worse by competition among local jurisdictions with little regional cooperation.[12]

The *brownfields* issue is another example of the need for regional strategies. Brownfields are abandoned, contaminated, or underused land that are often found in inner cities. In contrast, *greenfields* are relatively pristine undeveloped land–usually found at the edge of a metropolitan area or in a rural area. A company deciding whether to invest in building or modernizing a plant in a city center or building on rural or suburban

242

open space weighs many factors. The economic opportunities presented by brownfield redevelopment are numerous, but are often overshadowed by other considerations. Land use and infrastructure policies have a significant impact on development decisions. Brownfield sites are often not competitive with undeveloped suburban or rural areas because the true costs of development are not clear. Developers often do not consider the infrastructure costs of undeveloped areas, such as the cost of sewers, roads, and electrical lines that need to be built to support the growth. If the cost of cleaning up brownfields is borne by the developer but the cost of roads and utilities needed to serve greenfield development is borne by government, the scales tip to favor development of greenfields. If the uncertainties of time and the liabilities associated with brownfield development is greater, the scales can tip further. If the tax burden for development in a newer, more affluent suburb is less than in an urban center, the case for greenfield development could be substantial. While development is a private decision made by individuals and businesses, it is greatly influenced by governmental policies that are not always readily apparent.

The benefits of developing open space are experienced one house or one business at a time. These benefits are tangible and immediate. The costs are harder to measure. In contemplating the use of open land for residential or industrial development, an awareness and appreciation of what might be lost and of the environmental costs should be taken into account. Visionary planner Frederick Law Olmsted described urban parks as the lungs of a city. This concept also applies to rural regions. Forests, farmland, mountains, plains, deserts, and swamps give the nation vital breathing room. New development should be based upon the *carrying capacity* of a region, which is the environment's finite ability to support life and renew itself.[13]

Given the importance of the physical design of communities and their infrastructure, it is essential that communities continue to work cooperatively to understand and evaluate the potential long-term consequences of decisions made. State and federal governments should work collaboratively with communities to devise ways to measure these consequences in order to help local governments make better decisions.

Design, by definition, involves planning and making deliberate decisions. This occurs at different scales in the context of a community. The following recommendations are organized along these scales of design. The first scale relates to the design of buildings and other structures within the community. The second relates to the physical layout of streets, transportation, residences, stores, and workplaces in the community. The third ties the community to others in the region.

Action: Building Design and Rehabilitation:

There should be significant efforts to design and rehabilitate buildings so they use energy and natural resources efficiently, enhance public health and the environment, preserve historic and natural settings, and contribute to a sense of community identity. Federal, state, and local governments should work with builders, architects, developers, contractors, manufacturers, community groups, and others to develop and enhance design tools that can be used to improve the efficiency and liveability of buildings. Such tools should include models for building codes, zoning ordinances, and permit approval processes for buildings, public infrastructure, and landscapes. Model building codes should consider energy efficiency, durability, and the use of nontoxic materials. Indoor air quality should also be considered, as well as the use of recycled and recyclable materials. Landscaping codes should encourage the use of native plants that can reduce the need for fertilizers, pesticides, and water. Zoning codes should facilitate designs that promote human interaction.[14]

Disseminate Design Information: These design tools should be widely disseminated in an effort to make the information easily accessible to local decision-makers in interested communities. The local communities can then use the new model codes as a starting point to refine their own codes. By adapting them to reflect local conditions and values, communities can begin to reorient local planning to incorporate designs for sustainable communities.[15]

Inventory Historic Buildings: Groups in communities that have made historic preservation a priority can inventory and prioritize historic properties and identify financing to rehabilitate these buildings. Local governments can enact ordinances to preserve historic buildings and remove incentives that encourage demolishing them. They can create incentives for rehabilitating and adapting historic buildings for new uses, where appropriate.[16]

Initiative: Habitat for Humanity/Jordan Commons:

Homestead Habitat for Humanity, a non-profit ecumenical Christian organization whose mission is to encourage private home ownership for low-income families, hopes to alleviate some of the housing shortages caused by Hurricane Andrew in Dade County, Florida. The effort is through Jordan Commons, a pilot project in community building. Jordan Commons will provide 187 single-family homes built with government support, $15 million in private donations, and the work of individual volunteers and future homeowners working side by side. As in all Habitat projects, homeowners will reflect the ethnic and racial composition of their community. At Jordan Commons, approximately 40 percent of the owners will be African-American, 40 percent Latino, and 20 percent white. In addition to providing quality housing, the Jordan Commons project aims to tackle a much larger challenge. It hopes to use new principles in design and community planning to build a thriving neighborhood. The streets are designed for people. The roads will be narrow and the tree-shaded sidewalks wide. All homes will have front porches. Three small parks will allow children to play near their homes. The town center will draw homeowners out onto their sidewalks. This focal point of the community will be a 10,000 square foot recreation center. Additional community buildings will house a day-care center, a food co-op, continuing education programs, and an after-school program—all aimed at supporting families and encouraging social interaction.

Jordan Commons also plans to design environmentally sound homes. Scientists from Florida International University and the Florida Solar Energy Center have developed a list of energy-efficient approaches for building homes. With these innovations, the new homes are expected to be 38 to 48 percent more energy efficient than most homes of comparable size. Water heating will be supplied primarily through solar systems, and water will be recaptured and, after treatment, returned to the groundwater system. Alternative transportation will be encouraged through bike paths and racks, as well as a shaded bus stop station along nearby U.S. Route 1. Underlying all of the thoughtful planning and family-friendly design is one central goal: citizen participation.[17]

Action: Community Design:

Considerable efforts should be made to design new communities and improve existing ones to use land more efficiently. The improvements should strive to promote mixed-use and mixed-income development. Efforts should be made to retain public open space and to provide diverse transportation options. Local jurisdictions should structure or revise their local zoning regulations and permit processes to encourage development located along corridors which are near a range of transportation alternatives. There should also be positive efforts to develop and rehabilitate brownfield sites. Zoning codes should be revised to allow mixed-use development which includes residences, businesses, recreational facilities, and households with a variety of incomes within close proximity![18]

Design Assistance: Federal and state governments, businesses, and private organizations should offer the assistance of multidisciplinary design teams to local jurisdictions that want help with sustainable community design. These design teams should include leading experts in a broad range of fields, including architecture, transportation, land use, energy efficiency, development, and engineering. Design teams should work with state and local governments and community residents with related experience. The mission of the design teams should be to design, develop, and make accessible to communities the latest available alternatives to sprawl development, models for regional cooperation, and sustainable building practices.[19]

Location-efficient Mortgages: The federal government should work with lenders to expand research and application of location-efficient mortgages. Such mortgages are designed to increase the borrowing power of potential homebuyers in high-density locations where there is easy access to mass transportation. A potential borrower could qualify for a larger loan amount based on their expected use of mass transit. Their higher borrowing power is based on their anticipated higher disposable income from a reduction in—or total absence of—automobile payments, insurance, and maintenance.[20]

Integrated Development: Federal and state governments—in consultation with local government, private industry, and non-governmental organizations—should support local planning that integrates economic development, land use, and social concerns. These local planning initiatives

246

should be designed to engage significant public participation. The principles of integrated planning and public participation were included in the federal Intermodal Surface Transportation Efficiency Act, and should be reaffirmed during the act's reauthorization. The community use of integrated planning should be expanded as requirements for federal and state funding and tax incentives. For communities to receive funds for economic development, housing, transportation, and environmental programs, they should begin to be required to adopt planning processes that include a broader range of the public and which integrate environmental, economic, and social equity concerns.[21]

Community Traffic Design: The federal government can also provide incentives for communities to meets national air quality standards under the Clean Air Act. Communities can be given credit toward attainment of air standards when they use community design to lower overall traffic by adopting zoning codes, building codes, and other changes that act to reduce pollution from motor vehicles and energy use.[22]

Equitable Design: All levels of government should work with community groups and private industry to ensure that no segment of society bears a disproportionate share of environmental risks in a community. Collaborative public-private partnerships should periodically conduct an evaluation of community benefits. Action on such evaluations should ensure that desirable transportation and infrastructure investments–such as those in roads, buildings, and water projects–do not disproportionately deliver greater benefits to wealthier, more politically active communities and disproportionately fewer benefits to poorer, less politically active, or minority communities.[23]

Action: Community Growth Management:

Unchecked development has accompanied the rapid growth and prosperity in many communities over the past three decades. Suburban sprawl has taken a toll on society as well as on the landscape. There is a dramatic increase in the number of automobiles and in the time spent in traffic jams. Irreplaceable prime agricultural land and forest land have been lost. Taxes and other costs for individuals and businesses have increased to provide new infrastructure. Sprawl has often widened the distance between where people live and work. It has also resulted in the abandonment of investments in older communities, which continue to suffer long-term decline.

These negative effects of sprawl make a compelling argument to create more compact and efficient communities. The net effect of less sprawl would be to improve the business climate, conserve agricultural land and natural areas, and revitalize cities. To meaningfully reduce sprawl, however, will require bold community action, innovative public policies, new business practices, and active individual efforts.[24]

Reduce Sprawl: There should be significant new efforts to manage the geographical growth of existing communities and the siting of new ones to decrease sprawl and conserve open space. Community design should respect nature's carrying capacity and provide protection from natural hazards. States and communities should evaluate the added costs of providing infrastructure in greenfield or relatively undeveloped areas. There should be a thorough examination of current subsidies and market incentives in the financing of capital costs of infrastructure–such as sewers and utilities–for development of land bordering metropolitan areas.[25]

Land Acquisition: All levels of government and non-governmental organizations can conserve open space through acquisition of land and/or development rights. For example, public water departments can budget to acquire the land necessary to protect public water supplies. Private land trusts can expand their acquisition of wetlands or other valuable open space. Local governments and counties can create community partnerships to develop regional open space networks. Urban growth boundaries can be used as part of a regional framework to discourage sprawl developments that threaten a region's environmental carrying capacity.[26]

Community Impact Analyses: Local governments and counties can work together to use community impact analyses and other information on the environmental carrying capacity of a region as the foundation for land use planning and development decisions.[27]

Reform of Government Policies: All levels of government should identify and eliminate governmental incentives that encourage development in areas vulnerable to natural hazards. Some of such incentives are subsidized floodplain insurance and subsidized utilities in newly-developed areas. The federal government should redirect any federal policies that encourage low-density sprawl to instead foster investment in existing communities. The federal government should also encourage a shift in government transportation spending away from new highway construction and toward highway maintenance and repair, and the expansion of mass transportation options.[28]

Promoting Economic Development and Jobs

Sustainable development is premised on improving how society meets human needs for all people in a manner which is consistent with protecting the natural environment. A strong local economy is at the core of a sustainable community because the economic development and jobs created are the vehicles for meeting human needs. People must be able to provide for the basic necessities of food and shelter for themselves and their families. The economy of the nation as a whole depends significantly on the success of its many interconnected local and regional economies. In recent years, dramatic changes in the global economy have resulted in major shifts in local economies as both national and local markets have adjusted to the trends. In some cases, the nation has become more competitive. In the process, however, many local economies have lost numerous jobs and opportunities. In other cases, the very future of some communities has become endangered.

Government has an obligation to address the human consequences of policy decisions—on environmental, trade, or defense issues—that result in job losses in a community. For example, economic assistance and retraining has been provided to fishermen whose income has been drastically reduced because unsustainable fishing has necessitated strict conservation measures. Assistance has also been given to communities where military bases have closed. Some assistance has been provided for areas that have been adversely affected by trade agreements.

Strategies to create strong, diversified local economies are needed to weather and take advantage of fundamental shifts in national and international economies. The communities that prosper will be those that develop strategies to make the unique strengths of their people and their place a source of competitive advantage. Local economic health is often strengthened by partnerships between industry, employees, educators, and government. These efforts can create an environment that promotes entrepreneurship, innovation, and small business growth.

The only natural resource that can be considered unlimited is human intellectual capacity. Thus, training and lifelong learning are absolutely essential components if sustainable communities are to develop a flexible, well-educated workforce. Education and training are perhaps the most valuable elements of any economic development strategy because they are the only way to build the intellectual capacity necessary for a trainable and employable workforce. This capacity, in turn, allows a community to adapt to the fundamental shifts in national and international economies. Partnerships that involve employers, unions, educators, and workers are the keys to ensuring that employees can take advantage of the opportunities offered by emerging industries.

Communities should adopt an approach to community-wide economic development which promotes maximum resource and energy efficiency. A central factor of any local development strategy is encouraging those businesses and industries that are at the forefront of environmental economic opportunities. Economic growth is achieved and human needs are better met with improved efficiency and environmental performance. Environmental technologies promise both cleaner traditional industries and an important opportunity for creating jobs for the future which are based on cleaner and more efficient technologies. Strategies for development should include investments in resource efficiency to improve the profitability of local small businesses. Other promising ideas include the use of solid waste to develop community-based recycling businesses. Support for eco-industrial parks are another avenue. Pursuing such concepts will require imagination and effort. Initially, extra resources will be necessary, but the rewards can be significant. The benefits and avoided costs that will accrue to society from more efficient use of existing resources can provide the basis for an economic expansion that will increase economic prosperity for all. By preventing pollution, reusing and recycling materials, and conserving energy, new technologies can increase profits, protect and create jobs, and reduce threats to the environment.

There are also opportunities to target the benefits from regulatory flexibility to encourage social equity and economic development. An example is a *cash-for-clunkers* program in which companies that own industrial sources of air pollution can purchase and scrap older, more polluting cars rather than make expensive investments in pollution control in their facilities. Such a program benefits industry by allowing a more cost-effective method for reducing overall air pollution. It also benefits the environment by removing some of the highest polluting cars from the road. This type of program could provide further social benefits if some of the economic savings were used to provide training and jobs to low-income workers to repair older vehicles to meet air quality requirements.[29]

Urban communities around the country are also working to redevelop brownfield sites to improve public health and the economic competitiveness of these sites and surrounding neighborhoods. Cleveland, Detroit, and Chicago are examples of cities that are cleaning up brownfield sites as a strategy for revitalizing their local economies. By targeting economic development in otherwise wasted brownfield areas, these cities are hoping to create jobs, generate tax revenue, and improve the environmental quality of the inner city. They are working to identify and eliminate barriers to redeveloping brownfield sites and to create partnerships among city, state, and federal environmental agencies, residents, local businesses, and lenders. They are also using various tax rebates and financial incentives to attract and retain business activity in these areas.

Action: Creating Diversified Local Economies:

There should be efforts to create diversified local economies which are built on unique local advantages to tap expanding markets and technological innovation. As part of a broader community-driven strategic plan, communities should conduct an inventory and assessment of its economic, natural, and human resources to identify its unique comparative advantages and strategic niche in the larger regional economy.[30]

Labor Force Development: State and federal governments should promote labor force development when they fund projects for transportation, public housing, and sewer and water systems. Incentives can be created within a community for hiring local workers and for providing skills training for workers. Federal, state, and local governments should assist low-income workers–through various programs–to improve their access to education and training. Governments can also adopt tax and development strategies that are targeted at the creation of jobs in new markets. Federal and state governments should review and strengthen labor standards by ensuring an adequate minimum wage, proper health and safety standards, and greater flexibility in work hours to allow more time for community participation and parenting.[31]

Action: Training and Lifelong Learning:

Public and private training programs should be expanded and coordinated to enable all people to improve their skills to match future job requirements. Businesses, unions, schools, students, and local governments should develop and integrate training programs to ensure that workers—especially those who need it most—have the necessary skills to take advantage of current and future economic development opportunities. They should work together to integrate current programs and acquire funding from private industry, schools, and government. Training programs that should be expanded include school-to-work arrangements, apprenticeships, community service programs, summer employment, and job corps opportunities. Federal and state governments should help those who want to pursue further education by providing individuals with tax deductions for tuition, assistance with financing, or other incentives.[32]

Action: Environmental Economic Development:

There should be increased efforts to capitalize on economic development opportunities that target environmental technologies, recycling, and pollution prevention to create jobs. Federal and state agencies should work with industry to create a one-stop shop for financial and technical assistance to small businesses. This would identify cost-effective investments in resource efficiency and help make pollution prevention a standard practice. The federal government should work with lenders to develop ways to substantiate the outcomes of investments in resource efficiency.

Federal and state agencies should also assist communities that want to create eco-industrial parks. Assistance should include making relevant information available, allowing flexibility in permitting and zoning while ensuring that environmental goals are met or exceeded. Local communities can adopt programs to reuse materials and collect and recycle secondary materials diverted from municipal solid waste. Such programs can provide opportunities for new businesses, generate high-skill jobs, produce revenue from recycling collection and processing, and conserve landfill space. The federal government should work with state and local governments to establish related guidelines, develop model programs, and create incentives to promote recycling-related manufacturing.[33]

Initiative: Clean Cities Recycling:

Clean Cities Recycling, Inc. is a non-profit community development corporation formed as a joint venture involving 2-Ladies Recycling, Inc., of Hobart, Indiana; the Gary Clean City Coalition, a community-based environmental organization; and Brothers Keeper of Gary, a shelter for homeless men. The firm has set up 10 drop-off centers at grocery stores, where they collect clean, separated household recyclables–glass, aluminum, steel cans, newspaper, cardboard, and some plastics. This innovative program provides job training, work experience, and letters of recommendation to homeless shelter residents.[34]

Action: Redevelopment of Brownfield Sites:

Nationally, there must be action to revitalize brownfields–contaminated, abandoned, or underused urban land–by making them more attractive for redevelopment. This can be done by reducing regulatory barriers and insuring that suburban and rural greenfields development reflects the true costs of new infrastructure. All levels of government should work in partnership with community residents, environmental organizations, community development corporations, industry, and businesses to redevelop brownfield sites by creating incentives for environmental cleanup. There should also be efforts to reorient existing state and federal economic development funding and programs to include these sites. The federal government should work with states, counties, and communities to develop tools that specifically compare the local economic and environmental costs of developing a greenfield versus redeveloping a brownfield site.

Federal and state agencies should encourage investment in brownfield redevelopment by using the *polluter pays* principle. This principle can be used to assure prospective purchasers and lenders that they will not be held liable for environmental cleanup costs when they did not contribute to past contamination of the sites.[35]

Regional and State-wide Initiatives:

Some of the most innovative sustainability efforts are happening at the regional, state, and local levels. In recent years, the northwest region of the United States has experienced significant population growth, conflicts over the use of natural resources, a changing economic base, and emerging economic partnerships with Canada and Pacific Rim countries. In response to these changes, a number of communities and organizations in the region have demonstrated leadership in fostering sustainable approaches to development. Community leaders in the northwest have established the Pacific Northwest Regional Council. The role of the Regional Council is to foster regional cooperation among federal and state agencies, tribal governments, businesses, non-governmental organizations, and communities as they work to promote sustainable development.[36]

Several U.S. states have also initiated statewide efforts to ensure long-term sustainability. In 1995, Minnesota passed the Sustainable Forest Resources Act, which calls for the formation of public-private partnerships to protect and manage Minnesota's forest ecosystems. The same year, the state passed the Metropolitan Livable Communities Act which established a multi-million dollar program to redevelop brownfields and set metropolitan-wide goals for affordable housing. In 1996, the state passed sustainable development legislation that encourages state agencies to incorporate sustainability into their activities. This legislation also directs the state Office of Strategic and Long-Range Planning to develop a sustainability guide for local communities, including model ordinances, to encourage local governments to take a broader-than-usual view of problems and potential solutions. In addition, the 1996 Environmental Regulatory Innovations Act provides industries, government agencies, and even entire communities with greater flexibility in meeting regulatory requirements, in exchange for improved environmental performance.

The Minnesota Sustainable Development Initiative oversees a government-wide assessment of how well each state agency or program is doing in implementing sustainability principles. Among these principles is the belief that no entity has the right to shift the costs of its behavior to other individuals, communities, states, nations, or future generations. To help assess its progress toward sustainability, Minnesota has developed Minnesota Milestones, a series of social, economic, and environmental goals that the state is striving to achieve. Minnesota is the first state to implement sweeping sustainability legislation and to embark on a statewide effort to ensure that sustainable development becomes a reality.

It is likely that Minnesota's efforts will serve as a model for other states in the years to come.[37]

In recent years, Oregon has faced unprecedented challenges due to population growth, changing economic markets, and resource crises in both the timber and salmon industries. Citizens from across Oregon wanted to ensure that their communities would thrive in the coming years, and the state legislature responded by forming the Oregon Progress Board. This group is charged with developing a vision for the future of Oregon and assessing progress in realizing this vision. The Board selected a set of 259 benchmarks that could serve as indicators of the state's well-being. The indicators address major long-term issues the state is facing such as family stability, its capacity to support a growing population, quality of life and the environment, and the promotion of a strong and diverse economy. The indicators also address immediate, critical issues such as declines in endangered wild salmon stocks and rising teen pregnancy rates. Oregon's benchmarks have fostered a new spirit of collaboration across the state and been an effective tool for measuring the state's progress toward sustainable development. These benchmarks will provide insights into which programs and policies best serve the needs of communities across the state.[38]

Local Initiatives:

Some of the most inspiring examples of sustainable development are at the local level. Communities across the country are taking the initiative to improve the quality of life of their citizens by identifying unique local strengths, utilizing local resources, preventing pollution, reducing wastes, and creating opportunities for local residents to excel and prosper. The following initiatives are just a few of the many ongoing efforts in U. S. communities.

Since 1990, the city of Sarasota has conducted three conferences on community sustainability to address the issues associated with urban growth. As a result, city residents have become more aware of the principles and practices of sustainability. With the help of many volunteers and consultants, the city has developed the *Sarasota Vision Plan*, which will guide development through the year 2040. The city's Economic Development Board is using the proceeds of an occupational license tax to help implement the plan, and the private sector is providing matching funds.

The City and County of Sarasota worked with Mote Marine Laboratory to be included in the U.S. EPAs National Estuarine Program. This has led to assessments of pollution in Sarasota Bay, recommendations on how to restore the Bay, and specific remedial actions.[39]

The Midwest floods of 1993 nearly destroyed the small town of Pattonsburg, Missouri. When the waters subsided, residents joined together to consider strategies for preventing such disasters in the future. Working with a federally supported design team, the community decided that the best option was to move the entire town to higher ground. In an extraordinary demonstration of vision, the community seized the opportunity of relocation to design a completely new town that would incorporate the principles and technologies of sustainable development. The community adopted a *Charter of Sustainability*–a set of principles to guide its development–and building codes to ensure the efficient use of energy and resources. In addition, the Sustainable Economic Development Council was established with private funds to recruit environmentally-responsible industries to the town. The town has been designed to be pedestrian-friendly and to maximize the southern exposures to each home, making it possible for residents to use passive solar heating. A system of artificial wetlands will be used to collect and treat polluted urban runoff, reducing the costs of sewer construction. A methane recovery system will be used to convert the wastes from local swine farms into energy. Pattonsburg is a notable example of how a rural community pulled together in the face of tragedy to create a more sustainable future for themselves and their children.[40]

In the St. Louis area, a bi-state metropolitan planning organization known as the East-West Gateway Coordinating Council has developed a 20-year regional transportation plan. This plan provides a framework for linking the region's transportation investments with the economic, environmental and social needs of the community. Since adopting the plan, the Council has launched a variety of transportation-related projects. One project is designed to improve inner city workers' access to jobs, health care, and social opportunities. Another project is an assessment of community conditions and opportunities within the 18-mile Metrolink rail line corridor and the identification of investment priorities.[41]

In the city of Cleveland, Ohio, the *Neighborhood Economy Initiative* is being launched to create jobs by transforming a million square feet of

industrial buildings in Cleveland neighborhoods into economic incuba-
tors. In addition, Cleveland Tomorrow is working with Neighborhood
Progress Inc.–a partnership organization involving neighborhood organizations, corporations, banks, foundations, and government–to involve all
residents in the revitalization of the city. Community leaders have envisioned a completely revitalized downtown but brownfields have posed a
significant barrier to redevelopment. Cleveland has received funding
from the U.S. EPA to implement two demonstration projects to streamline the redevelopment of at least three brownfields sites. The city of
Cleveland and Cuyahoga County have also embarked on an aggressive
development effort in downtown Cleveland which will result in a new
baseball park, a new arena for basketball and hockey, and the redevelopment of the inner harbor. The new development is quickly becoming a
source of community pride and is drawing residents back to the city and
reducing the incentives for suburban development.[42]

The story of Chattanooga, Tennessee, is one of the greatest turn-
around stories of sustainable development. In 1969, Chattanooga was
designated as having the worst air pollution of any city in the United
States, and it was facing economic decline, unemployment, crumbling infrastructure, racial conflicts, and poor schools. Beginning in 1984, the
city invited all members of the community to participate in a series of
planning projects to develop a common vision for meeting Chattanooga's
economic, environmental, and social needs. These projects led to an unprecedented level of community involvement and cooperation between
civic leaders, government agencies, industry, non-governmental organizations and individuals. Today, public-private partnerships are tackling a
wide range of issues such as redeveloping the downtown and the riverfront, revitalizing neighborhoods, providing education and job training,
preventing air and water pollution, and conserving natural habitat.[43]

Seattle, Washington, has reached its geographic limits of growth, but
its population continues to grow. Seattle has a history of economic vitality, social tolerance, responsive government, environmental stewardship,
and civic pride. It is frequently ranked as one of the "most livable" cities
in the country, but like other major U.S. cities, Seattle faces significant
challenges in the years to come. One of the key concerns for Seattle's
long-term quality of life is population growth. The population in King

County is expected to grow by more than 20,000 people each year between 1995 and 2010.

Since 1990, Sustainable Seattle, a volunteer network and civic forum, has held open public meetings to examine key issues of sustainable development and to develop a set of indicators that can be used to assess progress. In general, these Sustainable Seattle indicators suggest that the area's economic and cultural resources are strong, but that environmental quality and social conditions may be worsening. The Seattle Commons, a citizen-led project is also working to redevelop the South Lake Union area, with support from the city government. The goal of this project is to create a neighborhood that includes parks, high-wage jobs, low-income housing, and pedestrian-friendly streets–a neighborhood that can thrive and sustain itself for the long term. In addition, the city government has initiated three major efforts to promote sustainability: the *Mayor's Environmental Action Agenda*, the *Seattle Comprehensive Plan*, and the *Neighborhood Planning Project*. The Environmental Action Agenda was developed with input from a citizen advisory board and provides a framework for addressing key environmental priorities. The Seattle Comprehensive Plan is designed to create urban village centers within Seattle, while reducing sprawl in the surrounding rural areas. The Neighborhood Planning Project. will involve more than 30 Seattle neighborhoods in a process to develop plans that respond to their unique needs and the city's overall sustainability goals.[44]

Non-governmental Initiatives:

Non-governmental organizations can play an important role in supporting the sustainability efforts of local communities. The Nature Conservancy's Center for Compatible Economic Development has developed the *Citizen's Guide to Achieving a Healthy Community, Economy, & Environment* with support from U.S. EPAs Office of Sustainable Ecosystems and Communities. The document is designed to foster locally-based development that supports a strong economy, a healthy environment, and a high quality of life. The guide presents two major case studies–the Clinch Valley of Virginia and the ACE Basin in South Carolina–and provides a series of outlines and questions to help communities assess and build on their unique strengths. By sharing information about some of the key elements of and strategies for success, the guide can serve as a starting point for communities as they take steps toward a sustainable future.[45]

The American Institute of Architects (AIA) Committee on the Environment provides a forum for compiling, exchanging, and disseminating the environmental information that is essential to creating sustainable buildings and communities. The AIAs *Environmental Resource Guide* provides a comprehensive compendium of information on environmentally responsive design with a focus on the environmental effectiveness of building materials. The AIA also sponsors environmental design workshops to educate citizen groups about design alternatives and provide information on available resources. The workshops also foster linkages between the community, architectural professionals, and government agencies and accelerate the adoption of sustainable development principles and practices.[46]

The Sustainable Communities Network–a partnership of fifteen nonprofit organizations–was created to connect citizens across the country with the resources they need to implement local sustainable development programs and approaches. It is co-directed by CONCERN, Inc., in Washington, D.C.; and by the Community Sustainability Resource Institute in Arden, North Carolina. The network provides information through its World Wide Web site (www.sustainable.org) and is providing a valuable mechanism for citizens and communities to share their experiences and gain access to a wide range of sustainable development resources, libraries, databases, and networks worldwide.[47]

The Joint Center for Sustainable Communities was proposed by the National Association of Counties and the U.S. Conference of Mayors to address the unique needs of local officials in promoting sustainable development. The Center will help them address the problems facing their communities by providing a range of technical assistance, training, sustainable development information, and funding for community visioning and collaborative planning activities. It will also conduct a series of public meetings to explore policies that contribute to building healthy communities. Based on these meetings, it will develop and present policy alternatives to interested government leaders, industries, and nongovernmental organizations. The Center will also help communities develop compacts between cities and counties to create partnerships and to break down the barriers that impede the efficient delivery of services.[48]

Federal Extension Service Initiative:

Federal extension services provide a ready mechanism for disseminating and exchanging information about sustainable development. A national community Sustainable Development Extension Network is being established to utilize existing federal extension services to address community needs concerning sustainability. The network is coordinated at the federal level, but implementation of sustainable practices occurs at the local level and depends on the resources, initiative, and commitment of the communities themselves. The network involves the U.S. EPA, the U.S. Department of Agriculture Cooperative Extension System, and numerous U.S. Department of Commerce programs (including the National Oceanic and Atmospheric Administration Sea Grant Marine Advisory Service, the Technology Administration Manufacturing Extension Partnership, the NASA Space Grant Program, and the Small Business Administration Small Business Development Centers). This will be the first time all of these extension services have joined together to fulfill a single mission—educating communities about sustainable development.[49]

These and other innovative actions by communities, states, regions, non-governmental organizations, and the federal government are confirming the conclusion that communities and regions can become more sustainable by engaging in coordinated efforts to develop and implement cooperative environmental, social, and economic strategies. The communities themselves hold the keys to success, but federal and state governments can be important partners in supporting their efforts to achieve a sustainable America.

Chapter 11

International Leadership in Sustainable Development

The future of the United States–its security, its prosperity, and its environment–is inextricably linked to the world. American firms and workers compete in a global economy shaped by global trends. The lives of Americans are increasingly affected by global environmental change. In an era of weapons of mass destruction, savage terrorism, and sophisticated transnational crime, national security is directly tied to conditions and events around the globe. The United States influences other nations by the force of its example, the power of its economy, and the strength of its arms. The model of American democracy and prosperity has shaped the hopes of many millions of people. The demands of U.S. markets and the products of U.S. industries influence the economic course of much of the world. With one of the highest standards of living in the world, the United States is the largest producer and consumer in history. With fewer than 5 percent of the world's population, the nation consumes nearly 25 percent of the planet's resources. This high standard of living and huge economy has also made the United States the world's largest producer of waste.[1]

The United States is a world leader–often *the* world leader–whether it chooses to exercise leadership or not. Other nations hesitate to act to address international issues of security, development, or the environment unless the United States takes the lead. Issues of development, environment, and human security are as surely interrelated globally as they are locally. This country will not prosper, nor will freedom thrive, in a violent and unstable world. Poverty, inequity, and environmental destruction corrode the bonds of stability and progress that hold civilization together. Human society can only achieve the universal aspiration for social and economic betterment in a world where environmental protection and a more equitable distribution of the fruits of progress are the norm. Improvement in people's lives worldwide will benefit this country economically, environmentally, and socially by alleviating many important sources of global conflict.

There is another compelling reason for U.S. leadership internationally: certain problems can only be addressed through global cooperation. The control of nuclear weapons or the creation of conditions for freer trade requires agreement among nations. The same is equally true of global environmental problems. Previous chapters have emphasized the importance of local communities and individual responsibility in moving the United States toward a more sustainable path. However, some issues affecting individuals and communities can only be solved if nations agree upon common goals and shared responsibilities.

The issues that demand international action include not only damage to ocean ecosystems and deforestation, but also—most importantly—changes in the atmospheric chemistry and composition that influence the global climate and loss of biological diversity. Each of these changes is proceeding at an accelerating rate with consequences that are difficult to predict with certainty or precision. Moreover, none of these phenomena can be quickly reversed after their consequences have been fully understood.

Around the globe people who depend on the sea for a living are already witnessing a decline in the productivity of many of the world's most valuable fisheries. The fishermen of many nations have competed for declining stocks of tuna, salmon, cod, and many other fish—a competition that recently flared into violent confrontation and international conflict. The collapse of many of these fisheries has brought misery to communities in the United States and elsewhere. No single nation can—by itself—limit fish catches to the levels necessary to sustain the fisheries. All nations must agree to abide by the same rules in order to save the shared resource.[2]

Forests–particularly tropical forests–play a critical role in maintaining the diversity, productivity, and resilience of global ecosystems. Forests are also important national resources subject to sensitive issues of sovereignty. In response both to global markets for tropical hardwoods and domestic demand for land and materials, many countries are rapidly cutting their forests. Individual nations understandably resist calls to preserve their forests to provide global benefits. Only cooperative solutions based on global agreements will work.[3]

Cooperation has worked effectively in structuring a phaseout of chlorofluorocarbons (CFCs)–the human-made gases which are destroying the Earth's ozone layer. U.S. industries have responded to clear international goals and economic incentives with a flurry of successful technological innovations that have put them ahead of the agreed-upon international schedule for the phase-out of CFCs.[4]

Human activities are also increasing the concentrations of so-called greenhouse gases. The global scientific consensus predicts a warming of 0.80 F to 3.5 F by the year 2100, although the resulting effects are much less clear. U.S. emissions of carbon dioxide–the primary greenhouse gas due to human activity–make up approximately 25 percent of global emissions of this gas. The per capita U.S. emissions rate is higher than that of any other major industrialized country and many times that of any developing country. In the future, however, emissions from the developing world will grow rapidly as their economies grow, and atmospheric concentrations of greenhouse gases consequently will rise. Without changes, emissions from developing nations will eventually surpass those from industrial nations. It is clear that the United States cannot solve the problem of climate change alone. But it also is clear that unless the industrialized nations demonstrate the benefits of a different development path, there will be little incentive for the rest of the world to follow.[5]

Threats to the global stock of biodiversity represent another global environmental challenge. Although the risks and implications for the United States (as well as its own contribution to the problem) may seem uncertain, the economic and environmental effects could be profound. Economic benefits from wild species make up an estimated 4.5 percent of the U.S. gross domestic product. Fisheries contribute about 100 million tons of food worldwide. One-fourth of all prescriptions dispensed in the United States contain active ingredients extracted from plants, and more than 3,000 antibiotics are derived from microorganisms. Further, nature tourism generates an increasing percentage of tourism revenues worldwide. Yet, for all its value, biodiversity is often not considered in many economic development plans. Tropical forests house between 50 and 90 percent of all species on Earth, but because of forest clearing, 5 to 10 percent of the tropical forest species may be faced with extinction within the next 30 years. As with climate change, one nation cannot solve the problem alone, and the potential for economic harm is huge.[6]

In accepting the challenges of leadership posed by its wealth, strength, and technology, the United States must first adopt effective domestic policies to achieve sustainable development so that it can demonstrate that a better path to progress is possible. Falling short of its own goals may signal to the world the ineffectiveness of free institutions to create environmentally sound economic development that equitably distributes the benefits of growing prosperity. If the United States believes that free institutions are the best means for pursuing human aspirations, it must show that these institutions can respond to the great changes taking place.

More than 100 nations have established national councils on sustainable development similar to the U.S. President's Council on Sustainable Development. They seek to create consensus and shape policies to bring together economic, environmental, and social goals. Some, like the Canadian and Australian Roundtables, began their work several years before the U.S. Council. Most have been organized in response to the 1992 Earth Summit, the United Nations Conference on Environment and Development. Each of the councils is addressing the relationship of human well-being, economic progress, and the environment within the fabric of the conditions, needs, heritage, and politics of its own country. Their council representatives have said—in many different ways—that if the United States fails, they cannot succeed; but that if the United States embraces the idea of sustainability, they believe their own nations will as well.[7]

Because the United States is linked to the world by inter-related economic, environmental, and security interests, it cannot simply turn

264

inward. The nation must lead the world in the transition to global sustainability. It can create markets for U.S. technology, foster equitable conditions under which U.S. industries and workers can compete, and build fair agreements for action to address global problems that affect the United States and its citizens. International engagement for sustainability is a task for government in its relations with other governments, but it is also a task for other parts of society.

For decades, and with considerable success, America has provided aid to nations to encourage development, fight disease, build democracy, and reduce environmental damage. The majority of that aid has come from government, but U.S. philanthropic organizations also have channeled billions of dollars of voluntary contributions into national and global efforts to meet human needs and protect the future. Leading U.S. companies have also been influential in moving their industries toward openness and the application of consistent codes of responsible global conduct. Non-governmental organizations have helped to spur the creation of strong independent voices in debates on development, environment, and social policies around the world. Both official and unofficial roles are essential to the process of international change. There must be several elements to this national engagement.[8]

The United States has both reason and responsibility to develop and carry out global policies that support sustainable development. The United States must promote economic and national security by actively participating in and leading cooperative international efforts to encourage democracy, support scientific research, and enhance economic development that preserves the environment and protects human health.

Action: Support Development Assistance Agencies:

One element of this participation is U.S. support for strong and effective bilateral and multilateral development assistance agencies. Through organizations such as the U.S. Agency for International Development, the United Nations, the Global Environment Facility, and the various international organizations charged with helping implement international environmental accords, the United States can demonstrate its commitment to global development paths that make sense for both this country and the rest of the world. The United States can also continue to play a key role in helping developing countries confront the critical problems this nation has already solved at home, such as the removal of lead from gasoline and the development of environmental assessment techniques. Financial support is one way for the United States to make credible, substantive, and analytical contributions to the work of multilateral institutions and encourage broader participation by other countries.[9]

Action: Convention on Biological Diversity:

The United States is a signatory to the international conventions or treaties that are designed to promote common actions to reduce the risks of climate change and biodiversity loss—two of a growing list of international accords to address global environmental concerns. Yet, the United States has not ratified the U.N. Convention on Biological Diversity—the only major industrialized country that has not done so—even though ratification is supported by a broad cross section of U.S. industry and environmental groups. As a result, the United States faces the risk of not being able to participate in the treaty or help shape the treaty's evolution. Further, the United States may forgo potential economic benefits from the import of genetic resources. The international environmental treaties may not be perfect from many different perspectives, but they do offer a framework for nations to use to move forward together when there is little incentive to move alone. America will derive the greatest benefit in support of its economic and environmental interests by participating in these treaties as well as in the full range of international development assistance processes. The federal government should cooperate in key international agreements—from ratifying the U.N. Convention on Biological Diversity to taking the lead in achieving full implementation of specific commitments made in international environmental agreements to which the United States is a party.[10]

Initiative: International Waterfowl Protection:

Ten years ago, North American waterfowl populations had plummeted to record lows. More than half—and by some estimates much more—of 215 million acres of U.S. wetlands habitat within the lower 48 states had disappeared since the arrival of the first European settlers. Across Canada, estimates of wetlands losses for different areas range from 29 to 71 percent over the same period.[11]

Because efforts to safeguard migratory waterfowl cannot succeed without international cooperation, the governments of the United States,

Canada, and Mexico have been working on a strategy to protect, restore, and enhance waterfowl habitat. In 1986, Canada and the United States established the North American Waterfowl Management Plan, which recognizes that the recovery of waterfowl populations depends on maintaining wetland ecosystems throughout the North American continent. Mexico became a participant in this plan in 1994![12]

The strength of the North American Waterfowl Management Plan lies in the partnerships it encourages among federal, state, provincial, and local governments; businesses; conservation organizations; and individual citizens. To date, this wide array of public and private partners has undertaken 12 joint ventures involving habitat and two directed toward individual species—Arctic nesting geese and black ducks. None of these projects has been mandated by regulation and participation is voluntary. Since 1986, over half a billion dollars has been invested in plan projects. One of the great successes of the plan is that its conservation impact expands beyond just waterfowl and protects all sorts of wetlands wildlife and species.[13]

Action: International Environmental Research:

This nation must not diminish either the importance of scientific research for domestic and international fronts or the importance of the U.S. role in such research. To develop treaties to deal with new concerns and issues effectively, the scientific understanding of the problems and the possible responses to them must continue to be improved. Therefore, the United States should continue to support research and encourage other nations to participate more in international research on critical issues which are relevant to health and the environment. The federal government—assisted by non-governmental organizations and private industry—should increase scientific research and data collection which is related to global environmental challenges. Credible, complete, and peer-reviewed research and data are central to guiding U.S. policy and international deliberations.[14]

Action: Global Trade:

This nation should also continue to promote and encourage global trading systems that mutually reinforce environmental protection and other social development goals. In recent years, initial steps have been taken to incorporate environmental provisions into regional and multilateral agreements designed to reduce trade barriers and improve equitable access to global markets. These agreements may serve to enhance U.S. economic well-being and to promote, in a broader sense, greater global stability. Much still needs to be done, however, in reconciling trade and environmental objectives in an increasingly integrated world economy. This is not just a job for governments, but requires the resources and commitment of the industrial community and the private sector as a whole. Improved economic health and political stability can provide greater resources for environmental protection and a more effective coordinated global approach to the challenges that the nations of the world face together.

The federal government should continue its efforts to ensure that international trade agreements do not threaten the validity of scientifically supported domestic health, safety, or environmental standards. It must also be vigilant in ensuring that trade agreements continue to encourage the parties to improve their environmental and labor standards in fostering trade and in attracting foreign investment. Government at all levels should work with industry to increase U.S. exports of environmental technologies. The aim of such exports should be to support and create new high-paying U.S. jobs and also to contribute to the development of technologies to clean up or prevent pollution and monitor the environment for better warning of natural disasters and climate change![15]

Initiatives: Environmental Technologies:

Environmental technologies are of growing worldwide interest, creating a vast market that U.S. firms are eager to tap. The U.S. Department of Commerce estimates that the global market is currently $400 billion, an amount that it projects could grow to $600 billion by the year 2010. In the United States alone, 1994 environmental spending was approximately 2.5 percent of the gross domestic product, or more than $165 billion. U.S. exports of environmental products and services are worth about $10 billion each year, supporting 170,000 domestic jobs here. While this is a substantial start, the Commerce Department and other U.S. government agencies see environmental technologies as a prime candidate for greater U.S. export opportunities and are working to help U.S. businesses sell their technologies overseas.[16]

Underpinning the financial and employment opportunities are the important societal gains that can come with more worldwide trade in environmental technologies. The world's poorest countries are in desperate need of more modern technology to help solve such urgent human health problems as unsafe drinking water and inadequate sewage treatment systems. Rapidly developing countries face growing environmental and human health risks stemming from dirty air and uncontrolled wastes. Finally, the most developed countries must continue to look for innovative technologies that allow for more cost-effective and efficient pollution protection and resource use.

Already, U.S. business and federal government partnerships have an impressive track record, even in hard-to-penetrate markets such as Asia. Hazardous wastes in Korea will be cleaned up by IT Corporation, a California-based company that recently won a $3.5 million contract with the Halla Corporation based in Korea. Many of Jakarta's canals and waterways are to be skimmed of debris and pollution, thanks to a $10 million contract between the Indonesian government and Aquatics Unlimited of California. Thailand is soon to have a new $2.5 million air pollution tracking system built by the Radian Corporation of Texas. And in China, two American wind turbine manufacturers, FloWind and Zond, have sales agreements totaling $312 million.[17]

Worldwide, the Commerce Department, in conjunction with the U.S. Department of Energy, the U.S. EPA, and other federal agencies, has helped U.S. companies win more than $1.6 billion in environmental contracts recently. New environmentally sound technologies for products, processes, and services create jobs and growth without environmental harm. Expanding world trade brings the benefits of these technologies and knowledge to the rest of the world. Together, they create a reinforcing cycle of sustainable development.[18]

Several federal agencies are providing programmatic and funding support for technological research and development. The U.S. Department of Energy *Industries of the Future* Program is designed to use scarce research and development resources by investing in areas that have potentially high payoffs for the public or in areas that are too risky for individual companies to assume the risks alone. The program focuses on seven industries in which improvements in technology are expected to yield significant benefits for the environment and the economy: forest and paper, steel, aluminum, metal casting, glass, chemicals, and petroleum refining. These industries provide the basic materials that are needed by the entire U.S. manufacturing sector, but they also consume 81 percent of the energy used in manufacturing and generate 80 percent of the wastes. The program is designed to stimulate the development and use of technologies that will increase energy efficiency and lower the costs associated with environmental protection and regulatory compliance.[19]

The U.S. Department of Commerce Technology Administration's *Manufacturing Extension Partnership* helps small and medium sized businesses adopt new technologies. These companies often lack the resources and expertise needed to incorporate new technologies into their production processes. The Partnership provides technical assistance, financing, training, and other services to these companies. By adopting new technologies, Partnership clients have often been able to meet environmental regulations in ways that lead to cost savings, reductions in wastes, and better utilization of waste products.[20]

The *Rapid Commercialization Initiative* was established by the U.S. Department of Commerce Technology Administration in cooperation with the U.S. Department of Defense, the U.S. Department of Energy and U.S. EPA. It is designed to strengthen cooperation among private industry, the states, and federal agencies to help bring environmental technologies to market more rapidly and efficiently. The program is focused on identifying and reducing barriers that impede market entry and on furthering the commercialization of four categories of environmental technologies: avoidance of pollution, control of pollution, monitoring and assessment of pollution, and remediation and restoration of polluted areas. This initiative provides companies with assistance in finding appropriate sites for demonstrating and testing possible commercial environmental technologies. It also provides assistance in verifying the performance and associated costs of new technologies and in facilitating the issuance of permits.[21]

In April 1995, the National Science and Technology Council released the *National Environmental Technology Strategy*. The Council is a cabinet-level group, chaired by the President, which is responsible for coordinating science, space, and technology policies throughout the government. The Strategy was developed over a two-year period, with input from Congress, the states, communities, industry, academia, NGOs, and interested citizens. It builds on an earlier document, *Technology for a Sustainable Future*, which outlined some of the challenges America faces–facilitating technological innovation, encouraging new approaches to environmental management, and working with other countries to develop and use environmentally-friendly technologies.[22]

Action: Global Climate Change:

The Earth has a blanket of gases that keeps its temperature at an average of about 60° F. Without this natural greenhouse effect, the Earth's average temperature would be about O° F, and the Earth itself would be frozen solid. Life as we know it would not be possible. The greenhouse effect is the result of naturally occurring gases in the atmosphere, principally water vapor, carbon dioxide, methane, and nitrous oxide. These gases trap some of the Earth's outgoing infrared radiation and, like a vast blanket, keep the Earth warmer than it otherwise would be. With the industrialization that has occurred over the past 150 years, the atmospheric concentrations of greenhouse gases have increased, and new greenhouse gases (such as the CFCs that deplete the ozone layer) have been added to the atmosphere. The most important greenhouse gas influenced by human activity is carbon dioxide. Concentrations of carbon dioxide have increased by about 30 percent over preindustrial levels. Buildup of this gas results primarily from the burning of fossil fuels and deforestation.[23]

The buildup of greenhouse gases in the atmosphere is expected to lead to an enhanced greenhouse effect popularly referred to as global warming. Because of the enormous complexity of the Earth's climate system, it is not possible to predict with certainty the temperature rise or other effects that will occur as concentrations of greenhouse gases increase. Generally though, models predict that global warming will lead to higher surface temperatures and to a rise in sea levels. They also suggest more severe droughts and/or floods in some places and the possibility of more extreme rainfall events. The Earth has warmed by about 1° F since preindustrial times, and the international scientific community now believes that the balance of evidence suggests a discernable human influence on global climate.[24]

Efforts to reduce the risks of global warming include initiatives to reduce man-made emissions of greenhouse gases domestically and through cooperative efforts with other countries. One such initiative is the recently developed pilot program, the *United States Initiative on Joint Implementation*. In addition, efforts should be pursued to mitigate potential effects of global warming and to adapt to those effects. Since the world depends on fossil fuels (which account for most carbon dioxide emissions) for 90 percent of its energy, the implications of global warming could be profound. If the risks of warming are judged to be too great, then nothing less than a drastic reduction in the burning of coal, oil, and natural gas would be necessary.[25]

Action: International Leadership:

The federal government should increase support for effective and efficient bilateral and multilateral institutions as a means to achieve national sustainable development goals. The federal government should ensure open access for, and participation of, non-governmental organizations and private industry in international agreements and decision-making processes. Private industry should continue to move toward voluntarily adopting consistent goals that are protective of human health and the environment in its operations around the world. All elements of society can promote voluntary actions to build commitments and incentives for resource efficiency, stewardship, information sharing, and collaborative decision-making processes. Finally, the United States should support the U.N. Commission on Sustainable Development as a forum for nations to report on their progress in moving toward sustainability?[26]

Initiatives: Global Youth Forums:

Around the globe, more and more youth are becoming aware of environmental issues. As concern for the future grows among the youth of the world—a group that today represents half of the world's population—they are becoming a strong voice in the effort to raise social and environmental consciousness. Conferences like the 1994 and 1995 Global Youth Forums, sponsored by the U.N. Environment Programme and S.C. Johnson & Son, Inc. provide a means to build partnerships, share ideas, and work toward achieving common goals. The 1995 forum was attended by approximately 2,000 youth representatives from over 75 countries who ranged between 8 and 25 years old. Youth presentations included a video encouraging communities to recycle aerosol cans, classrooms fueled by alternative energy, youths organizing environmental clubs, establishing an environmental pen pal network, lobbying the government for land for a bird sanctuary, educating homeless families on health and environmental issues, and developing a model for an energy efficient house. At the 1994 Forum, the conference participants ratified Ten Commitments which articulate what they believe needs to be done to achieve a sustainable world. As the rationale for these commitments states, "Ours is a generation unique in the history of our world. Growing up in a reality of ozone holes and global warming, mass extinctions and widespread poverty, we have learned fear, but have confronted it time after time with hope and education. As caring citizens of this planet, we commit ourselves to restoring and preserving our world and to rebuilding our dreams of tomorrow—pure waters, vast wildlands, clean air and cities free of poverty."[27]

Constructing an imaginative and creative scenario for development into the 21st century depends on our faith, our confidence, and our trust in youth. If sustainability is to be a persuasive theme, people must find satisfying, alternative values and patterns of behavior. Achieving sustainability depends on motivating people in a positive way to replace non-sustainable practices with sustainable behaviors.

Implementing the many recommendations suggested in this book will be exceedingly difficult, but it can be accomplished. Success in realizing the goals of sustainable development in the United States will depend on the joint efforts of many actors—industry, non-governmental organizations, academic institutions, federal and state agencies, communities, and individuals. Each alone is important, but to succeed they must all work together. Success will require leadership from every part of society. Bold leadership efforts by government officials, businesspeople, community leaders, environmental activists, labor organizers, educators, and individual citizens will all be necessary to create a sustainable America. It will also require new institutions—such as the Joint Center for Sustainable Communities and the Northwest Regional Council—that can translate the abstract concepts of sustainable development into tangible results at local, state, and regional levels. Another part of the answer will be to establish a focus for sustainable development at the highest levels of government—in all agencies and departments, both state and federal.

Still another part of the answer is for the President's Council on Sustainable Development to continue its examination of specific policies and approaches.

The United States must move boldly to implement strategies for sustainable development within its own borders, but its efforts must not stop there. Many sustainability issues–such as population growth, deforestation, pollution, climate change, and biodiversity–are global and can only be addressed by working closely with our partners around the world. America must participate fully in international discussions, and implement global strategies for sustainable development. As America approaches the 21st century, it has an opportunity to make a strong national commitment to develop sustainable approaches for the next millennium. America must become the global leader in the development and implementation of bold and innovative strategies to build a sustainable world: a world in which concern for the environment is part of decision-making at all levels of society; a world in which a secure future with shelter, food, education, and meaningful employment is available for every citizen; a world in which fairness and justice are the common attributes of social life.

Ultimately, however, it is individuals who will determine whether the nations of the world will embark on a sustainable path. It is individuals who will decide whether to act sustainably in their own lives. It is individuals who will influence corporate behavior. It is individuals who will serve as the leaders of communities and nations and help move them toward sustainability. In the end, what we do as individuals–or what we fail to do–will determine whether humanity begins to live sustainably. One by one, our individual actions will provide the sum total of human behaviors that will determine our collective future. Right or wrong, the individual actions taken by Americans in the next few years will lead the world into the next millennium. The consequences of those actions will be the legacy that our children will inherit.

Notes

Introduction Notes:

1. *Agenda 21: Program of Action for Sustainable Development*, Rio Declaration on Environment and Development (New York: United Nation, undated). See also Daniel Sitarz, ed., *Agenda 21: The Earth Summit Strategy to Save Our Planet* (Boulder, Colo.: Earth Press, 1993); Executive Order No. 12852, 29 June 1993, amended 19 July 1993, 42 U.S.C. 4321.
2. The World Commission on Environment and Development (The Brundtland Commission), *Our Common Future* (Oxford: Oxford University Press, 1987), p. 43.
3. United Nations Population Division, *Long-Range World Population Projections: Two Centuries of World Population Growth 1950-2150* (UN: New York, 1992), p. 22; World Resources Institute, *World Resources 1994-95*, prepared in collaboration with the U.N. Environmental Program and the U.N. Development Program (New York: Oxford University Press, 1994), pp. 256, 267, 284-285; U.S. Department of Commerce, *Statistical Abstract of the United States 1994* (Washington, D.C.: Government Printing Office, 1994); U.N. Food and Agricultural Organization (FAO), *Rome Consensus on World Fisheries* (presented at FAO Ministerial Conference on Fisheries, Rome, Italy, 14-15 March 1995).
4. The President's Council on Sustainable Development, *Sustainable America: A New Consensus for Prosperity, Opportunity, and a Healthy Environment* (Washington, D.C., 1996), pp. i-ii.
5. Ibid., pp. v-vi.

Chapter 1 Notes:

1. President's Council on Sustainable Development, *Population and Consumption Task Force Report* (Washington D.C.), p. 3.
2. U.S. Department of Energy, Energy Information Administration, *Monthly Energy Review*: October 1995, DOE/EIA-0035(95/10) (Washington, D.C., October 1995), p. 16, fig. 1.8 and table 1.9.
3. World Bank, *World Tables 1995* (Baltimore, Md: The Johns Hopkins University Press, 1995), pp. 28-29, table 7; *Statistical Abstract of the United States 1994*, p. 470, table 716; U.S. Department of Commerce, Bureau of the Census, *World Population Profile: 1994* (Washington, D.C.: Government Printing Office, 1994), p. A-1, table 1; *World Resources 1994-95*, p. 268, table 16.1.

4. *Sustainable America: A New Consensus for Prosperity, Opportunity, and a Healthy Environment*, pp. 4-5.
5. World Conservation Monitoring Center, *Global Biodiversity: Status of the Earth's Living Resources* (New York: Chapman & Hall, 1992), p. 253, table 18.3; *World Resources 1994-95*, p. 305; and World Resources Institute, *Global Biodiversity Strategy: Guidelines for Action to Save, Study, and Use Earth's Biotic Wealth Sustainably and Equitably* (Washington, D.C.: World Resources Institute, 1992), p. 7.; Walter V. Reid et al., *Biodiversity Prospecting: Using Genetic Resources for Sustainable Development* (Washington, D.C.: World Resources Institute, 1993), p. 7.; Eduardo A. Loayza, *A Strategy for Fisheries Development* (Washington, D.C.: World Bank, 1992), p. xi; U.N. Food and Agriculture Organization (FAO), *Bulletin of Fishery Statistics: Fishery Fleet Statistics* (Rome, 1988); *FAO Yearbook Fisheries Statistics 1993*, vol. 76 (Rome, 1993), p. xi, "World Catch."
6. *Population and Consumption Task Force Report*, p. 5; *Statistical Abstract of the United States 1994*, p. 446, table 684; and p. 862, table 1366; U.S. Department of Energy, Energy Information Administration, *International Energy Annual: 1993*, DOE/EIA-0219(93) (Washington, D.C.: Government Printing Office, 1995), p. vii; U.S. Department of the Interior, Bureau of Mines, "Changing Minerals and Material Use Patterns" (presented at the Annual General Meeting of the Academia Europaea, Parma, Italy, 23-25 June 1994), figs. 5-1 and 5-2. OCED Environmental Performance Reviews-Netherlands (Paris, 1995), p. 78, fig. 4.2.
7. *World Tables 1995*, pp. 76-77, table 19; and *Statistical Abstract of the United States 1994*, p. 446, table 684; U.N. Conference on Trade and Development, *Handbook of International Trade and Development Statistics 1989* (New York: United Nations, 1990), pp. 2-3, tables 1.1 and 1.2.; Anthony Ramirez, "Automation Drives Surge in Currency Trading Volume," *New York Times*, 20 September 1995, sec. D, p. 3.
8. *Sustainable America: A New Consensus for Prosperity, Opportunity, and a Healthy Environment*, p. 6-13.
9. Ibid., p. 14.
10. Ibid., p. 15.
11. Ibid., p. 16
12. Ibid., p. 17
13. Ibid., p. 18

14. Ibid., p. 19
15. Ibid., p. 20
16. Ibid., p. 23
17. Ibid., p. 21
18. Ibid., p. 22

Chapter 2 Notes:
1. *Statistical Abstract of the United States 1994*, p. 446.; *World Resources 1994-95*, p. 15. U.S. Department of Commerce, Bureau of the Census, *World Population Profile: 1994* (Washington, D.C.: Government Printing Office, 1994), p. 9, fig. 6; *International Energy Annual: 1993*, p. vii.
2. *Sustainable America: A New Consensus for Prosperity, Opportunity, and a Healthy Environment*, p. 143; *World Resources 1994-95*, p. 15-16.
3. Population Reference Bureau, *World Population Data Sheet 1995*. Alan Durning, *How Much Is Enough? The Consumer Society and the Future of the Earth* (New York: W.W. Norton & Company, 1992), pp. 50-51.
4. *Population and Consumption Task Force Report*, p. 33; Population and Consumption Scoping Task Force, *Preliminary Report* (in memorandum form) dated 1 April 1994; John Young and Aaron Sachs, "The Next Efficiency Revolution: Creating a Sustainable Materials Economy," *Worldwatch Paper #121* (Washington, D.C.: Worldwatch Institute, 1994), p. 14; *World Resources 1994-95*.
5. *World Resources 1994-95*, pp. 15-16.
6. New Road Map Foundation, *All-Consuming Passion: Waking Up from the American Dream* (Seattle, Washington, 1993).
7. *Statistical Abstract of the United States 1994*, pp. 584-85; Energy Information Administration, U.S. Department of Energy, *Energy Use and Carbon Emissions: Some International Comparisons* (Washington, D.C., 1994), pp. 37, 39, and 40.
8. *Sustainable America: A New Consensus for Prosperity, Opportunity, and a Healthy Environment*, p. 47; *Population and Consumption Task Force Report*, p. 37; President's Council on Sustainable Development, *Eco-efficiency Task Force Report*, p. 31.
9. *Sustainable America: A New Consensus for Prosperity, Opportunity, and a Healthy Environment*, p. 47; *Population and Consumption Task Force Report*, p. 37; President's Council on Sustainable Development, *Eco-efficiency Task Force Report* (Washington, D.C.), pp. 29-30.
10. *Sustainable America: A New Consensus for Prosperity, Opportunity, and a Healthy Environment*, pp. 61-69; *Population and Consumption Task Force Report*, pp. 41-49.
11. *Sustainable America: A New Consensus for Prosperity, Opportunity, and a Healthy Environment*, pp. 45-46; President's Council on Sustainable Development, *Energy and Transportation Task Force Report* (Washington, D.C.), p. 46-47

12. *Statistical Abstract of the United States 1994*, p. 330, table 504; and p. 331, table 505.
13. Robert Repetto, Roger Dower, Robin Jenkins, and Jacqueline Geoghegan, *Green Fees: How a Tax Shift Can Work for the Environment and the Economy* (Washington, D.C.: World Resources Institute, 1992), pp. 3-12; and testimony of Roger Dower, World Resources Institute, 3 March 1995 Task Force Roundtable.
14. Ibid. pp. 3-12
15. Joanne Freund Lesher, "Pursuing Ecological Tax Reform in the United States," (mimeographed report) January 1995; Organization for Economic Cooperation and Development, *Taxation and the Environment: Complementary Policies* (Paris, 1994); Organization for Economic Cooperation and Development, *Managing the Environment: The Role of Economic Instruments* (Paris, 1994); and *Green Fees: How a Tax Shift Can Work for the Environment and the Economy*.
16. *Population and Consumption Task Force Report*, p. 67
17. Ibid., p. 67
18. *Sustainable America: A New Consensus for Prosperity, Opportunity, and a Healthy Environment*, p. 47; *Population and Consumption Task Force Report*, pp. 37 and 67; *Eco-efficiency Task Force Report*, p. 31; *Managing the Environment: The Role of Economic Instruments*; David Pearce, "Sustainable Consumption Through Economic Instruments," *Symposium: Sustainable Consumption*, report on a symposium held 19- 20 January 1994, in Oslo, Norway, pp. 84-90; and Robert Stavins and Bradley Whitehead, "Dealing with Pollution: Market-Based Incentives for Environmental Protection," *Environment*, September 1992, pp. 7-11, and 29-41; *Green Fees: How a Tax Shift Can Work for the Environment and the Economy*; and testimony of Roger Dower, World Resources Institute, 3 March 1995 Population and Consumption Task Force Roundtable.
19. *Sustainable America: A New Consensus for Prosperity, Opportunity, and a Healthy Environment*, pp. 45-46.
20. *Sustainable America: A New Consensus for Prosperity, Opportunity, and a Healthy Environment*, p. 47; *Population and Consumption Task Force Report*, pp. 37-38 and 68; "Pursuing Ecological Tax Reform in the United States"; *Taxation and the Environment: Complementary Policies*, *Managing the Environment: The Role of Economic Instruments*; and *Green Fees: How a Tax Shift Can Work for the Environment and the Economy*.
21. *Sustainable America: A New Consensus for Prosperity, Opportunity, and a Healthy Environment*, p. 47; *Population and Consumption Task Force Report*, pp. 37 and 68; *Eco-efficiency Task Force Report*, pp. 29-30.
22. Poll commissioned by the National Consumers League, conducted by New Jersey-

based Bruskin/Goldring Research, and reported in *Greenwire* in late April 1995.

23. Testimony of Norman Dean, President, Green Seal, 3 March 1995 Task Force Roundtable. Study by researchers at the University of Utah, Oregon State University, and the University of Illinois, and reported in *Greenwire* in late April 1995.

24. *Population and Consumption Task Force Report*, p. 43.

25. Ibid., p. 43.

26. *Sustainable America: A New Consensus for Prosperity, Opportunity, and a Healthy Environment*, p. 42; *Population and Consumption Task Force Report*, p. 69; *Eco-efficiency Task Force Report*, pp. 21-53; Personal communications with David Harwood, Office of the Under-Secretary of State for Global Affairs, U.S. Department of State, May and June 1995; Testimony of Norman Dean, President, Green Seal, 3 March 1995 Population and Consumption Task Force roundtable.

27. *Population and Consumption Task Force Report*, p. 45.

28. Ibid., pp. 46 and 71.

29. *All-Consuming Passion; Waking Up from the American Dream; How Much Is Enough?*, p. 128.

30. Personal communications with David Harwood, Office of the Under-Secretary of State for Global Affairs, U.S. Department of State, May and June 1995.

31. *All-Consuming Passion: Waking Up from the American Dream*.

32. *Population and Consumption Task Force Report*, pp. 47 and 71.

33. Merck Family Fund poll result from personal communication with Betsy Taylor, Executive Director, Merck Family Fund, 19 June 1995.

34. *Population and Consumption Task Force Report*, pp. 47 and 71.

35. Ibid., pp. 47 and 71.

36. Testimony by David Gershon, President, Global Action Plan, 11 January 1995 Task Force Roundtable; David Gershon and Robert Gilman, *Household Ecoteam Workbook: A Six-Month Program to Bring Your Household into Environmental Balance* (Woodstock, New York: Global Action Plan for the Earth, 1992).

Chapter 3 Notes:

1. The President's Council on Sustainable Development, *The Road to Sustainable Development: A Snapshot of Activities in the United States of America* (Washington D.C., 1997), p. 4; World Resources Institute, *Has Environmental Protection Really Reduced Productivity Growth?* (Washington D.C.: World Resources Institute, 1996).

2. *Sustainable America: A New Consensus for Prosperity, Opportunity, and a Healthy Environment*, pp. 38-43; *Eco-efficiency Task Force Report*, pp. 17-19; *The Road to Sustainable Development*, p. 10.

3. *Population and Consumption Task Force Report*, pp. 50-54.

4. *Sustainable America: A New Consensus for Prosperity, Opportunity, and a Healthy Environment*, pp. 48-51; *Eco-efficiency Task Force Report*, pp. 20-22.

5. *Population and Consumption Task Force Report*, p. 44.

6. *Eco-efficiency Task Force Report*, p. 1-9.

7. *Sustainable America: A New Consensus for Prosperity, Opportunity, and a Healthy Environment*, p. 60.

8. Ibid., pp. 67-68.

9. Ibid., pp. 65-66.

10. *Eco-efficiency Task Force Report*, p. 27.

11. *Sustainable America: A New Consensus for Prosperity, Opportunity, and a Healthy Environment*, pp. 38-40.

12. Ibid., pp. 38-39.

13. Ibid., p. 40; *Eco-efficiency Task Force Report*, p. 17.

14. *Sustainable America: A New Consensus for Prosperity, Opportunity, and a Healthy Environment*, p. 40; *Eco-efficiency Task Force Report*, p. 17.

15. *Sustainable America: A New Consensus for Prosperity, Opportunity, and a Healthy Environment*, p. 80; *Eco-efficiency Task Force Report*, p. 17.

16. *Sustainable America: A New Consensus for Prosperity, Opportunity, and a Healthy Environment*, p. 40; *Eco-efficiency Task Force Report*, p. 18.

17. *Population and Consumption Task Force Report*, p. 75.

18. *The Road to Sustainable Development*, p. 5.

19. Ibid., p. 6.

20. Ibid., pp. 6-7.

21. Ibid., pp. 7-8.

22. Ibid., p. 8.

23. Ibid., pp. 8-9.

24. Ibid., pp. 16-17.

25. Ibid., pp. 17-18.

26. Ibid., pp. 18-19.

27. *Sustainable America: A New Consensus for Prosperity, Opportunity, and a Healthy Environment*, p. 42; U.S. Environmental Protection Agency, *Introducing The Green Lights Program*, fact sheet, EPA 430-F-93-050, November, 1993; Chemical Manufacturer's Association, *Responsible Care fact sheet*; and Environmental Defense Fund, "Agreement on a Joint McDonald's/EDF Task Force to Address McDonald's Solid Waste Issues," 1 August 1990, reproduced in McDonald's Corporation and EDF Waste Reduction Task Force, *Final Report*, April 1991.

28. *Green Fees: How a Tax Shift Can Work for the Environment and the Economy*, p. 15. Jennifer Seymour Whitaker, *Salvaging the Land of Plenty: Garbage and the American Dream* (New York: William Morrow and Co., Inc., 1994), pp. 103-04; Megan Ryan, "Packaging a Revolution," *World Watch*, September/October 1993, pp. 28-34; Megan Ryan, "Update:

Packaging a Revolution," *World Watch*, July/August 1994, p. 9;

29. *Sustainable America: A New Consensus for Prosperity, Opportunity, and a Healthy Environment*, p. 50; *Population and Consumption Task Force Report*, pp. 51 and 72.

30. *Salvaging the Land of Plenty: Garbage and the American Dream*, pp. 200-2 and 230.

31. Personal communications with David Harwood, Office of the Under-Secretary of State for Global Affairs, U.S. Department of State, May and June 1995.

32. *Sustainable America: A New Consensus for Prosperity, Opportunity, and a Healthy Environment*, p. 42; *Eco-efficiency Task Force Report*, p. 19.

33. *Population and Consumption Task Force Report*, pp. 53 and 73; *Green Fees: How a Tax Shift Can Work for the Environment and the Economy*, pp. 15 and 34.

34. *Salvaging the Land of Plenty: Garbage an the American Dream*, p. 107.

35. *Green Fees: How a Tax Shift Can Work for the Environment and the Economy*, pp. 16-29.

36. *Population and Consumption Task Force Report*, p. 73.

37. *Salvaging the Land of Plenty: Garbage an the American Dream*, pp. 121-122.

38. *Population and Consumption Task Force Report*, pp. 54-55 and 74.

39. *Sustainable America: A New Consensus for Prosperity, Opportunity, and a Healthy Environment*, p. 44; *Eco-efficiency Task Force Report*, pp. 20-22.

40. *Sustainable America: A New Consensus for Prosperity, Opportunity, and a Healthy Environment*, p. 44; Clean Air Act Amendments of 1990, Pub. L. 101-549, 104 Stat. 2399; *Eco-efficiency Task Force Report*, p. 19.

41. *Sustainable America: A New Consensus for Prosperity, Opportunity, and a Healthy Environment*, p. 48.

42. *Eco-efficiency Task Force Report*, pp. 20-21; Clean Air Act Amendments of 1990.

43. *Sustainable America: A New Consensus for Prosperity, Opportunity, and a Healthy Environment*, p. 50.

44. The Resource Conservation and Recovery Act (RCRA) of 1976, 42 U.S.C. 6901 et seq. (1994); *Population and Consumption Task Force Report*, pp. 44-45; Personal communications with David Harwood, U.S. Department of State, May and June 1995.

45. U.S. Environmental Protection Agency, "*Comprehensive Guidelines for Procurement of Products Containing Recovered Materials and Issuance of a Draft Recovered Materials Advisory Notice*; Proposed Rule and Notice," Federal Register, 20 April 1994, p. 18851-914.

46. *Population and Consumption Task Force Report*, p. 70.

47. *Sustainable America: A New Consensus for Prosperity, Opportunity, and a Healthy Environment*, p. 42; *Population and Consumption Task Force Report*, p. 70.

48. *Eco-efficiency Task Force Report*, Appendix A, p. 4.

49. Ibid., Appendix A, pp. 4-5.

50. *Eco-efficiency Task Force Report*, p. 1; The Business Council for Sustainable Development, *Changing Course* (Cambridge, Mass.: The MIT Press, 1992), p. 10.

51. *Sustainable America: A New Consensus for Prosperity, Opportunity, and a Healthy Environment*, p. 33.

52. *Eco-efficiency Task Force Report*, Appendix A, p. 2.

53. *The Road to Sustainable Development*, pp. 39-40.

54. Ibid., p. 40.

55. Ibid., p. 10; *Sustainable America: A New Consensus for Prosperity, Opportunity, and a Healthy Environment*, p. 104.

56. *Eco-efficiency Task Force Report*, Appendix B4, p. 1.

57. Ibid., p. 3; *The Road to Sustainable Development*, pp. 11-12.

58. *Eco-efficiency Task Force Report*, Appendix B4, p. 2; *The Road to Sustainable Development*, pp. 12-13.

59. *The Road to Sustainable Development*, p. 13.

60. *Sustainable America: A New Consensus for Prosperity, Opportunity, and a Healthy Environment*, p. 104.

61. *Eco-efficiency Task Force Report*, p. 23.

62. *The Road to Sustainable Development*, p. 59.

63. Ibid., p. 61.

64. *Sustainable America: A New Consensus for Prosperity, Opportunity, and a Healthy Environment*, p. 62-64; The Toxic Release Inventory, Emergency Planning and Community Right-to-Know Act of 1986, 42 U.S.C. 11001-50 (1994).

65. *Sustainable America: A New Consensus for Prosperity, Opportunity, and a Healthy Environment*, pp. 67-68; *Eco-efficiency Task Force Report*, pp. 24-25.

66. U.S. Department of Commerce, Bureau of Economic Analysis, "Integrated Economic and Environmental Satellite Accounts" and "Accounting for Mineral Resource Issues and Bureau of Economic Analysis' Initial Estimates," *Survey of Current Business*, April 1994.

67. *Eco-efficiency Task Force Report*, p. 24-25.

68. Ibid., pp. 24-25.

69. *Sustainable America: A New Consensus for Prosperity, Opportunity, and a Healthy Environment*, p. 69.

70. Ibid., p. 69.

71. Ibid., pp. 60-65; *Eco-efficiency Task Force Report*, pp. 25-26; Organization for Economic Cooperation and Development, *Environmental Indicators* (Paris, 1994); J.A. Bakkes et al., *An Overview of Environmental Indicators: State of the Art and Perspectives* (Nairobi: U.N. Environment Program, 1994); and Albert Adriaanse, *The Development of Environmental Performance Indicators in the Netherlands* (paper presented to the President's Council on Sustainable Development, Eco-Efficiency Task Force, The Netherlands, May 1994); Albert Adriaanse, *Environmental Policy Performance Indicators: A Study on the Development of Indicators for Environmental Policy in the Netherlands* (The Hague: Dutch Ministry of Housing, 1993).

72. *The Road to Sustainable Development*, p. 25.

73. The President's Council on Sustainable Development, *Public Linkage, Dialogue, and Education Task Force Report*, p. 56.

74. Ibid., p. 56.

75. *Sustainable America: A New Consensus for Prosperity, Opportunity, and a Healthy Environment*, p. 66.

76. *Eco-efficiency Task Force Report*, p. 28.

77. Ibid., p. 27.

78. Ibid., p. 27.

79. Ibid., p. 28.

80. Ibid., p. 28.

Chapter 4 Notes:

1. *Sustainable America: A New Consensus for Prosperity, Opportunity, and a Healthy Environment*, p. 142; U.N. Department for Economic and Social Information and Policy Analysis, *World Population Prospects-1994 Revision* (New York: United Nations, 1995), pp. 103-04, table 50; *Statistical Abstract of the United States 1994* , p. 9, table 4; U.N. Conference on Environment and Development, *United States of America National Report* (Washington, D.C.: Council on Environmental Quality, 1992), p. 26; and Jennifer Cheeseman Day, *Population Projects of the United States, by Age, Sex, Race, and Hispanic Origin: 1993 to 2050*, U.S. Department of Commerce, Bureau of the Census, Current Population Report (Washington, D.C.: Government Printing Office, 1993), table 1.a.

2. U.S. Health and Human Services, "Advance Report of Final Mortality Statistics, 1992," *Monthly Vital Statistics Report 43*, no. 6 (Hyattsville, Md.: National Institute for Health Statistics, 1994); and *Monthly Vital Statistics Report 43*, no. 5.

3. *Sustainable America: A New Consensus for Prosperity, Opportunity, and a Healthy Environment*, p. 145; Institute of Medicine, *The Best Intentions: Unintended Pregnancy and the Well-Being of Children and Families*, S. Brown and L. Eisenberg, eds. (Washington, D.C.: National Academy Press, 1995); Alan Guttmacher Institute, "Women and Reproductive Health in the United States," *Facts in Brief* (New York, 1994); Patricia Donovan, *The Politics of Blame: Family Planning, Abortion, and the Poor* (Washington, D.C.: The Alan Guttmacher Institute, 1995), p. 20; Population Reference Bureau, "Population Update," *Population Today*, June 1995, p. 6. Testimony by Jacqueline Forrest, Research and Planning Division, Alan Guttmacher Institute, 27 October 1994 Task Force roundtable; Stanley Henshaw and Jacqueline Forrest, *Women at Risk of Unintended Pregnancy, 1990 Estimates: The Need for Family Planning Services, Each State and County* (New York: The Alan Guttmacher Institute, 1993) and L.S. Peterson, "Contraceptive Use in the United States: 1982-1990," Advance Data from *Vital and Health Statistics*, No. 260 (Washington, D.C.: National Center for Health Statistics, 1995), in consultation with Barbara Cohen, Office of Population, U.S. Department of Health and Human Services.

4. National Family Planning and Reproductive Health Association, "*Facts About the National Family Planning Program*," (Washington, D.C., undated); Testimony of Jacqueline Forrest, 27 October 1994 Population and Consumption Task Force Roundtable.

5. *Sustainable America: A New Consensus for Prosperity, Opportunity, and a Healthy Environment*, p. 149; Calculation by the Population and Consumption Task Force; and Personal communication with Stanley Henshaw, Alan Guttmacher Institute, New York, 6 June 1995; *The Politics of Blame: Family Planning Abortion and the Poor*, p. 9.

6. *Sustainable America: A New Consensus for Prosperity, Opportunity, and a Healthy Environment*, pp. 142-146 and 152; *Population and Consumption Task Force Report*, pp. 15-16 and 61-66; *Statistical Abstract of the United States 1994*, pp. 9-10, tables 4-6.

7. Paul Demeny, "Pronatalist Policies in Low-Fertility Countries: Patterns, Performance, and Prospects," *Below-Replacement Fertility in Industrial Societies: Causes, Consequences, Policies: A Supplement to Vol. 12 of Population and Development Review*, 1986, pp. 335-58.

8. Ibid., p. 335-338.;

9. *USA by Numbers: A Statistical Portrait of the United States*, p. 59; *Statistical Abstract of the United States 1994*, p. 78.

10. *Population and Consumption Task Force Report*, p. 13.

11. Ibid., p. 13.

12. International Conference on Population and Development, *Programme of Action*, A/CONF 171/13, (New York: United Nations, 18 October 1994).

13. *World Population Data Sheet 1995*; Population Reference Bureau, "Population Update," *Population Today*, June 1995, p. 6. Testimony of Susan Martin, Director, U.S. Commission on Immigration Reform, 27 October 1994 Population and Consumption Task Force roundtable.

14. Philip Martin and Elizabeth Midgley, "Immigration to the United States: Journey to an Uncertain Destination," *Population Bulletin*, September 1994, p. 23; *Statistical Abstract of the United States 1994*, p. 78; *World Population Data Sheet 1995*.

15. Testimony of Jennifer Day, Demographer and Statistician, U.S. Bureau of the Census, 27 October, 1994 Population and Consumption Task Force roundtable.

16. *Below-Replacement Fertility in Industrial Societies: Causes, Consequences, Policies: A Supplement to Vol 12 of Population and Development Review*, 1986, pp. 217-238.

17. National Audubon Society, *Population and the American Future Twenty Years Later: Revisiting the Rockefeller Commission Report* (Boulder, Colorado: Human Population and Resource Use Department, 1994), pp. 27 and 31.

18. *Population and Consumption Task Force Report*, p. 19; *Statistical Abstract of the United States 1994*, p. 78.

19. Personal communication with Felicia Stewart, M.D., Deputy Assistant Secretary for Population Affairs, U.S. Department of Health and Human Services, 14 June 1995; Testimony of Jule Hallerdin, Director of Medical Affairs, Planned Parenthood Federation of America, 3 March 1995 Population and Consumption Task Force Roundtable.

20. *Sustainable America: A New Consensus for Prosperity, Opportunity, and a Healthy Environment*, p. 146.

21. Ibid., p. 146; D. Daley and R. Gold, "Public Funding for Contraceptive, Sterilization, and Abortion Services, Fiscal Year 1992," *Family Planning Perspectives* 25, no. 6 (December 1993), p. 248; The Alan Guttmacher Institute, "The U.S. Family Planning Program Faces Challenges and Change," *Issues in Brief* (Washington, D.C., 1995).

22. National Family Planning and Reproductive Health Association, "Facts About the National Family Planning Program" (Washington, D.C., undated); *The Politics of Blame: Family Planning, Abortion, and the Poor*, p. 5.

23. Rachel Gold and Daniel Daley, "Public Funding of Contraceptive, Sterilization, and Abortion Services, Fiscal Year 1990," *Family Planning Perspectives*, September/October 1991, pp. 204-211.

24. *Sustainable America: A New Consensus for Prosperity, Opportunity, and a Healthy Environment*, pp. 146-147; *Population and Consumption Task Force Report*, pp. 20 and 61; *The Politics of Blame: Family Planning, Abortion, and the Poor*, p. 34; Testimony of Judith Desamo, Executive Director, National Family Planning and Reproductive Health Association, 3 March 1995 Population and Consumption Task Force Roundtable; "Public Funding of Contraceptive, Sterilization, and Abortion Services, Fiscal Year 1990," *Family Planning Perspectives*, September/October 1991, pp. 204-211.

25. *Sustainable America: A New Consensus for Prosperity, Opportunity, and a Healthy Environment*, pp. 146-147; The Alan Guttmacher Institute, *Uneven and Unequal: Insurance Cover and Reproductive Health Service* (Washington, D.C., 1994); Testimony of Judith Desamo, 3 March 1995 Population and Consumption Task Force Roundtable.

26. *Sustainable America: A New Consensus for Prosperity, Opportunity, and a Healthy Environment*, p. 147; *Population and Consumption Task Force Report*, pp. 20 and 61; Carl Djerassi, "The Bitter Pill," *Science*, 28 July, 1989, pp. 356-361; testimony of Jule Hallerdin, Director of Medical Affairs, Planned Parenthood Federation of America, 3 March 1995 Population and Consumption Task Force Roundtable.

27. *Population and Consumption Task Force Report*, pp. 61-62.

28. Ibid., pp. 21 and 62; Testimony of Judith Desamo, 3 March 1995 Population and Consumption Task Force Roundtable.

29. *Population and Consumption Task Force Report*, p. 21 and 62; Testimony of Jule Hallerdin, Director of Medical Affairs, Planned Parenthood Federation of America, 3 March 1995 Population and Consumption Task Force Roundtable.

30. *Population and Consumption Task Force Report*, p. 62.

31. *Population and Consumption Task Force Report*, p. 62; Judith Jacobsen, "Promoting Population Stabilization: Incentives for Small Families," *Worldwatch Paper 54* (Washington, D.C.: Worldwatch Institute, 1983).

32. *Sustainable America: A New Consensus for Prosperity, Opportunity, and a Healthy Environment*, p. 147; *Population and Consumption Task Force Report*, pp. 24 and 63; Testimony of Margaret Pruitt Clarke, President, Advocates for Youth, 3 March 1995 Population and Consumption Task Force Roundtable; Alan Guttmacher Institute, "Women and Reproductive Health in the United States," *Facts in Brief* (New York, 1994). 33. Testimony of Jacqueline Forrest, 27 October 1994 Population and Consumption Task Force Roundtable; Testimony of Jule Hallerdin, 3 March 1995 Population and Consumption Task Force Roundtable.

34. Testimony of Margaret Pruitt Clarke, President, 3 March 1995 Population and Consumption Task Force Roundtable.

35. Ibid.

36. Testimony of Jule Hallerdin, 3 March 1995 Population and Consumption Task Force Roundtable.

37. Alan Guttmacher Institute, *Sex and America's Teenagers* (Washington, D.C., 1994), p. 20.

38. *Population and Consumption Task Force Report*, p. 26.

39. Ibid., p. 63.

40. Ibid., p. 63.

41. *Sustainable America: A New Consensus for Prosperity, Opportunity, and a Healthy Environment*, p. 147; *Population and Consumption Task Force Report*, p. 63.

42. *Population and Consumption Task Force Report*, p. 63.

43. Ibid., p. 62.

44. Ibid., p. 62.
45. *Sustainable America: A New Consensus for Prosperity, Opportunity, and a Healthy Environment*, p. 148; *Population and Consumption Task Force Report*, p. 26.
46. *Sustainable America: A New Consensus for Prosperity, Opportunity, and a Healthy Environment*, p. 149; *The Politics of Blame: Family Planning, Abortion, and the Poor*, p. 9; Testimony of Jule Hallerdin, 3 March 1995 Population and Consumption Task Force Roundtable.
47. *Sustainable America: A New Consensus for Prosperity, Opportunity, and a Healthy Environment*, p. 149; *Population and Consumption Task Force Report*, p. 64.
48. *Sustainable America: A New Consensus for Prosperity, Opportunity, and a Healthy Environment*, p. 149; *Population and Consumption Task Force Report*, p. 64.
49. *Sustainable America: A New Consensus for Prosperity, Opportunity, and a Healthy Environment*, p. 149; *Population and Consumption Task Force Report*, p. 64.
50. *Sustainable America: A New Consensus for Prosperity, Opportunity, and a Healthy Environment*, p. 151; *Population and Consumption Task Force Report*, p. 27.
51. *Sustainable America: A New Consensus for Prosperity, Opportunity, and a Healthy Environment*, p. 150.
52. Personal communication with Public Information Office of the U.S. Bureau of the Census, 6 June 1995; Testimony of Susan Martin, 27 October 1994 Population and Consumption Task Force Roundtable; *Population Bulletin*, September 1994, pp. 21-23.
53. U.S. Department of State, Bureau of Population, Refugees, and Migration, U.S. *National Report to the International Conference on Population and Development* (Washington, D.C., 1994), p. 30; *Population Bulletin*, September 1994, pp. 12-14.
54. Testimony of Susan Martin, 27 October 1994 Population and Consumption Task Force Roundtable; *Population Bulletin*, September 1994, p. 4; Testimony of Ellen Percy Kraly, Department of Geography, Colgate University, 27 October 1994 Population and Consumption Task Force Roundtable; Testimony of Michael Teitelbaum, Vice Chair, U.S. Commission on Immigration Reform, 3 March 1995 Population and Consumption Task Force Roundtable.
55. *Sustainable America: A New Consensus for Prosperity, Opportunity, and a Healthy Environment*, p. 152.
56. Ibid., p. 153; *Population and Consumption Task Force Report*, p. 65.
57. *Sustainable America: A New Consensus for Prosperity, Opportunity, and a Healthy Environment*, p. 153; *Population and Consumption Task Force Report*, p. 65.
58. *Sustainable America: A New Consensus for Prosperity, Opportunity, and a Healthy Environment*, p. 153; *Population and Consumption Task Force Report*, p. 65.
59. *Population and Consumption Task Force Report*, p. 65.
60. *USA by Numbers: A Statistical Portrait of the United States*, p. 24; *U.S. National Report to the International Conference on Population and Development*, p. 5; Population and Consumption Scoping Task Force, Preliminary Report (in memorandum form) dated 1 April 1994, pp. 1-2; *High Country News*, "Grappling with Growth," 5 September 1994.
61. *Population and Consumption Task Force Report*, p. 61.
62. Ibid., pp. 30 and 66.

Chapter 5 Notes:
1. *Population and Consumption Task Force Report*, p. 7; Population and Consumption Scoping Task Force, Preliminary Report 1 April 1994, p. 6; National Research Council, *Alternative Agriculture* (Washington, D.C., 1989); *World Resources 1994-1995*; New Road Map Foundation, *All-Consuming Passion: Waking Up from the American Dream*.
2. *Sustainable America: A New Consensus for Prosperity, Opportunity, and a Healthy Environment*, p. 111; U.S. Department of the Interior, Bureau of Land Management, *Ecosystem Management in the BLM: From Concept to Commitment*, BLM/SCGI-94/005-1736 (Washington, D.C., 1994), p. 2.
3. *Statistical Abstract of the United States 1994*, p. 225, table 354.
4. U.S. Department of Agriculture, Natural Resources and Environmental Division, Economic Research Service, *AREI Updates: Land Trusts*, No. 13 (Washington, D.C., 1995).
5. The Conservation Reserve Program, Food Security Act of 1985, Title XII, Pub. L. 99-198, 99 Stat. 1354; Interagency ecosystem Management Task Force, *The Ecosystem Approach: Healthy Ecosystems and Sustainable Economies-Volume II-Implementation Issues* (Washington, D.C.: U.S. Department of Commerce, 1995), pp. 110-11; U.S. Department of Agriculture, Natural Resources Conservation Service, *Summary Report*, 1992; *National Resources Inventory Graphic Highlights* (Washington, D.C., 1995), p. 1.
6. *Sustainable America: A New Consensus for Prosperity, Opportunity, and a Healthy Environment*, p. 115; Government Performance and Results Act of 1993, 31 U.S.C. 1115-19 (1995).
7. *Sustainable America: A New Consensus for Prosperity, Opportunity, and a Healthy Environment*, p. 115.
8. Ibid., p. 117.
9. Ibid., p. 117-118.
10. Ibid., p. 118.
11. Ibid., p. 118-119.
12. Ibid., p. 119.
13. *Statistical Abstract of the United States 1994*, p. 225, table 354; Endangered Species Act, 16 U.S.C. 1531 et seq. (1982); and Bruce A. Stein et al., "Status of U.S. Species: Setting Conservation Priorities," in U.S. Department of

the Interior, National Biological Service, *Our Living Resources-A Report to the Nation on Distribution, Abundance, and Health of U.S. Plants, Animals, and Ecological Systems* (Washington, D.C., 1995), pp. 399-400.

14. Douglas S. Powell et al., *Forest Resources of the United States*, No. 234 (Fort Collins, Colo.: U.S. Department of Agriculture, Forest Service, Rocky Mountain Forest and Range Experimentation Station, 1994), p. 132.

15. *Sustainable America: A New Consensus for Prosperity, Opportunity, and a Healthy Environment*, pp. 122-123.

16. Ibid., p. 123.

17. Ibid., p. 123

18. Ibid., p. 123

19. *Population and Consumption Task Force Report*, p. 48.

20. Ibid., p. 48.

21. Merck Family Fund poll, personal communication with Betsy Taylor, Executive Director, Merck Family Fund, 19 June 1995.

22. "Religious Communities and Population Concerns", (Population Reference Bureau, April 1994), p. 3-5.

23. "Religious Communities and Population Concerns", pp. 10-17; Poll results from personal communication, Daniel Devlin-Foltz, Pew Global Stewardship Initiative, 10 May 1995.

24. *Population and Consumption Task Force Report*, p. 49

25. Ibid., p. 71.

26. *Sustainable America: A New Consensus for Prosperity, Opportunity, and a Healthy Environment*, p. 130; *Forest Resources of the United States*, 1992.

27. Presented by Eldon Ross, Associate Deputy Chief for research for the U.S. Forest Service, to the Second Ministerial Conference on the Protection of Forests in Europe, Helsinki, Finland, 16-17 June 1993, p. 4.

28. Scott Wallinger, "A Commitment to the Future American Forest and Paper Association Sustainable Forestry Initiative," *Journal of Forestry* 93, no. 1 (January 1995): 16-19.

29. *Sustainable America: A New Consensus for Prosperity, Opportunity, and a Healthy Environment*, p. 131.

30. *The Road to Sustainable Development*, p. 19.

31. *Sustainable America: A New Consensus for Prosperity, Opportunity, and a Healthy Environment*, p. 132; W. Nehlsen, J.E. Williams, and J.A. Lichatowich, "Pacific Salmon at the Crossroads: Stocks at Risk From California, Oregon, Idaho, and Washington," *Fisheries* 16, no. 2 (1991): 4-21; *Habitat Protection Activity Report 1991-1993*; and *Proposed Recovery Plan for Snake River Salmon*.

32. *Sustainable America: A New Consensus for Prosperity, Opportunity, and a Healthy Environment*, p. 133; *The Road to Sustainable Development*, p. 38.

33. *Sustainable America: A New Consensus for Prosperity, Opportunity, and a Healthy Environment*, p. 135-136.

34. *Sustainable America: A New Consensus for Prosperity, Opportunity, and a Healthy Environment*, p. 135-136.

35. U.S. Department of Agriculture, Natural Resources Conservation Service, *1992 National Resources Inventory Backgrounder* (Washington, D.C., 1995).

36. *Sustainable America: A New Consensus for Prosperity, Opportunity, and a Healthy Environment*, p. 136.

37. Ibid., p. 137.

38. Ibid., p. 139.

Chapter 6 Notes:

1. *Sustainable America: A New Consensus for Prosperity, Opportunity, and a Healthy Environment*, p. 125; President's Council on Sustainable Development, *Sustainable Agriculture Task Force Report*, p. 1; U.S. Department of Agriculture, *1990 Fact Book of Agriculture* (Washington, D.C., 1991), pp. 124-125, tables 19, 20; Marc Ribudo, U.S. Department of Agriculture, Economic Research Service, *Water Quality Benefits from the Conservation Reserve Program Agricultural Economic Report no.* 110606 (Washington, D.C., 1989).

2. *Sustainable America: A New Consensus for Prosperity, Opportunity, and a Healthy Environment*, p. 125-126; U.S. Department of Agriculture, Economic Research Service, *Agricultural Resources and Environmental Indicators*, no. 705 (Washington, D.C., 1994), pp. 1-16.

3. U.S. Environmental Protection Agency, Office of Water, *National Water Quality Inventory*, 1992 Report to Congress 841-R-94-001 (Washington, D.C., 1994).

4. U.S. Department of Agriculture, *National Agricultural Statistical Survey*, U.S. Number of Farms 1910-1993 (Washington, D.C.).

5. *Sustainable America: A New Consensus for Prosperity, Opportunity, and a Healthy Environment*, p. 127; *Sustainable Agriculture Task Force Report*, p. 3.

6. U.S. Department of Agriculture, Natural Resources Conservation Service, *Summary Report, 1992-National Resources Inventory* (Washington, D.C., 1994), p. 5.

7. *Sustainable Agriculture Task Force Report*, p. 6.

8. Ibid., p. 6; *Sustainable America: A New Consensus for Prosperity, Opportunity, and a Healthy Environment*, p. 129.

9. U.S. Department of Agriculture, Natural Resources Conservation Service, *National Resources Inventory: Graphic Highlights of Natural Resources Trends in the United States Between 1982 and 1992* (Washington, D.C., 1995), p. 3.

10. The Conservation Reserve Program, Food Security Act of 1985, Title XII, Pub. L., 99-198, 99 Stat. 1354; Interagency Ecosystem Management Task Force, *The Ecosystem*

Approach: Healthy Ecosystems and Sustainable Economics-Volume II-Implementation Issues (Washington, D.C.: U.S. Department of Commerce, 1995), pp. 110-11; *Summary Report, 1992 National Resources Inventory Graphic Highlights*, p. 1.

11. *Sustainable America: A New Consensus for Prosperity, Opportunity, and a Healthy Environment*, p. 129

12. *Sustainable Agriculture Task Force Report*, p. 7.

13. *Sustainable America: A New Consensus for Prosperity, Opportunity, and a Healthy Environment*, p. 129.

14. Ibid., p. 129; *Sustainable Agriculture Task Force Report*, p. 6.

15. *Sustainable America: A New Consensus for Prosperity, Opportunity, and a Healthy Environment*, p. 129.

16. *Sustainable Agriculture Task Force Report*, p. 8.

17. Paul Faeth, *Growing Green: Enhancing the Economic and Environmental Performance of U.S. Agriculture* (Washington, D.C.: World Resources Institute, 1995), p. 17.

18. *Sustainable Agriculture Task Force Report*, p. 9.

19. Ibid., p. 9.

20. Ibid., p. 10; *Sustainable America: A New Consensus for Prosperity, Opportunity, and a Healthy Environment*, p. 129.

21. *Sustainable America: A New Consensus for Prosperity, Opportunity, and a Healthy Environment*, p. 129; American Farmland Trust, *Farming on the Edge: A New Look at the Importance and Vulnerability of Agriculture Near American Cities* (Washington, D.C., 1994).

22. *Sustainable Agriculture Task Force Report*, p. 12.

23. Ibid., p. 13.

24. U.S. Department of Commerce, Bureau of the Census, *Historical Statistics of the United States: Colonial Times to 1970* (Washington, D.C.), p. 523, table K595-608; U.S. Department of Agriculture, *Dairy Outlook* (Washington, D.C., 1995).

25. *Sustainable America: A New Consensus for Prosperity, Opportunity, and a Healthy Environment*, p. 129; *Sustainable Agriculture Task Force Report*, pp. 14-15.

26. *Sustainable Agriculture Task Force Report*, p. 16.

Chapter 7 Notes:

1. *Sustainable America: A New Consensus for Prosperity, Opportunity, and a Healthy Environment*, pp. 26-30.

2. Ibid., p. 28-29; *Eco-efficiency Task Force Report*, p. 13; *World Resources 1994-95*, p. 15; *Statistical Abstract of the United States 1994*, p. 587, table 924.

3. *Sustainable America: A New Consensus for Prosperity, Opportunity, and a Healthy Environment*, pp. 28-29; *Eco-efficiency Task Force Report*, p. 15.

4. *Sustainable America: A New Consensus for Prosperity, Opportunity, and a Healthy Environment*, pp. 28-31.

5. Ibid., p. 31; *Eco-efficiency Task Force Report*, p. 14.

6. *Sustainable America: A New Consensus for Prosperity, Opportunity, and a Healthy Environment*, p. 31; *Eco-efficiency Task Force Report*, p. 15

7. *Eco-efficiency Task Force Report*, pp. 14-15.

8. *Sustainable America: A New Consensus for Prosperity, Opportunity, and a Healthy Environment*, pp. 29-31; *Eco-efficiency Task Force Report*, p. 11.

9. *Eco-efficiency Task Force Report*, Appendix B5, p. 11.

10. *Sustainable America: A New Consensus for Prosperity, Opportunity, and a Healthy Environment*, p. 34.

11. *Eco-efficiency Task Force Report*, p. 39

12. *Sustainable America: A New Consensus for Prosperity, Opportunity, and a Healthy Environment*, pp. 34-35; *Eco-efficiency Task Force Report*, p. 15.

13. *Sustainable America: A New Consensus for Prosperity, Opportunity, and a Healthy Environment*, p. 34.

14. Ibid., p. 34.

15. Ibid., p. 35.

16. Ibid., p. 35.

17. Ibid., p. 61.

18. Ibid., p. 53.

19. Ibid., p. 53.

20. Ibid., p. 26.

21. *The Road to Sustainable Development*, p. 41.

22. Ibid., p. 41-42.

23. Ibid., p. 42.

24. Ibid., p. 24.

25. Ibid., p. 24.

26. Ibid., p. 25.

27. Ibid., p. 25.

28. Ibid., p. 25.

29. Ibid., p. 26.

30. Ibid., p. 26.

31. Ibid., p. 26-27.

Chapter 8 Notes:

1. *Sustainable America: A New Consensus for Prosperity, Opportunity, and a Healthy Environment*, p. 143; *World Resources 1994-95*, p. 15 and p. 16, table 1.9, and p. 341, table 21.6; U.S. Department of Commerce, Bureau of the Census, *World Population Profile: 1994* (Washington, D.C.: Government Printing Office, 1994), p. 9, fig. 6; U.S. Department of Energy, Energy Information Association, *International Energy Annual: 1993*, DOE/EIA-0219(93) (Washington, D.C.: Government Printing Office, 1995), p. vii; Organization for Economic Cooperation and Development, *OECD Environmental Performance Review-Netherlands* (Paris, 1995), p. 69, fig. 3.4; U.N. Environment Program, *Environmental Data Report 1993-94* (Oxford: the Alden Press, 1993), pp. 347-48, table 8.2.; President's

Council on Sustainable Development, *Energy and Transportation Task Force Report*, p. iii.

2. U.S. Congress, Office of Technology Assessment, *Industry, Technology, and the Environment: Competitive Challenges and Business Opportunities* (Washington, D.C., 1994), p. 190; *Statistical Abstract of the United States 1994*, p. 237, table 376 and p. 590, table 929; President William J. Clinton and Vice President Albert Gore, Jr., *The Climate Change Action Plan* (Washington, D.C.: The White House, 1993), p. 15.

3. *Sustainable America: A New Consensus for Prosperity, Opportunity, and a Healthy Environment*, p. 49; *Energy and Transportation Task Force Report*, p. 23.

4. *Sustainable America: A New Consensus for Prosperity, Opportunity, and a Healthy Environment*, p. 54; U.S. Department of Commerce, *The Effect of Imports of Crude Oil and Refined Petroleum Products on the National Security* (Washington, D.C., 1994), p. ES-4.

5. *Sustainable America: A New Consensus for Prosperity, Opportunity, and a Healthy Environment*, p. 54; *Energy and Transportation Task Force Report*, pp. 29-33.

6. *Energy and Transportation Task Force Report*, pp. 5-7; *Monthly Energy Review*, February 1996, U.S. Department of Energy, Energy Information Agency (Washington, D.C., 1996), p. 25, table 2.2; *Annual Energy Outlook 1995*, p. 100, table B2 and p. 109, table B8.

7. *Energy and Transportation Task Force Report*, p. 9.

8. *Energy and Transportation Task Force Report*, p. 10; Intergovernmental Panel on Climate Change, *Climate Change 1994-Radiative Forcing of Climate Change*, J.T. Houghton et al., eds. (Cambridge: Cambridge University Press, 1995), p. 43; Intergovernmental Panel on Climate Change, *Summary for Policy Makers*-Working Group I, draft (Washington D.C., 1995); Intergovernmental Panel on Climate Change: *Climate Change-IPCC Scientific Assessment*, J.T. Houghton, G.J. Jenkins, and J.J. Ephraums, eds. (Cambridge: Cambridge University Press, 1990); Climate Change 1992. *The Supplementary Report to the Scientific Assessment*, J.T. Houghton, B.A. Callander, and S.K. Varney, eds., (Cambridge: Cambridge University Press, 1992).

9. G. Marland, R.J. Andres, and T.A. Boden, "Global, Regional, and Natural CO2 Emissions," in T.A. Boden et al., eds., *Trends '93: A Compendium of Data on Global Change* (Oak Ridge, Tenn.: Oak Ridge National Laboratory, 1994), pp. 505-84; World Resources 1994-95 p. 202, table 11.7; International Energy Agency, *World Energy Outlook 1995* (Paris: Organization for Economic Cooperation and Development/International Energy Agency, 1995), pp. 48-49, 50.

10. U.S. Department of Energy, Energy Information Administration, *Annual Energy Review 1993* (Washington, D.C., 1994), p. 17, table 1.7.

11. *Energy and Transportation Task Force Report*, p. 24-25; *Annual Energy Review 1993*, p. 17, table 1.7.

12. *Energy and Transportation Task Force Report*, p. 26

13. Ibid., p. 25; U.S. Department of Energy, National Energy Strategy 1991/1992, *Technical Annex 2: Integrated Analysis Supporting the National Energy Strategy* (Washington, D.C.: Government Printing Office, 1991), p. 11, table 2-2, and p. 22, table 3-2.

14. *Sustainable America: A New Consensus for Prosperity, Opportunity, and a Healthy Environment*, p. 49; *Energy and Transportation Task Force Report*, p. 27; Edward Moscovitch, "DSM and the Broader Economy: The Economic Impacts of Utility Efficiency Programs," *The Electricity Journal*, May 1994: 15.

15. *Sustainable America: A New Consensus for Prosperity, Opportunity, and a Healthy Environment*, p. 49; *Energy and Transportation Task Force Report*, pp. 42-43.

16. *Energy and Transportation Task Force Report*, pp. 42-45.

17. *Sustainable America: A New Consensus for Prosperity, Opportunity, and a Healthy Environment*, p. 49.

18. *The Road to Sustainable Development*, pp. 15-16.

19. American Wind Energy Association, *1994 Wind Energy Status Report* (Washington, D.C., 1994), p. 2.

20. *Annual Energy Outlook 1995*, p. 99, table B1; and p. 146, table C17.

21. *Annual Energy Review 1993*, p. 13, table 1.5; and p. 263, table 10.1; *Annual Energy Outlook 1995*, p. 125, table C1; and pp. 145-46, table C17.

22. *Energy and Transportation Task Force Report*, pp. 23, 27-28, and 40; *Annual Energy Review 1993*, p. 233, table 8.2; and p. 237, table 8.4; *Annual Energy Outlook 1995*, p. 100, table B2; and p. 109, table B8.

23. *Energy and Transportation Task Force Report*, pp. 26 and 38; J. Yancher, "The U.S. Electricity Outlook," *Electrical World*, January 1995.

24. *Energy and Transportation Task Force Report*, pp. 38-41.

25. Ibid., pp. 40-41.

26. Ibid., pp. 24, 39-40; U.S. Department of Energy, Energy Information Administration, *Renewable Resources in the US. Electricity Supply* (Washington, D.C., 1993), p. 6.

27. *Energy and Transportation Task Force Report*, pp. 40-41.

28. *The Climate Change Action Plan*, Action Descriptions p. 1.

29. *Energy and Transportation Task Force Report*, p. 61-62.

30. *Sustainable America: A New Consensus for Prosperity, Opportunity, and a Healthy Environment*, p. 49; *The Road to Sustainable Development*, pp. 29-30; Federal Highway Administration, *Nationwide Personal*

Transportation Survey 1990: NPTS Databook, vol. I (Washington, D.C., 1993), p. 4-107, table 4.64.

31. *Energy and Transportation Task Force Report*, pp. 27-28, 62-63; Personal communication from Elizabeth Campbell, U.S. Department of Energy, Office of Policy, January 1995.

32. The National Coal Council, *Clean Coal Technology for Sustainable Development*, (Washington, D.C., 1994), pp. I and 5.; Personal communication from Elizabeth Campbell, January 1995.

33. *Energy and Transportation Task Force Report*, pp. 63-64.

34. Ibid., p. 82.

35. *Sustainable America: A New Consensus for Prosperity, Opportunity, and a Healthy Environment*, p. 54; *Energy and Transportation Task Force Report*, p. 13; *The Effect of Imports of Crude Oil and Refined Petroleum Products on the National Security*, p. ES-4.

36. U.S. Department of Energy, *Transportation Energy Data Book*-Edition 15 (Washington, D.C. 1995), p. 2-42, table 2.24; U.S. Department of Commerce, Partnership for a New Generation of Vehicles Secretariat, *PNGV Program Plan*, 23 August 1995, p. 5-3.

37. *Statistical Abstract of the United States 1994*, p. 97, table 39.

38. *Sustainable America: A New Consensus for Prosperity, Opportunity, and a Healthy Environment*, p. 54; *Energy and Transportation Task Force Report*, p. 29.

39. *The Effect of Imports of Crude Oil and Refined Petroleum Products on the National Security*, p. ES-3 and ES-4.

40. Ibid., pp. ES-4, II-25, table II-10, and II-11.

41. *Energy and Transportation Task Force Report*, p. 51.

42. Ibid., p. 34; *Nationwide Personal Transportation Survey 1990:* Summary of Travel Trends, p. 18, table 7; Federal Highway Administration, *Nationwide Personal Transportation Survey 1990: NPTS Databook*, vol. I, p. 4-107, table 4.64; Michael D. Meyer, "Alternative Methods for Measuring Congestion Levels," *Curbing Gridlock: Peak Period Fees to Relieve Congestion*, pp. 52-55; *Statistical Abstract of the United States 1994*, p. 631, table 1013; *Green Fees: How a Tax Shift Can Work for the Environment and Economy*, p. 48.

43. *Energy and Transportation Task Force Report*, p. 52; Congressional Budget Office, *High-Tech Highways. Intelligent Transportation Systems and Policy* (Washington, D.C.: Government Printing Office, 1995).

44. *Energy and Transportation Task Force Report*, p. 51.

45. *Green Fees: How a Tax Shift Can Work for the Environment and Economy*, pp. 36, 42, 45, and 47.

46. LINK Resources Corp., *US. Home Office Overview, 1994* (New York, 1994), p. 25.

47. *Energy and Transportation Task Force Report*, p. 32; *Supplement to the Annual Energy Outlook 1995*, tables 1, 32, 47, 52 and 53; *Transportation and Energy Data Book*: Edition 13 (Washington, D.C., 1993), tables 2.12 and 2.14.

48. *Sustainable America: A New Consensus for Prosperity, Opportunity, and a Healthy Environment*, p. 54.

49. *PNGV Program Plan*; *The Road to Sustainable Development*, p. 14.

50. Ibid., p. 14-15.

51. Ibid., p. 15.

52. *Energy and Transportation Task Force Report*, p. 29

53. Intermodal Surface Transportation Efficiency Act of 1991, Pub. L. 102-240, 105 Stat 1914; Clean Air Act Amendments of 1990, Pub. L. 101-549, 104 Stat. 2399.

54. *Nationwide Personal Transportation Survey 1990: 1990 NPTS Databook*, vol. I, p. 4-41, table 4.23 and p. 4-89, table 4.53.

55. 55. U.S. Congress, Office of Technology Assessment, *Saving Energy in U.S. Transportation* (Washington, D.C., 1994), p. 89.

56. *Energy and Transportation Task Force Report*, p. 64; *The Road to Sustainable Development*, p. 32.

57. *Energy and Transportation Task Force Report*, p. 81

Chapter 9 Notes:

1. *Public Linkage, Dialogue, and Education Task Force Report*, p. 10; "Goals and Priority Action Projects: Environmental Education about Fish and Wildlife Conservation" (Troy, Ohio: North American Association for Environmental Education, 1994), p. 2; "National Forum on Nonpoint Source Pollution, Water: Taking a New Tack on Nonpoint Water Pollution" (Washington, D.C.: The National Geographic Society and The Conservation Fund, 1995), p. 11; and Susan Cohen, "The Warm Zone," *The Washington Post Magazine*, July 16, 1995: 16.

2. *Sustainable America: A New Consensus for Prosperity, Opportunity, and a Healthy Environment*, pp. 70-71; *Public Linkage, Dialogue, and Education Task Force Report*, pp. 17-20.

3. *Sustainable America: A New Consensus for Prosperity, Opportunity, and a Healthy Environment*, p. 73; *Public Linkage, Dialogue, and Education Task Force Report*, pp. 21, 25-45.

4. *Sustainable America: A New Consensus for Prosperity, Opportunity, and a Healthy Environment*, p. 74; *Public Linkage, Dialogue, and Education Task Force Report*, p. 26.

5. *Public Linkage, Dialogue, and Education Task Force Report*, p. 27.

6. Ibid., p. 27.

7. Ibid., p. 29; *Sustainable America: A New Consensus for Prosperity, Opportunity, and a Healthy Environment*, p. 74.

8. Ibid., p. 74.

9. *Public Linkage, Dialogue, and Education Task Force Report*, pp. 29-30.

285

10. Ibid., p. 30.
11. Ibid., p. 30.
12. Ibid., p. 30.
13. Ibid., p. 30.
14. Ibid., p. 31.
15. Ibid., p. 31.
16. Ibid., p. 31.
17. Ibid., p. 31.
18. Ibid., p. 32 and 34.
19. Ibid., p. 32.
20. Ibid., p. 32.
21. Ibid., p. 35 and 37; National Center for Educational Statistics, *Digest of Educational Statistics 1992* (Washington, D.C, 1994), p. 13.
22. *Public Linkage, Dialogue, and Education Task Force Report*, p. 32 and 36; *We Got the Whole World in Our Hands: A Youth Interpretation of Agenda 21* (Louisville, 1993). Also see Daniel Sitarz, ed, *Agenda 21: The Earth Summit Strategy to Save Our Planet* (Boulder, Colo.: Earth Press, 1993).
23. *Public Linkage, Dialogue, and Education Task Force Report*, p. 36.
24. Ibid., p. 36; 7. Randy Champeau et. al., *A Summary of the Status and Needs of Environmental Education in Wisconsin K-12 Schools*, presented at the 24th annual conference of the North American Association for Environmental Education, Portland, Maine, September 1995.
25. *Public Linkage, Dialogue, and Education Task Force Report*, p. 36; 8. Tufts University, *Environmental Programs* (Medford, Mass, 1994), pp. 2-3.
26. *Public Linkage, Dialogue, and Education Task Force Report*, p. 37.
27. Ibid., p. 37.
28. *Sustainable America: A New Consensus for Prosperity, Opportunity, and a Healthy Environment*, p. 74; *Public Linkage, Dialogue, and Education Task Force Report*, p. 38; Public Linkage, Dialogue, and Education Task Force, *Workshop on the Principles of Sustainability in Higher Education*, (Essex, MA, February 24-27, 1995), p. 17.
29. *Public Linkage, Dialogue, and Education Task Force Report*, pp. 39 and 45; Diane MacEachern, *Save Our Planet: 750 Everyday Ways You Can Help Clean Up the Earth* (New York: Dell Publishing, 1990), p. 138; Holly Brough, "Environmental Studies: Is It Academic?," *World Watch*, 5, 1 (January/February 1992) pp. 32-33.
30. *Public Linkage, Dialogue, and Education Task Force Report*, p. 41.
31. Ibid., p. 40.
32. Ibid., p. 44.
33. Ibid., p. 39
34. Ibid., p. 41
35. Ibid., p. 40.
36. Ibid., p. 43; *Sustainable America: A New Consensus for Prosperity, Opportunity, and a Healthy Environment*, p. 74; Campus Earth Summit, *Blueprint for a Green Campus: The Campus Earth Summit Initiatives for Higher Education* (New Haven, 1995).

37. The Roper Organization, *America's Watching, Public Attitudes Toward Television*, commissioned by the Network Television Association and the National Association of Broadcasters (New York, 1995), p. 17; *Public Linkage, Dialogue, and Education Task Force Report*, pp. 47-49; *Sustainable America: A New Consensus for Prosperity, Opportunity, and a Healthy Environment*, pp. 76-77.
38. *Sustainable America: A New Consensus for Prosperity, Opportunity, and a Healthy Environment*, p. 78; *Public Linkage, Dialogue, and Education Task Force Report*, p. 49; U.S. Department of Education, Office of Educational Research and Improvement, National Center for Education Statistics, *The Condition of Education* (Washington, D.C.: Government Printing Office, 1994), p. 68; P.A. Wright, G.W. Mullins, and M. Watson, "Market Segmentation of Interpretive. Participants at National Park Sites" (San Diego: San Diego State University, 1988); John Disinger, "National Environmental Education Report to Congress" (National. Environmental Education Advisory Council, 10 March 1993), p. 19.
39. *Public Linkage, Dialogue, and Education Task Force Report*, p. 50.
40. Ibid., p. 50.
41. Ibid., p. 50.
42. Ibid., p. 51.
43. Ibid., p. 51.
44. Ibid., p. 52.
45. Ibid., p. 55.
46. Ibid., p. 54.
47. *Sustainable America: A New Consensus for Prosperity, Opportunity, and a Healthy Environment*, p. 78; *America's Watching, Public Attitudes Toward Television*, p. 17.
48. *Public Linkage, Dialogue, and Education Task Force Report*, pp. 55-56.
49. Ibid., p. 57; *Sustainable America: A New Consensus for Prosperity, Opportunity, and a Healthy Environment*, p. 77.
50. *Public Linkage, Dialogue, and Education Task Force Report*, p. 58.
51. *Public Linkage, Dialogue, and Education Task Force Report*, p 61; *Agenda 21: Program of Action for Sustainable Development*. See also Daniel Sitarz, ed., *Agenda 21: The Earth Summit Strategy to Save Our Planet* (Boulder, Colo.: Earth Press, 1993).
52. *Public Linkage, Dialogue, and Education Task Force Report*, pp. 61-63.
53. Ibid., p. 63.
54. Ibid., p. 63.
55. Ibid., p. 64.
56. Ibid., p. 66-74; *Sustainable America: A New Consensus for Prosperity, Opportunity, and a Healthy Environment*, p. 78.
57. *Sustainable America: A New Consensus for Prosperity, Opportunity, and a Healthy Environment*, p. 81; *Public Linkage, Dialogue, and Education Task Force Report*, pp. 76-77.
58. *Sustainable America: A New Consensus for Prosperity, Opportunity, and a Healthy*

Environment, p. 81; *Public Linkage, Dialogue, and Education Task Force Report*, p. 76.
59. *Public Linkage, Dialogue, and Education Task Force Report*, p. 77.
60. Ibid., p. 77.
61. Ibid., p. 78-79
62. Ibid., p. 79.
63. Ibid., p. 79.
64. Ibid., p. 81-82; *Sustainable America: A New Consensus for Prosperity, Opportunity, and a Healthy Environment*, p. 81; Lynnell Hancock et al, "The Haves and the Have-Nots," *Newsweek*, 27 February 1995: 51-52; U.S. Department of Education, Interagency Technology Task Force, *Technology Learning Challenge* (Washington, D.C.: Government Printing Office, 1995), p. 2; Software Publishers Association, *Software Publishers Association Market Report* (1994-95 school year), Education Section (Washington, D.C, 1995), p. 105; Andrew Pollack, "A Cyberspace Front in a Multicultural War," *New York Times*, 6 August 1996: front page business section.
65. *Public Linkage, Dialogue, and Education Task Force Report*, p. 82-83.
66. Ibid., p. 82-83.
67. Ibid., p. 83.
68. Ibid., p. 84.
69. Ibid., p. 83.
70. Ibid., p. 84.
71. Ibid., p. 84.
72. Ibid., p. 84.
73. Ibid., p. 84.
74. Ibid., p. 84.
75. Ibid., p. 84-85.
76. Ibid., p. 85.
77. **78**. *Sustainable America: A New Consensus for Prosperity, Opportunity, and a Healthy Environment*, p. 75; *The Road to Sustainable Development*, p. 27; *Public Linkage, Dialogue, and Education Task Force Report*, p. 86.
78. *Sustainable America: A New Consensus for Prosperity, Opportunity, and a Healthy Environment*, p. 81; *Public Linkage, Dialogue, and Education Task Force Report*, p. 87; Daniel Sitarz, ed., *Agenda 21: The Earth Summit Strategy to Save Our Planet* (Boulder, Colo.: Earth Press, 1993).
79. *Sustainable America: A New Consensus for Prosperity, Opportunity, and a Healthy Environment*, p. 81; *Public Linkage, Dialogue, and Education Task Force Report*, pp. 91-92; David B. Rockland, "Where Are the Gaps in Environmental Education?" *EPA Journal* August 1995: 12-13.
80. *Public Linkage, Dialogue, and Education Task Force Report*, p. 92.
81. Ibid., p. 92.
82. Ibid., p. 93.
83. Ibid., p. 94.
84. Ibid., p. 94.
85. Ibid., p. 94.
86. Ibid., p. 95.,

Chapter 10 Notes:
1. *Sustainable America: A New Consensus for Prosperity, Opportunity, and a Healthy Envi-*
ronment, p. 88; *Statistical Abstract of the United States 1994*, p. 97, table 39.
2. *Sustainable America: A New Consensus for Prosperity, Opportunity, and a Healthy Environment*, p. 90.
3. Ibid., p. 90.
4. Ibid., p. 90.
5. Ibid., p. 90.
6. Ibid., p. 91.
7. Ibid., p. 91; Omnibus Budget Reconciliation Act of 1993, Pub. L. 103-66, 107 Stat. 312.
8. *Sustainable America: A New Consensus for Prosperity, Opportunity, and a Healthy Environment*, p. 91.
9. Ibid., p. 92; U.S. Environmental Protection Agency, *Wetlands Fact Sheet #4: Economic Benefits of Wetlands* (Washington, D.C., 1993), p. 1.
10. *Sustainable America: A New Consensus for Prosperity, Opportunity, and a Healthy Environment*, p. 93.
11. Ibid., p. 93.
12. Ibid., p. 94.
13. Ibid., p. 94; Frederick Law Olmstead, Jr., and Theodora Kimball, eds., *Forty Years of Landscape Architecture: Central Park* (Cambridge: MIT Press, 1973), p. 45.
14. *Sustainable America: A New Consensus for Prosperity, Opportunity, and a Healthy Environment*, p. 95.
15. Ibid., p. 95.
16. Ibid., p. 95.
17. Ibid., p. 96; Homestead Habitat for Humanity, *Concept and Background, Jordan Commons: A Pilot Program for Sustainable Community-Building* (Homestead, Fla., 1995).
18. *Sustainable America: A New Consensus for Prosperity, Opportunity, and a Healthy Environment*, p. 97.
19. Ibid., p. 97.
20. Ibid., p. 97.
21. Ibid., p. 97.
22. Ibid., p. 97.
23. Ibid., p. 97.
24. Ibid., p. 94 and 100
25. Ibid., p. 99.
26. Ibid., p. 99.
27. Ibid., p. 99.
28. Ibid., p. 99.
29. Ibid., p. 101; U.S. Congress, Office of Technology Assessment, *Retiring Old Cars: Programs to Save Gasoline and Reduce Emissions* (Washington, D.C.: Government Printing Office, 1992); Environmental Law and Policy Center, *Components of a Model Accelerated Vehicle Retirement Program*, report to the Energy Foundation (Chicago, 1994); President's Commission on Environmental Quality, *Partnership to Progress: The Report of the President's Commission on Environmental Quality* (Washington, D.C., 1993), pp. 30-31.
30. *Sustainable America: A New Consensus for Prosperity, Opportunity, and a Healthy Environment*, p. 103.
31. Ibid., p. 103.
32. Ibid., p. 104.

33. Ibid., p. 104.
34. Ibid., p. 104.
35. Ibid., p. 106
36. *The Road to Sustainable Development*, p. 43.
37. Ibid., p. 44-45.
38. Ibid., p. 45.
39. Ibid., p. 46-47.
40. Ibid., p. 47.
41. Ibid., p. 47-48.
42. Ibid., p. 48.
43. Ibid., p. 49-50.
44. Ibid., p. 50-51.
45. Ibid., p. 19-20.
46. Ibid., p. 20.
47. Ibid., p. 52.
48. Ibid., p. 53.
49. Ibid., p. 28.

Chapter 11 Notes:
1. *Sustainable America: A New Consensus for Prosperity, Opportunity, and a Healthy Environment*, p. 156; *World Resources 1994-95*; p. 268; *Statistical Abstract of the United States 1994*, p. 862.
2. *Sustainable America: A New Consensus for Prosperity, Opportunity, and a Healthy Environment*, p. 157; *Rome Consensus on World Fisheries.*
3. World Resources Institute, *Global Biodiversity Strategy: Guidelines for Action to Save, Study and Use Earth's Biotic Wealth Sustainably and Equitably*, prepared in collaboration with the U.N. Environmental Program and The World Conservation Union (Washington, D.C.: World Resources Institute, 1992), p. 7, citing C.D. Thomas, "Fewer Species," *Nature* 347 (1990): 237.
4. *Sustainable America: A New Consensus for Prosperity, Opportunity, and a Healthy Environment*, p. 158; Intergovernmental Panel on Climate Change, *Summary for Policy Makers-Working Group I draft.*
5. *Sustainable America: A New Consensus for Prosperity, Opportunity, and a Healthy Environment*, p. 158-159; Intergovernmental Panel on Climate Change, *Climate Change 1994* (Cambridge: Cambridge University Press, 1994) p. 43.; Intergovernmental Panel on Climate Change (IPCC), *Climate Change: The IPCC Scientific Assessment*, J.T. Houghton, G.J. Jenkins, and J.J. Ephraums, eds. (Cambridge: Cambridge University Press, 1990), p. xi.
6. *Sustainable America: A New Consensus for Prosperity, Opportunity, and a Healthy Environment*, p. 159; *Global Biodiversity Strategy*, p. 2 and 4; *FAO Yearbook Fisheries Statistics 1993*, vol. 76 (Rome, 1993), p. xi, "World Catch"; Walter V. Reid et al., *Biodiversity Prospecting: Using Genetic Resources for Sustainable Development* (Washington, D.C.: World Resources Institute, 1993), p. 7.
7. *Sustainable America: A New Consensus for Prosperity, Opportunity, and a Healthy Environment*, p. 160;

8. *Sustainable America: A New Consensus for Prosperity, Opportunity, and a Healthy Environment*, pp. 160-161.
9. Ibid., p. 163.
10. Ibid., p. 165; The United States signed the Biodiversity Convention on 4 June 1993. See U.N. Office of Legal Affairs, United Nations-- *Multilateral Treaties Deposited With Secretary-General*, Status as of 31 December 1994 With Supplements, ST/LEG/SER.E/13 (New York: United Nations, 1994).
11. *Sustainable America: A New Consensus for Prosperity, Opportunity, and a Healthy Environment*, p. 154; U.S. Fish and Wildlife Service, *North American Waterfowl Management Plan Fact Sheet* (Washington, D.C., 1995); Council on Environmental Quality, *Environmental Quality: The Twenty-Fourth Annual Report* (Washington, D.C.: Government Printing Office, 1993), pp. 96 and 99; and U.S. Fish and Wildlife Service, *1994 Update to the North American Waterfowl Management Plan-Expanding the Commitment* (Washington, D.C., 1994), p. 2.
12. *Sustainable America: A New Consensus for Prosperity, Opportunity, and a Healthy Environment*, p. 154.
13. Ibid., p. 154.
14. Ibid., p. 165.
15. Ibid., p. 165.
16. Ibid., p. 166; U.S. Department of Commerce, International Trade Administration, citing estimate by Environmental Business International, Inc., *Environmental Business Journal*, August 1995: pp. 1-5; *Statistical Abstract of the United States 1994*, p. 235 table 373; and p. 446, table 684.
17. *Sustainable America: A New Consensus for Prosperity, Opportunity, and a Healthy Environment*, p. 166.
18. Ibid., p. 166.
19. *The Road to Sustainable Development*, p. 29.
20. Ibid., p. 29.
21. Ibid., p. 30.
22. Ibid., p. 30.
23. *Sustainable America: A New Consensus for Prosperity, Opportunity, and a Healthy Environment*, p. 163; The discussion of climate change is based on the Intergovernmental Panel on Climate Change studies listed in notes 4 and 5 for this chapter. In addition, there are other major studies on global climate change. See National Research Council (NRC), *Energy and Climate* (Washington, D.C.: National Academy of Sciences, 1997); NRC, *Carbon Dioxide and Climate: A Scientific Assessment* (Washington, D.C.: National Academy of Sciences, 1979); NRC, *Changing Climate: Report of the Carbon Dioxide Assessment Committee* (Washington, D.C.: National Academy Press, 1983); NRC, *Global Change and Our Common Future: Papers From a Forum* (Washington, D.C.: National Academy Press, 1989); NRC, *Ozone Depletion, Greenhouse Gases, and Climate Change* (Proceedings of Joint

Symposium by the Board on Atmospheric Sciences and Climate and the Committee on Global Change, Commission on Physical Sciences, Mathematics and Resources) (Washington, D.C.: National Academy Press, 1989); National Academy of Sciences, *Policy Implications of Greenhouse Warming: Mitigation, Adaption, and the Science Base* (Washington, D.C.: National Academy Press, 1992); U.S. Congress, Office of Technology Assessment, *Preparing for an Uncertain Climate-Volume 1*, OTA-O-567 (Washington, D.C.: Government Printing Office, 1993).

24. *Sustainable America: A New Consensus for Prosperity, Opportunity, and a Healthy Environment*, p. 163.

23. Ibid., p. 163; For more information on joint implementation, see President William J. Clinton and Vice President Albert Gore, Jr., *The Climate Change Action Plan* (Washington, D.C.: The White House, 1993), pp. 26-31.

25. *Sustainable America: A New Consensus for Prosperity, Opportunity, and a Healthy Environment*, p. 163.

26. Ibid., p. 163.

27. *Population and Consumption Task Force Report*, p. 102.

Appendix A

Additional Resources

**Alliance for Transportation and
Research Institute**
University of New Mexico
1001 University Boulevard SE, Suite 10
Albuquerque, NM 87106-4342
Phone:(505)246-6410 Fax:(505)246-6001

American Forum for Global Education
120 Wall Street, Suite 2600
New York, NY 10005
Phone:(212)742-8232 Fax:(212)742-8752

Applied Sustainability Enterprises
formerly *Global Tomorrow Coalition*
1200 G Street, NW, Suite 800
Washington, DC 20005
Phone:(202)434-8783 Fax:(703)532-2862

**Boston University Center for Energy and
Environmental Studies**
675 Commonwealth Avenue
Boston, MA 02215
Phone:(617)353-3083

Brown University
Brown Is Green Program
P.O. Box 1943
Providence, RI 02912
Phone:(401)863-1000 Fax:(401)863-3503

**Business Environment Learning and
Leadership (BELL)**
1101 17th Street, NW, Suite 502
Washington, DC 20036
Phone:(202)833-6556 Fax:(202)833-6228

Center for Citizen Advocacy
73 Spring Street #206
New York, NY 10012
Phone:(212)431-3922

**Center for Environmental
Citizenship/Campus Green Vote**
1731 Connecticut Avenue, NW, Suite 50
Washington, DC 20009
Phone:(202)234-5990 Fax:(202)234-5997

Center for Environmental Education
Blueprint for a Green School
400 Columbus Avenue
Valhalla, NY 10595
Phone:(914)747-8200 Fax:(914)747-8299

Center for Neighborhood Technology
2125 W. North Avenue
Chicago, IL 60647
Phone:(312)278-4800 Fax:(312)2783840
WWW: http://www.cnt.org/TNW/

Center for Sustainable Living, Inc.
Route 1, Box 107
Shenandoah Junction, WV 25442
Phone:(304)876-0740 Fax:(304)867-2783

Chicago Academy of Sciences
2060 North Clark Street
Chicago, IL 60614
Phone:(773)549-0606 Fax:(773)549-5199
WWW: http://www.chias.org

Chicago Public Schools
1819 W. Pershing Road
Chicago, IL 60609
Phone:(312)535-3700 Fax:(312)535-3721

**Citizens Network for Sustainable
Development/U.S. Network for Habitat II**
1025 Vermont Avenue, NW, Suite 301
Washington, DC 20001
Phone:(202)879-4286 Fax:(202)783-0444
WWW: http://www.odsnet.com/
habitatnetwk

City of Pattonsburg
Town Hall
P.O. Box 226
Pattonsburg, MO 64670
Phone:(816)367-4412 Fax:(816)367-2165
*see also Department of Energy, Center of
Excellence for Sustainable Development.*

City of Plymouth
Plymouth, WI 53073
Phone:(414)893-1271

Coastal Enterprises, Inc.
Project SOAR
P.O. Box 268 Water Street
Wiscasset, ME 04578
Phone:(207)882-7552 Fax:(207)887-7308

Color Me Green
56 Valley View Drive
Gorham, ME 04038
Phone:(207)839-6455

Columbian International Center
*American Institute of Urban and Regional
Affairs*
19251 Dunbridge Way
Gaithersburg, MD 20879
Phone:(301)948-4327 Fax:(301)948-4789

**Committee for the National Institute for
the Environment**
730 11th Street, NW #300
Washington, DC 20001-4521
Phone:(202)628-4303 Fax:(202)628-4311
WWW: http://www.cnie.org/nle

**Community Sustainability Resource
Institute**
P.O. Box 11343
Takoma Park, MD 20913
Phone/Fax:(301)588-7227

Concern, Inc.
1794 Columbia Road
Washington, DC 20009
Phone:(202)328-8160 Fax:(202)387-3378

Council on Economic Priorities
30 Irving Place
New York, NY 10003
Phone:(212)420-1133 Fax:(212)420-0988

Council on Environmental Quality
The White House
Executive Office of the President
722 Jackson Place, NW
Washington, DC 20503
Phone:(202)456-6224 Fax:(202)456-2710
WWW: http://www.whitehouse.gov

Earth Pledge Program
The Earth Pledge Book
Cronkhite Beach
Building 1055
Sausalito, CA 94965

EarthPress
705 West Main Street
Carbondale IL 62901
Phone: (618)457-3521 Fax: (618)457-2541

EARTHWATCH
680 Mt. Auburn Street Box 403
Watertown, MA 02272
Phone:(617)926-8200 Fax:(617)926-1973
WWW: http://www.earthwatch.org

EE-Link
WWW: http://nceet.snre.umich.edu/use.html
*see also National Consortium for
Environmental Education and Training*

Econet
2051 Parton Lane
Arcata, CA 95521
Phone:(707)822-7947

Eisenhower National Clearinghouse
1929 Kenny Road
Columbus, OH 43210-1063
Phone:(614)292-7784 Fax:(614)292-2066
WWW: http://www.enc.org

**Environmental Resources Information
Center (ERIC)**
Access Eric
1600 Research Boulevard, Mail Stop #5F
Rockville, MD 20850
Phone:800-LET-ERIC Fax:(301)309-2084
WWW: http://www.aspen.sys.com/eric

The Foundation for the Future of Youth
Peace Child International
11426 Rockville Pike, Suite 100
Rockville, MD 20852
Phone:(301)468-9431 Fax:(301)468-9612
WWW:http://www.shs.net:
8D/rescue/found.htm .

**Four Corners School of Outdoor
Education**
PO. Box 1029
Monticello, UT 84535
Phone:(801)587-2156 Fax:(801)587-2193

Friends of the Future
see St. Francis of Assisi School

The George Washington University
Institute for the Environment
2121 Eye Street, NW, Suite 603
Washington, DC 20052
Phone:(202)994-3366 Fax:(202)994-0723
WWW: http://www.gwu.edu/greenu

Georgia Institute of Technology
Center for Sustainable Technology
School of Civil Engineering
Atlanta, GA 303320355
Phone:(404)894-1444 Fax:(404)894-2281

**Global Action and Information Network
(GAIN)**
740 Front Street, Suite 355
Santa Cruz, CA 95060
Phone:(408)457-0130 Fax:(408)457-0133
WWW: http://www.gain.org/gain

Global Action Plan for the Earth
P.O. Box 428
Woodstock, NY 12498
Phone:(914)679-4830 Fax:(914)679-4834
WWW: http://www.hudsonvalley.com/GAP

Global Environment and Technology Foundation (GETF)
7010 Little River Turnpike, Suite 300
Annandale, VA 22003-3241
Phone:(703)750-6401 Fax:(703)750-6506
WWW: http://www.gxinet.com
http://www.gnet.org

Global Research Institute
705 West Main Street
Carbondale IL 62901
Phone:(618)457-24855 Fax:(618)457-2541

Global Rivers Environmental Education Network (GREEN)
721 East Huron Street
Ann Arbor, MI 48104
Phone:(313)761-8142 Fax:(313)761-4951

The GLOBE Program
744 Jackson Place, NW
Washington, DC 20503
Phone:(202)395-7600 Fax:(202)395-7611
WWW: http://www.info@ globe.gov

Government Information Locator Service for U.S. EPA
U.S. Environmental Protection Agency
WWW: http://www.epa.gov/gils

GreenWire
3129 Mt. Vernon Avenue
Alexandria, VA 22305
Phone:(703)518-4600 Fax:(703)518-8702
WWW: http://www.apn.com

The High School for Environmental Studies
444 West 56th Street
New York, NY 10019
Phone:(212)262-8113 Fax:(212)262-0702

Institute for Sustainable Communities
56 College Street
Montpelier, VT 05602-3115
Phone:(802)229-2900 Fax:(802)229-2919

The Island Institute
410 Main Street
Rockland, ME 04841
Phone:(207)594-9209 Fax:(207)594-9314

Jupiter Community High School
Environmental Research and Field Studies Academy
500 N. Military Trail
Jupiter, FL 33458
Phone:(407)743-6005 Fax:(407)744-7978

Management Institute for Environment and Business
1101 17th Street, NW, Suite 502
Washington, DC 20036
Phone:(202)833-6556 Fax:(202)833-6228

Menominee Sustainable Development Institute
College of the Menominee Nation
P.O. Box 1179
Keshena, WI 54135
Phone:(715)799-5614 Fax:(715)799-5638
WWW: http:www.menominee.com/sdi

Multimedia Development Laboratory
Safety, Health and Environmental Management Division (mail code: 3207)
Office of Administration
U.S. Environmental Protection Agency
401 M Street, S.W.
Washington, D.C. 20460
Phone:(202)260-1640 Fax:(202)260-0215

National Association of Physicians for the Environment
6410 Rockledge Drive, Suite 203
Bethesda, MD 20817
Phone:(301)571-9791 Fax:(301)530-8910

National Center on Education and the Economy
700 11th Street, NW
Washington, DC 20001
Phone:(202)783-3668 Fax:(202)783-3672

National Commission on Economic Conversion and Disarmament
1828 Jefferson Place, NW
Washington, DC 20036
Phone:(202)728-0815 Fax:(202)728-0826

National Consortium for Environmental Education and Training (NCEET)
430 East University, Dana Building
Ann Arbor, MI 48109-1115
Phone:(313)998-6726 Fax:(313)998-6580
WWW: http://www.eelink@mich.edu
WWW: http://www.nceet.snre.umich.edu/use.html

National Environmental Education Advancement Project (NEEAP)
College of Natural Resources
University of Wisconsin-Stevens Point
Stevens Point, WI 54481
Phone:(715)346-4179 Fax:(715)346-3819
WWW: http:www.uwsp.edu/acad/cnr/neeap.htm.

National Environmental Education Training Foundation
734 15th Street, NW, Suite 420
Washington, DC 20005
Phone:(202)628-8200 Fax:(202)628-8204

National Environmental Information Resources Center (NEIRC)
Institute for the Environment
The George Washington University
Washington, DC 20052
Phone:(202)994-3366 Fax:(202)994-0723
WWW: http://wwwgwu.edu/-greenu/

The National 4-H Council
7100 Connecticut Avenue
Chevy Chase, MD 20815
Phone:(301)961-2800 Fax. (301)961-2848

National Library for the Environment
1725 K Street, NW
Washington, DC 20006-1401
Phone:(202)628-4303 Fax:(202)628-4311
WWW: http://www.cnie.org/nle

National Science and Technology Council
Bridge to a Sustainable Future: National Environmental Technology Strategy
Office of Science and Technology Policy
Old Executive Building, Room 443
17th Street and Pennsylvania Avenue, NW
Washington, DC 20500
Phone:(800)368-6676

National Urban Internet
see Urban Technologies, Inc.

National Wildlife Federation
Campus Outreach Division
Ecodemia
1400 16th Street, NW
Washington, DC 20036-2266
Phone:(202)797-5435

The Nature Conservancy
1815 North Lynn Street
Arlington, VA 22209
Phone:(703)841-5300 Fax:(703)841-1283
WWW: http://www.tnc.org

New York University
Stern School of Business Management
Global Environmental Program
44 West Fourth Street, Suite 7-73
New York, NY 10012-1126
Phone:(212)998-0426

Noblesville, Indiana
Center for Urban Policy and the Environment
342 North Senate Avenue
Indianapolis, IN 46204
Phone:(317)261-3000

North American Association for Environmental Education
1255 23rd Street, NW, Suite 400
Washington, DC 20037
Phone:(202)884-8912 Fax:(202)884-8701

Office of Science and Technology Policy
Bridge to a Sustainable Future: National Environmental Technology Strategy
Office of Science and Technology Policy
Old Executive Building, Room 443
17th Street and Pennsylvania Avenue, NW
Washington, DC 20500
Phone:(800)368-6676
WWW :http// www.whitehouse.gov

Partnerships Supporting Education About the Environment
Education for Sustainability: An Agenda for Action.
see the U.S. Department of Education

Plymouth Institute and High Wind Association
W7136 County Road "U"
Plymouth, WI 53073
Phone:(414)528-8488
e-mail: highwind@wxecpc.com

President's Council on Sustainable Development
730 Jackson Place, NW
Washington, DC 20503
Phone:(202)4085296 Fax:(202)408-6839
WWW: http://www.whitehouse.gov/PCSD

Presidio Pacific Center
220 Sansome Street
San Francisco, CA 94104
Phone:(415)956-3686 Fax:(415)956-4996

Project SEED
see U.S. EPA. Environmental Ed. Division

Project Learning Tree
1111 19th Street, NW
Washington, DC 20036
Phone:(202)463-2472

Project WILD
5430 Grosvenor Lane
Bethesda, MD 20814
Phone:(301)493-5447

Public Technology, Inc.
The Urban Consortium
1301 Pennsylvania Avenue, NW
Washington, DC 20004-1793
Phone:(202)626-2400 or (800)852-4934
Fax:(202)626-2498
WWW: http://www.pti.nw.dc.us

Renewable Energy Policy Project
University of Maryland
3140 Tydings Hall
College Park, MD 20742
Phone:(301)403-4165 Fax:(301)405-4550

Rutgers University
Center for Urban Policy Research
33 Livingston Avenue Suite 400
New Brunswick, NJ 08901-1982
Phone:(908)932-3133 Fax:(908)932-2363
WWW: http://policy.rutgers.edu/cupr/
see U.S. Department of Housing and Urban Development, re: Indicators on Sustainable Cities.

San Francisco Bay Area EcoTeam Project
1000 Green Street PH#1
San Francisco, CA 94133
Phone:(415)5678657

Sarasota County
County Extension Agents
2900 Ringling Boulevard
Sarasota, FL 34237
Phone:(813)955-4240 Fax:(813)955-0413

Second Nature
44 Bromfield Street, 5th floor
Boston, MA 02108
Phone:(617)292-7771 Fax:(617)292-0150
WWW: http://www.2nature.org

Sierra Club National Headquarters
85 Second Street, 2nd Floor
San Francisco, CA 94105-3441
Phone:(415)977-5500 Fax:(415)977-5799
WWW: http://www.sierraclub.org

Smithsonian Institution
1100 Jefferson Drive, SW
Washington, DC 20560
Phone:(202)357-4792

Sonoma State University
Department of Environmental Studies and
Planning
1801 East Cotati Avenue
Rohnert Park, CA 94928
Phone:(707)664-2249

Southern Center for Environmental Justice
see Three Circles Center for Multicultural Environmental Education

Southern University
Center for Energy and Environmental
Studies
P.O. Box 9764
Baton Rouge, LA 70813
Phone:(504)771-4724 Fax:(504)771 4722

Southwest Network for Environmental and Economic Justice
P.O. Box 7399
Albuquerque, NM 87194
Phone:(505)242-0416 Fax:(505)242-5609

St. Francis of Assisi School
1938 Alfresco Place
Louisville, KY 40205
Phone:(502)245-7000 or (502)459-3088

State University of New York
Environmental Science and Forestry
#1 Forestry Drive
Marshall Hall, Room 107
Syracuse, NY 13210-2778
Phone:(315)470-6636 Fax:(315)470-6915

Student Conservation Association
P.O. Box 9867
Arlington, VA 22219
Phone:(703)524-2441 Fax:(703)524-2451

Sustainability Project (The)
4 Gavilan Road
Santa Fe, New Mexico 87505
Phone:(505)466-2052 Fax:(505)466-2052

Sustainable Community Roundtable
Creating a Sustainable Community in South Puget Sound
2129 Bethel Street, NE
Olympia, WA 98506
Phone:(360)754-7842

Sustainable Seattle
909 Fourth Avenue
Seattle, WA 98104
Phone:(206)382-5013

Sustainable Wisconsin
929 North Sixth Street
Milwaukee, WI 53203
Phone:(414)227-3270 Fax:(414)227-3168

Syracuse University
Crouse School of Management
Crouse Hinds, Suite 200
Syracuse, NY 10324
Phone:(315)443-3751 Fax:(315)443-5389

Three Circles Center for Multicultural Environmental Education
P.O. Box 1946
Sausalito, CA 94965
Phone:(415)331-4540 Fax:(415)331-4540

TI Group, Inc, Washington Office
National Alliance for Environmental Systems Engineering
2001 Jefferson Davis Highway
Suite 607-A
Arlington, VA 22202
Phone:(703)418-6090 Fax:(703)418-0946

Tides Foundation Economics Working Group
3407 34th Street, NW
Washington, DC 20016
Phone:(202)542-4800

Tufts University
Peace and Justice Studies
109 Eaton Hall
Medford, MA 02155
Phone:(617)628-5000 Fax:(617)627-3032

Tufts University
Fletcher School of Law and Diplomacy
Global Development and Environment Institute
Cabot Building
Medford, MA 02155
Phone:(617)627-3700 Fax:(617)627-3712
www. http://www.tufts.edu/fletcher/

United Nations
Department of Public Information
Room S-894
New York, NY 10017
Phone:(212)963-4556

University of Arizona
Recycling Office
P.O. Box 210049
Tucson, AZ 85721-0049
Phone:(520)621-1264 Fax:(520)621-6086

University of California at Berkeley
College of Natural Resources
101 Giannini Hall
Berkeley, CA 94720
Phone:(510)642-7171 Fax:(510)6424612

University of Louisville
*Institute for the Environment and
Sustainable Development (IESD)*
Louisville, KY 40292
Phone:(502)8526512 Fax:(502)852-8361

University of Michigan
School of Natural Resources and the
Environment
430 East University
Ann Arbor, MI 48109-1115
Phone:(313)764-6453 Fax:(313)936-2195
WWW: http://wqww.snre umich.edu

University of Oregon
Institute for a Sustainable Environment
130 Hendricks Hall
Eugene, OR 97403-1209
Phone:(503)346-3895 Fax:(503)346-2040

University of Vermont
Environmental Education Program
153 S. Prospect
Burlington, VT 05401
Phone:(802)656-4055

University of Washington
Center for Sustainable Communities
224 Gould Hall, Box 355726
Seattle, WA 98195
Phone:(206)543-7679

University of Wisconsin, Milwaukee
Center for Urban Community Development
161 West Wisconsin Avenue
Milwaukee, WI 53217-3985
Phone:(414)227-3280 Fax:(414)277-3168

University of Wisconsin, Stevens Point
Wisconsin Center for Environmental
Education
Stevens Point, WI 54481
Phone:(715)592-4619 Fax:(715)346-3025

**University Leaders for a Sustainable
Future**
Tufts University Environmental Literacy
Institute
Center for Environmental Management

177 College Avenue, Room 101
Medford, MA 01255
Phone:(617)627-3464 Fax:(617)627-3099
WWW: http://wwwUlsf.org

Urban Technologies, Inc.
5808 Bush Hill Drive
Alexandria, VA 22310
Phone:(703)922-7653 Fax:(703)924-9593

**U.S. Agency for International
Development**
320 21st Street, NW
Washington, DC 20523
Phone:(202)647-4000

U.S. Chamber of Commerce
1615 H Street, NW
Washington, DC 20062
Phone:(202)659-6000 Fax:(202)463-5836

U.S. Department of Agriculture
14th Street and Independence Avenue, SW
Washington, DC 20250
Phone:(202)720-2791

U.S. Department of Agriculture
Cooperative State Research, Education and
Extension Service (CSREES)
Natural Resources and Environmental
Management (NREM)
Agbox 2210 329
Aerospace Building
Washington, DC 20250-2210
Phone:(202)401-5351

U.S. Department of Commerce
Bureau of Economic Analysis
14th Street & Constitution Avenue, NW
Washington, DC 20230
Phone:(202)606-9900.

U.S. Department of Commerce
National Oceanic and Atmospheric
Administration (NOAA)
Sea Grant Program
#5222 14th St. & Constitution Avenue NW
Washington, DC 20230
Phone:(202)482-2663.

U.S. Department of Commerce
Office of Economic Conversion Information
(OECI)
14th Street &: Constitution Avenue NW
Washington, DC 20230
Phone:(800)345-1222

U.S. Department of Education
Office of the Deputy Secretary
600 Independence Avenue, SW
Washington, DC 20202
Phone:(202)401-1000 Fax:(202)401-3093
WWW: http://www.ed.gov.

U.S. Department of Energy
Center for Excellence for Sustainable
Development
P.O. Box 3048
Merrifield VA 22116
Phone:(800)357-7732
WWW: http://www.crest.org/doe/.
sustainable.

U.S. Department of Energy
Office of Energy Efficiency and Renewable
Energy
2801 Youngfield Street,
Suite 380
Golden, CO 80401
Phone:(303)231-5750

**U.S. Department of Housing and Urban
Development**
Office of Policy Development and Research
451 Seventh Street, SW
Washington, DC 20410
Phone:(202)708-3896 Fax:(202)619-8000

U.S. Department of the Interior
Water and Science Branch
1849 C Street, NW Mail stop 6640
Washington, DC 20240
Phone:(202)208-5691 Fax:(202)371-2815.

U.S. Department of State
2201 C Street, NW
Room 7250
Washington, DC 20520
Phone:(202)647-4000 Fax:(202)647-0753 .

U.S. Environmental Protection Agency
Safety, Health and Environmental
Management Division (mail code: 3207)
Office of Administration
401 M Street, SW
Washington, DC 20460
Phone:(202)260-1640 Fax:(202)260-0215
e-mail: jimeno.julius@epamail.epa.gov.

U.S. Environmental Protection Agency
Office of Communications, Education, and
Public Affairs (mail code: 1707)
Environmental Education Division
401 M Street, SW
Washington, DC 20460
Phone:(202)260-4965 Fax:(202)260-4095

U.S. Fish and Wildlife Service
National Education and Training Center
4401 N. FairFax Drive
MS 304 Webb
Arlington, VA 22203
Phone:(703)358-2504

**U.S. National Aeronautics and Space
Administration** (NASA)
300 E Street, SW
Washington, DC 20546
Phone:(202)358-0000 Fax:(202)358-3251
WWW: http://www.nasa.gov.

U.S. Postal Service
Environmental Policy Management
475 L'Enfant Plaza, SW
Washington, DC 20260-2810
Phone:(202)268-3364 Fax:(202)268-6016
WWW: http://www.usps.gov.

Vice President Albert Gore
White House
1600 Pennsylvania Avenue, NW
Washington, DC 20016
Phone:(202)456-1414
WWW: http://www.whitehouse.gov.

Widener University Law School
Harrisburg Campus 3800 Vartan Way
Harrisburg, PA 17110-9450
Phone:(717)541-3900 Fax:(717)541-3999
WWW: http://www.widner.edu.

World Resources Institute
Environmental Education Project
1709 New York Avenue, NW
Washington, DC 20006
Phone:(202)638-6300 Fax:(202)638-0036
WWW: http://www.wri.org.

Yale University
School of Forestry and Environmental
Studies
205 Prospect Street
New Haven, CT 06511
Phone:(203)432-5100 Fax:(203)432-5942
http://www.academic programs.

YWCA of the USA
Education for Global Responsibility
726 Broadway - 5th Floor
New York, NY 10003
Phone:(212)614-2700 Fax:(212)677-9716.

Zero Population Growth
1400 16th Street NW
Suite 320
Washington, DC 20036
Phone:(202)332-2200 Fax:(202)332-2302

Appendix B

Council Membership

297

ECO-EFFECIENCY TASK FORCE MEMBERSHIP

Carol Browner, Administrator U.S. Environmental Protection Agency
A.D. "Pete" Correll, Chairman and CEO, Georgia-Pacific Corp.
Fred Krupp, Executive Director, Environmental Defense Fund
D. James Baker, Under Secretary for Oceans and Atmosphere, U.S. Department of Commerce
Dick Barth, Chairman and CEO, Ciba-Geigy Corporation
Ronald Brown, Secretary, U.S. Department of Commerce
William Hoglund, Executive V.P. (Retired) General Motors Corporation
Samuel C. Johnson, Chairman, S.C. Johnson & Son, Inc.
David T. Buzzelli, Vice President, The Dow Chemical Company
Hazel O'Leary, Secretary U.S. Department of Energy
Scott Bernstein, President, Center for Neighborhood Technology
Ben Cooper, Vice President, Governmental Affairs Printing Industries of America
Deeohn Ferris, President, D.C. Office of Environmental Justice
Ben Henneke, President, Clean Air Action Corp.
Herb Beattie, Director of Corporate Development, Clean Air Action Corporation
Hubert H. "Skip" Humphrey III, Attorney General, Minnesota Attorney General's Office
Sherri Goodman, Undersecretary for Environmental Security, U.S. Department of Defense
Howard Klee, Director of Regulatory Affairs, Amoco Corporation
Susan Maxman, Former President, American Institute of Architects
Edgar Miller, Director of Policy and Programs, National Recycling Coalition
Mike Pierle, Vice President, Monsanto Company
Robert N. Stavins, Associate Professor of Public Policy Harvard University
Tom Rogers, Former Commissioner Santa Barbara County, California
Joanna Underwood, President, INFORM, Inc.
Pam Reed, Commissioner Texas Natural Resource Conservation Commission

ENERGY AND TRANSPORTATION TASK FORCE MEMBERSHIP

John H. Adams, Executive Director, Natural Resources Defense Council
Kenneth T. Derr, Chairman and CEO, Chevron Corporation
Hazel R. O'Leary, Secretary, U.S. Department of Energy
Christine E.M. Álvarez, Commissioner, Colorado Public Utilities Commission
Robert T. (Hap) Boyd, Director of Government & Regulatory Affairs, Zond Systems
Earl Blumenauer, Commissioner, Portland, Oregon
Nancy Brockway, National Consumer Law Center
Frank Carlile, Assistant Secretary, Florida Department of Transportation
Phil Carroll, CEO, Shell Oil Company
A.R. (Peter) Carpenter, President and CEO, CSX Transportation
Richard A. Clarke, Chairman and CEO, Pacific Gas and Electric Company
William Davis, Chairman, CEO, Niagara Mohawk Power
Henry (Hank) Dittmar, Director, Surface Transportation Policy Project
Thomas Donahue, Secretary Treasurer, AFL-CIO
Linn E. Draper Jr., Chairman, American Electric Power Company
Irl Englehardt, Chairman, President and CEO, Peabody Holding Company Inc.
Judith Espinosa, Former Secretary, New Mexico Environment Department
Jacky Grimshaw, Coordinator, Center for Neighborhood Technology
Martha S. Hogerty, President, Missouri Public Counsel
William E. Hoglund, Executive Vice President, General Motors Corporation
Fred D. Krupp, Executive Director, Environmental Defense Fund
Jonathan Lash, President, World Resources Institute
Kenneth L. Lay, Chairman and CEO, Enron Corporation
Mary Nichols, Assistant Administrator, U.S. Environmental Protection Agency
David Nemtzow, President, Alliance to Save Energy
Vincent O'Reilly, President, International Brotherhood of Electrical Workers
Federico Pena, Secretary, U.S. Department of Transportation
Michele A. Perrault, International Vice President, Sierra Club
Howard (Bud) Ris, Executive Director, Union of Concerned Scientists
Ellen Roy, Vice President, Intercontinental Energy Corporation Chairman, NAIEP
Jean Smith, Manager, South Central Arkansas Transit
S. Lynn Sutcliffe, CEO, SYCOM
Richard I. Trumka, President, United Mine Workers of America

POPULATION AND CONSUMPTION TASK FORCE MEMBERSHIP

John H. Adams, Executive Director, Natural Resources Defense Council
D. James Baker, Under-Secretary for Oceans and Atmosphere, U.S. Department of Commerce
Richard Barth, CEO of CIBA-Geigy Corporation
Ron H. Brown, Secretary of U.S. Department of Commerce
Dianne Dillon-Ridgley, National Co-Chair, Citizen's Network for Sustainable Development

298

Fred D. Krupp, Executive Director, Environmental Defense Fund
Michelle A. Perrault, International Vice President, Sierra Club
Theodore Strong, Executive Director, Columbia River Inter-Tribal Fish Commission
Timothy E. Wirth, Under-Secretary for Global Affairs, U.S. State Department
Margaret Pruitt Clark, Advocates for Youth
Clifford Cobb, Redefining Progress
David Crocker, University of Maryland
George Gerbner, University of Pennsylvania
David Gershon, Global Action Plan for the Earth
Neva Goodwin, Tufts University
Wade Greene, Rockefeller Financial Services
Jeanne Haws, AVSC International
Judith Jacobsen, University of Denver
Vicki Robin, New Road Map Foundation
Jeffrey Rogers, City Attorney, Portland, Oregon
James Martin-Schramm, Luther College
Felicia Stewart, U.S. Department of Health and Human Services
Betsy Taylor, Merck Family Fund
Georgina Verdugo, Mexican-American Legal Defense and Education Fund

PUBLIC LINKAGE, DIALOGUE, AND EDUCATION TASK-FORCE MEMBERSHIP
Judith M. Espinosa, (former) Secretary of the Environment; State of New Mexico
Michele A. Perrault, International Vice President; Sierra Club
Dianne Dillon-Ridgley, Co-Chair; Citizens Network for Sustainable Development
Madeleine M. Kunin, Deputy Secretary; U.S. Department of Education
Samuel C. Johnson, Chairman; S.C. Johnson & Son, Inc.
Jonathan Lash, President; World Resources Institute
Timothy E. Wirth, Under Secretary for Global Affairs; U.S. Department of State
Ray C. Anderson, Chairman and Ceo; Interface, Inc.
Scott Bernstein, President; Center for Neighborhood Technology
Harry J. Pearce, Vice Chairman; Board of General Motors Corporation
M. Susan Savage, Mayor of Tulsa, Oklahoma
Randall Franke, Chairman; Marion County Commission
Nancy Anderson, Fletcher School of Law and Diplomacy; Tufts University
Matt Arnold, Management Institute for Environment and Business
Michael Baker, Environmental Education Division; U.S. Environmental Protection Agency
Gregory Bischak, National Commission on Economic Conversion and Disarmament
Ronald Blackwell, UNITE
David Blockstein, Committee for the National Institute for the Environment
Ann Boren, San Francisco Bay Area EcoTeam Project
Barbara Bramble, National Wildlife Federation
Steve Brown, Council of State Governments
Ruth Caplan, Economics Working Group/Tides Foundation
Randy Champeau, University of Wisconsin
Tony Cortese, Second Nature
Jackie Cummins, National Conference of State Legislatures
Tom Curtis, National Governors' Association
Herman Daly, University of Maryland
Michael Dorsey, Student, Yale University
Anne Ehrlich, Stanford University
Dave Gatton, U.S. Conference of Mayors
Kathleen Gavin, Institute for Sustainable Communities
David Gershon, Global Action Plan for the Environment

SUSTAINABLE AGRICULTURE TASK FORCE MEMBERSHIP
John H. Adams, Executive Director; Natural Resources Defense Council
Richard Barth, Chairman, President, and CEO; Ciba-Geigy Corporation
Richard E. Rominger, Deputy Secretary; U.S. Department of Agriculture
Carol M. Browner, Administrator; U.S. Environmental Protection Agency
A.D. Correll, Chairman and CEO; Georgia Pacific Corporation
John Hagaman, President and CEO; DowElanco
Samuel C. Johnson, Chairman; S.C. Johnson & Son, Inc.
Jonathan Lash, President; World Resources Institute
John C. Sawhill, President and CEO; The Nature Conservancy

Index

301